Additional Praise for *Women at Church*

"Neylan McBaine's voice is uniquely important. She speaks as a unifier, knowledgeable of gender issues and attentive to all perspectives. I particularly like her questions—some paradoxical ("How do we respect the traditions, practices, and truths of our earliest progenitors, while holding sacred the rebel explosion of the Restoration?"); some rhetorical ("How can we dismiss others' pain simply because we do not feel it ourselves?"); some inviting introspection in all of our conversations about gender ("Who will feel closer to God if my ideas are implemented?"). Women at Church invites respect of all for all, and particularly for any woman who identifies herself as a member of the 'armies of SHElaman' , standing as a witness for Christ in any circumstance and transcending argument with love."

> — MARGARET BLAIR YOUNG, co-author of *Standing on the Promises*

"In *Women at Church*, Neylan McBaine artfully addresses the perception of Mormon feminism from the perspective of an orthodox believer; weaving their stories in with those who have traditionally been maligned for identifying concerns surrounding the position of women in the LDS Church. Rather than pose church members as opposing factions, Neylan draws us closer together in a narrative that highlights our potentially common goals. The book is accessible and offers a way forward for faithful seekers to highlight the contributions of women in the Church and empower all people in the spirit of equity in the Gospel of Christ."

> — LINDSAY HANSEN PARK, founder of the Feminist Mormon
> Housewives Podcast

"With her keen insights, Neylan McBaine has emerged as a leading voice in a necessary conversation. *Women at Church* brings attention to gender issues while offering innovative solutions. A truly remarkable resource that belongs in every Latter-day Saint home!"

> — JULIANN REYNOLDS, co-founder and member of the Board of Directors
> of FairMormon

WOMEN AT CHURCH

WOMEN AT CHURCH

MAGNIFYING LDS WOMEN'S LOCAL IMPACT

Neylan McBaine

GREG KOFFORD BOOKS
SALT LAKE CITY, 2014

Greg Kofford Books
P.O. Box 1362
Draper, UT 84020
www.gregkofford.com
facebook.com/gkbooks

Also available in ebook.

A companion website to this volume can be found at
womenatchurch.com

2018   17   16   15   14   5   4   3   2   1

_____

Library of Congress cataloging information available upon request.

For Esme, Auden, and Dalloway,
my future Mormon women

Contents

Acknowledgements, ix
Introduction, xiii

Part I: Identifying the Divide

1. Misbegotten Males, 3
2. A Brief History of the Conversation about Women, 7
3. Why Should I Be Concerned about How Women Feel at Church? 17
4. Why Are Some Women in Pain? 31
5. Are We Practicing What We Preach? 61

Part II: Exploring Solutions

6. Getting Down to Work, 67
7. Identify the Audience and Walk in their Shoes, 69
8. Are We Asking the Right Questions? 73
9. Prayer, 83
10. People, 89
11. Process, 125
12. Perseverance, 167
13 We Are Not Alone, 173

References Cited, 179

Acknowledgements

No book about a community can succeed without the contributions and support of that community. For that support, I thank the hundreds if not thousands of women and men who have shared their stories with me over the past several years as I launched the Mormon Women Project, built up that collection of interviews, and became a voice for celebrating women in the Church. There have been casual emails, formal interviews, and heartfelt conversations; I have made dear friends in the process. I am also grateful to all those who answered my requests for interviews in the process of writing this book. They opened their hearts to me, revisited old wounds, stripped away their pride to honestly evaluate painful situations, and allowed me to probe into their leadership and communication strengths and weaknesses. Regardless of the format or formality or length of our acquaintance, I have been deeply moved time and time again by the strength, dedication, and faith of our membership. We truly have remarkable women and men in this Church, and it has been my privilege to touch souls with a handful of them.

This book would not have happened without prodding from Brad Kramer of Greg Kofford Books who gave me the confidence to plunge in, and Riley M. Lorimer who helped me shape my thoughts. Riley is a consummate editor, thinker, and counselor, and I was grateful to have her on my team. Steve Evans and the team at *By Common Consent* graciously allowed me to post a call for stories on their blog, as did *Feminist Mormon Housewives*. Individuals spread the news far and wide that I was looking for real world examples, and it is because of their efforts that I had such rich sources to work from.

My work colleagues at Boncom offered support and thoughtful conversation throughout the process of writing this book. For being a valuable sounding board, I thank Andrea Radke-Moss, who inspires me with her commitment to our shared faith in the gospel and in women. For introducing me to the work of R. Marie Griffith, I thank Joanna Brooks. For an expert look at tone and structure, Amy Jameson was invaluable. Whitney Johnson gave me practical tips for writing a book while juggling a full-time job and children at home. Cathy Chamberlain shared insights from her career spent researching women in and out of the Church, and I am also grateful for her encouragement and friendship. Clayton Christensen has been an inspiration, as he has been to many, but I am particularly grateful for a conversation he had with the LDS students at Harvard Business School in 2008 in which he pointed out that many of our most beloved church programs started as grassroots efforts of "disruptive innovation." That conversation opened a door in my thinking about the subject of women in the Church. I am also indebted to his talk at the 2012 Boncom conference about "asking the right questions."

There are many who have supported me and inspired me to think more deeply, not just in the process of writing this book, but in developing my voice on women's issues generally. I am particularly indebted to Ruth Todd, who initially recommended me to FairMormon as a speaker for the 2012 conference while she was working for the Church's Public Affairs department. Scott Gordon, Steve Densley, John Lynch, and Juliann Reynolds of FairMormon have been consistent and appreciated cheerleaders of my voice. The work and personal encouragement of Valerie Hudson and Bonnie Ballif-Spanvill are humbling to me. My sisters from our 2010 Patheos.com podcast, The Round Table, remain inspiring sources for broad viewpoints and consistent support: Kathryn Soper, Chelsea Shields Strayer, Lisa Butterworth, Saren Loosli, and Emily Jensen. Kristine Haglund's enthusiasm about publishing the 2012 FairMormon talk in *Dialogue: A Journal of Mormon Thought* helped me take myself seriously. Kate Holbrook of the Church History Library and the members of her discussion group have inspired me to better understand Church history and deeply informed sections of this book. Jeremy Hunt of the San Francisco Institute of Religion gave me speaking opportunities that prompted me to flesh out some of the ideas in this book. Maxine Hanks, Fiona Givens, and Margaret Blair Young have been teachers, mothers, friends, and mentors; their wisdom and kindness and closeness to the Lord have strengthened me.

Those who have built up the Mormon Women Project (MWP) alongside me have become trusted advisors and friends. Barbara Christiansen has been with the MWP from the start and serves as our treasurer. Scott

Lunt served as our original webmaster and nurtured the site from its infancy. Chrysula Winegar is an interview subject, dear friend, and our social media manager. Janelle Higbee graciously took over our demanding interview publication schedule while I took a hiatus to write this book. Key interview producers like Annette Pimentel, Krisanne Hastings Knudsen, Kathryn Peterson, Lydia Defranchi, among many others, are the lifeblood of the project. Melissa McQuarrie and Rosalyn Eves have copy-edited scores of our interviews. Patti Cook creates fundraising events that strengthen the MWP brand (which allows us to raise the funds we need to continue the project) and brings both fun and organizational expertise to everything she touches. Lastly, Elizabeth Ostler has performed an outstanding labor of love leading the charge on creating WomenAtChurch. com, the online extension of this book. Along with Meredith Nelson and Heather Steed, they have created a place where we can all share our stories of women being magnified at church.

A lifelong debt of gratitude is due to Beverly Campbell who is one of the heroes of my youth and continues to be a beloved mentor. She teaches me to pursue my full potential while still acknowledging and relying on the source of all goodness. My stepfather, James E. Ford, has been reading my writing, the good and bad, since college; for honest feedback, mind-opening discussions and hours of proofreading, I thank him. My mom, Ariel Bybee, will always be the greatest Mormon woman in my eyes. Faithful and indomitable to the end, she remains my original inspiration. My husband, Elliot C. Smith, gives me the peace that comes from being loved well. "Love sought is good, but given unsought better." For the unsought gift, I thank him.

Introduction

"Blessed are the peacemakers,
for they shall be called the children of God."
Matthew 5:9

This book is predicated on a single belief: that there is much more we can do to see, hear, and include women at church. In an effort to increase awareness of that belief and move all Church members to act on it, I have written this book as an inducement toward greater empathy for those who feel unseen, unheard, and unused, and a strategic guide to improving our gender cooperation in local Church governance.

I have written this book out of a sincere desire to help us as God's laborers to build His kingdom. As a Mormon woman myself and one privy to the feelings and insights of hundreds of other Mormon women I've interviewed, I know that being a woman in The Church of Jesus Christ of Latter-day Saints can be a joyous and fulfilling identity. Being a Mormon is, for me, as inextricably linked to my identity as being a woman. But my years working on gender issues have also made me aware that not all women feel the way I do and that some extraordinary souls are being lost because we, the stewards of God's kingdom on earth, fall short in embracing them.

I believe we already have the tools to see, hear, and include women more fully in the operation and governance of our wards and stakes. Even if nothing were to change in the structural hierarchy of local Church governance—even if being ordained to the priesthood remains entirely a male privilege and men continue to make up the majority of our ward and stake leadership and even if nothing were to change from the 2012 edition of the Church's *Handbook of Instructions 2*—I believe we have the opportunity and the responsibility to adapt our local practices to include our women more comprehensively. In fact, the 2012 *Handbook,* which is the general instruction book for how to administer the Church organization and is available to every member online and in print, includes an entire section on the potential for adaptation. Male and female local leaders can stretch their organizational and spiritual imagination's even further to embrace innovative solutions for the inclusion of women. For some, increasing visibility, voice, and usefulness on the local levels is playing whack-a-mole at symptoms. They believe this approach pushes aside the root cause of some women's struggle because it doesn't unseat men from having priesthood responsibility for women. I am convinced, however, that we can ease these adverse symptoms to a point where more women can be at peace with our current structure as we look to continued prophetic guidance.

I write from a belief that we are not doing all we can to fully recognize and utilize women's unique voices, experiences, opinions, and abilities; it is imperative that we do better. Perhaps you as the reader are deeply convinced of this already. Perhaps you are skeptical of this belief and have not seen proof of this in your own life. It is my job in this book to point out how we can do better, but it is also my job to convey that we *need* to do better for the future Church membership and spiritual health of our mothers, sisters, wives, and selves. Unfortunately, that means that a good portion of this book has to talk about a problem: that some women are feeling neglected, overlooked, and silenced in their Church experiences.

Understanding why these women are feeling the way they do is the necessary first step to solving the problem, and so we must face the sad stories and examples of compromised behavior. Dwelling on negative examples is not the way we Mormons like to do things, so I have thought long and hard about including the stories and examples that I do here. Even though we Mormons are a generally optimistic people and prefer to teach by positive example, additional authenticity and impact often come from discussing what is going wrong as well as what is going right. As I have learned while dealing with very heavy subjects like depression and abuse as the editor of the Mormon Women Project, a meaningful and well-placed tale of authentic experience can actually have a bolstering and comforting effect on others who might be similarly struggling. Honoring the suffering of one by telling her story is a way of honoring and relieving the suffering of all who have had similar experiences. I believe that the discouraging stories told here will serve to increase our empathy for those who are suffering and make us more vigilant against any similar thing happening in our own spheres of influence.

This book is neither written just for men, nor just for women; it is written for both. Tensions that arise around gender and responsibilities in Church administration are not a women problem, nor are they a men problem. In my years of working on gender issues, I have watched men come up with innovative, inclusive solutions as often as women. Similarly, I have noted that women confine other women, as frequently as men confine women. I have received more letters from men expressing concern about gender practices in the Church than I have from women—mostly from fathers, husbands, and bishops who are seeing their loved ones struggle. Both men and women are responsible for being aware of the challenges of gender cooperation and addressing them in their own ways. I make an attempt here to speak to both genders. I do not intend to vilify or condemn men in any way, especially those men who dedicate hours of their lives to serving in demanding, and often thankless, lay positions.

In this book, I am proposing a strategic approach to maturely and respectfully wrestle with the tensions of gender in local Church settings. This approach offers both female and male members of the Church a framework to approach changes in our gendered practices with faith, constructive innovation, and empathy. I hope that, with the help of this book, we can better evaluate possible pain points in current practices and propose solutions that uphold all mandated Church policies. This book has been designed to serve as an active tool in your ward, stake, or mission leadership, whether you are a man or a woman. I've liberally used real-world examples to illustrate the depth of pain that some women are feeling, the positive examples of solution-driven leadership that are happening all around us, and the negative examples of unresolved conflict. I hope these case studies will open our minds to how we might unwittingly be hurting each other and expand our spiritual imaginations to new solutions and resources.

In Part I, I offer a very brief overview of gender discussions in our Church's history in an effort to establish context for my ideas. I explore our collective responsibility to women who struggle and encourage each of us to take an empathetic stance. I also explain why I believe some women are struggling today and how those struggles are different from the challenges of earlier eras.

In Part II, I take a practical approach to magnifying women's impact in the local Church by examining specific practices and offering real-world examples of what is being explored in local settings around the country.

As part of the research for this book, I interviewed in person and via phone and email hundreds of men and women who are currently serving in stake or ward leadership callings, those who are not and have never had leadership callings, and those who have served in leadership callings in the past. I also draw on years of personal emails that I have received from individuals. I am deeply grateful to each person who contributed thoughts and experiences to me. Their stories are presented here with their permission and my thanks. When I refer to "leadership callings" in the book, I am generally referring to any man or woman who attends Ward Council meetings or who is in the presidency of an auxiliary organization.

What this book *isn't* is as important as what it is. This book is not an attempt to challenge or redefine gender doctrine, to offer scriptural exegesis on gender, or to posit ways doctrine could change to accommodate contemporary desires. This book does not deal with doctrine. It is also not an attempt to argue that everything in Church practices today reflects the best of all possible worlds. I am working under two assumptions. First, I believe our living prophet and apostles are the only people who can revolutionize our current gender doctrine. Second, gender practices in the Church today are not what they can be. Thus, my approach here should be very clear: accepting the doctrine and policies we have in place in the Church today, how can we help improve gender-cooperative practices on the local levels so as to relieve unnecessary tensions caused by cultural or historically normative practices?

This book is not meant to be an authoritative exploration of women's relationship to male priesthood authority. I am not an academician or a historian. I am not a theologian beyond the demands of discipleship, and I am not interested in this book becoming a platform for debates about the nature and administration of the priesthood. There are many good thinkers and theologians currently writing and speaking on priesthood, gender doctrine, and the comprehensive history of women in the Church. The References section at the end of this book indicates a number of books I have found enlightening; the Resources section at this book's website, womenatchurch.com, offers a more comprehensive list of writings and recordings I feel are helpful to gaining a richer understanding of the gender discussions. I have attempted here to give a lay of the land, and I approach the subject from my own professional background as a marketer and brand strategist, but I encourage anyone who wants to take on a full study of the subject to peruse the website's Resources section carefully.

Some will argue that it is those very doctrines and policies surrounding priesthood that create a less-than-ideal culture and that they need to be changed in order for anything to improve. I am aware of these arguments and am sympathetic to parts of them. If President Monson announced tomorrow that women would now be ordained to priesthood offices and thus equally eligible to be local and general leaders, I wouldn't complain. But I do not believe such a change would fix our challenges overnight. After all, we currently have one of the most progressive gender doctrines among any Western religion—an acknowledged female deity, a "fortunate fall" which lifts Eve from condemnation, a doctrine of divine love despite gender, and an endowment of divine power for women in the temple—and yet even these revolutionary beliefs have not inoculated us from gender challenges in our culture. Universal priesthood ordination would not safeguard us much more effectively, I believe, than our current doctrine already does.

Thus my approach assumes that we will have our current doctrine for quite some time yet, and that it is within this current reality that we must work to improve our experiences. My approach also assumes that the Church's *Handbook of Instructions 2* will be enforced for quite some time in an effort to streamline a global community and avoid the chaos of factionalized worship. Within these boundaries, however, there is ample room for us to imagine, innovate, experiment, and refine on the ward, stake, and mission levels. Inspiring and guiding this innovation is the aim of this book.

Who Is This Book For?

There are many members of the Church around the world who feel the identity and responsibilities of Mormon women are of either no cause for concern or else bring great peace. Our doctrine around the eternal nature of gender and the importance of mothers is, in many women's eyes, a unique theological gift resulting in worth, self-confidence, and self-definition. Many women find purpose in these doctrines and the roles they prescribe. The teaching that they are daughters of God, who loves them without their having to earn that love, results in a strong sense of personal worth. Many of these women happily leave to men the ecclesiastical structure of priesthood authority and the accompanying leadership roles; they also assume separate, less public, responsibilities themselves. Many mothers feel supported in their potentially isolating and thankless jobs, and in many homes there is a division of labor that works for both parties. Especially in developing countries, the gospel's empowerment of women has resulted in positive seismic shifts in the way women are respected, families are run, and men rise up to their responsibilities. I acknowledge and celebrate these fruits as real and beautiful and possible only because of the gospel of Jesus Christ.

One husband describes the way he's seen his wife rise to the challenge of being Primary president in their ward:

> I do have a wonderful wife who is not what I would consider a type-A personality, so not typically one who seeks out leadership or the spotlight, although she has never been one to shy away from a challenge. I watch her now as she leads the primary and marvel at the leadership skills and experience it affords her. I would definitely say she struggles with this role, but the struggle is more of a struggle to grow and learn as she performs her calling that takes her well outside her comfort zone. She has been the primary president now for almost 3 years, and her leadership and guidance has brought the primary organization to a wonderful place, both organizationally and spiritually.
>
> I equate her role to that of the president of a start-up company. She has somewhere between 20 to 30 teachers, advisers, scout leaders, and counselors all looking to her for direction. I think it has been a great experience for her, and I am hard pressed to imagine anywhere else she would be challenged to grow and stretch and simultaneously impact as many lives for good as she has through this calling. Especially for someone with her personality that wouldn't otherwise be seeking out leadership roles, short of starting her own company, she would not have the opportunity, and again her personality would not be one likely to pursue that.

But not all of our women find themselves so aligned with these attitudes. For a range of reasons discussed in this book, women in the Church today can feel a tension between what they are being taught at church or how they're being engaged at church, and what they feel is a true evaluation of their potential and worth. It is not uncommon for a member in the Church today—at least in the United States or developed countries—to know someone who is wrestling with what it means to be a Mormon woman.

This book is for men and women who either are themselves engaged in this wrestle or know someone who is. It is for women who have been sitting on the sidelines of the media conversation around Mormon women, not sure where they fit or what they feel, but they resonate with at least some of what has been said. It is for the women who can't understand why someone would be discontent in light of our glorious doctrine, but whose daughter or sister or friend or Relief Society sister may not be feeling so at ease. It is for the man who has ecclesiastical responsibility to call women to callings, work with women in counsel, teach with women, improve the lives of members and investigators with women, or live with women in the home. In short, I hope there is something useful here for every person who is or who knows a Mormon woman who must integrate her faith and her activity in the Church with a contemporary life.

I am aware that the challenges present in Mormon womanhood today are most pronounced in America and other developed nations. Members in countries where the Church has had a lengthy presence and where the society at large has progressive laws and customs with respect to women seem, anecdotally, most attuned to gender issues. In an effort to focus the conversation here, I am mostly concerned with practices in the American Church, and my interviews were almost exclusively with Americans.

Offering a Guiding Hand

In a 1990 BYU Women's Conference, Karen Lynn Davidson highlighted the blessings found in serving together in our church communities. She said,

> I'm grateful that our Father in Heaven instructs us to prove our worthiness not by living as hermits in holy isolation but by forming communities through our branches, wards, stakes. . . . In this way, our individual powers can supplement the powers that may be missing in someone else. . . . Sometimes in our ward the events on a typical Sunday are not perfectly predictable, but I realized long ago that efficiency is not usually the highest priority of our Father in Heaven.

We believe the Holy Ghost to be the great teacher. Some of the most beautiful phrases in scripture describe how the Spirit imparts wisdom to us: the Spirit "shall enlighten your mind," teach us "line upon line, precept upon precept," and lead us to know "the truth of all things." One of our greatest strengths as a Church is our lay administration. It demands that we are thrown into situations where we must work together for the spiritual welfare of those we serve, in high-stakes jobs with little to no training except for the guidance of the Spirit and a manual. It is remarkable that we do as well as we do.

But we have also been taught to seek out the resources that study and earthly scholarship have to offer when faced with life's challenges. Recently, Elder Jeffrey R. Holland emphasized how important it is to seek professional care, in addition to spiritual care, when managing unseen physical ailments such as depression. Figuring out interpersonal relations can sometimes feel as burdensome as a disease. We are assumed to have learned how to work with other people at home or in school assignments or on sports teams, but sometimes a guiding hand can be a welcome relief as we try to figure things out on our own. As with any kind of education, a new approach, a new technique, a new teacher can open doors to solutions that we never thought of before. Especially in areas that lack much formal training, such as the slightly intimidating and amorphous "be a good leader at church" job description, a structured approach can be particularly helpful.

I learned this lesson many years ago when my dear friend Saren Eyre Loosli and I realized as new mothers that there were no "professional development" workshops for mothers. We had both come from business industries where training and continuing education were integral parts of the corporate experience, but now as mothers we were expected to either self-teach or have a mother's intuition. Sure, there were books about what to expect, how to sleep train, and how to organize a kitchen, but practical advice for crafting the characters of our children seemed scarce. In many ways, the shaping of a child's character was shrouded in romanticism and mystery: we were supposed to provide a nurturing environment and unconditional love, and we felt like failures when that didn't just magically happen. How were nurturing and love supposed to play out in the day-to-day life of children's messes, busy schedules, conflicting personalities, jealousies, and emotional needs? To find the answers, we started a professional development retreat for mothers, which Saren has gone on to shape into the important and popular organization, Power of Moms.

In a similar vein, I see our work at Church shrouded in romanticism and mystery: let the Holy Spirit guide, as the Primary song says. With the Spirit, anything is possible. After all, we read of Nephi building a boat with no prior knowledge of how to accomplish such a feat. But we have other scriptural stories, like that of the Brother of Jared, that prove with just as much vigor that we sometimes need to work things out for ourselves: the Brother of Jared identifies a problem (i.e., there's no light in the barges) and asks God for help, but God sends him off to figure out a plan of his own. We are warned against taking "no thought save it was to ask me" (D&C 9:8). And Brigham Young said, "Whatever duty you are called to perform, take your minds with you, and apply them to what is to be done."

In this spirit, we can be grateful for an extra boost, a guiding hand to lead us to solutions we might not have thought of on our own, solutions we did not even know were possible. We seek priesthood blessings *and* medical help when faced with a physical problem. In the face of a spiritual challenge, such as ministering to and with women, we can take the same approach. I hope this book is that guiding hand.

* * *

In keeping with my desire to have this book benefit and strengthen the experiences of women in the Church, all of the profits from this book will go directly to the Mormon Women Project, a 501(c)3 organization I founded in 2010 as a continually expanding digital library of interviews with Mormon women from around the world. The Mormon Women Project can be found at www.mormonwomen.com. In addition, the conversations and ideas generated by this book can be communally shared at www.womenatchurch.com or by using #womenatchurch in social media postings. This book is not meant to be the end of the discussion, but a participant in an ongoing dialogue that transcends gender, longevity in the Church, and political or social leanings; instead this book focuses solely on our commonality under Christ. Please visit the website or use social media to share your own experiences and thoughts on women at church.

PART I
IDENTIFYING THE DIVIDE

PART I

Chapter One

Misbegotten Males

"Without the input of women, humanity sees with only one eye, hears with only one ear and thinks with only one half of the human mind."
Sister Joan Chittister, *National Catholic Reporter,*
December 11, 2013

One night in 2009, I lay in bed awake with an idea that I couldn't shake: I needed to tell Mormon women's stories. My six-month-old baby slept in the next room, her two older sisters down the hall; cars sped past our ground-floor Brooklyn apartment even in the dead of night. I had returned to my hometown of New York City after years away in San Francisco and Boston. I was tired of new acquaintances reacting with surprise that I could be an educated city-dweller and a Mormon woman too. After several years of being home with babies, I craved work that reconnected me with my office career. And in an instinctive, inspired way, I knew that telling Mormon women's stories was my calling.

Years before I actually heard it, I believed the pithy phrase by Marie Wilson from the White House Project: "You can't be what you can't see." I believed it because I had had examples of remarkable women in my youth and seeing how they engaged with the world around them helped me craft my own identity. I had seen what I wanted to be. They were women at Church: the mother of seven in a New York City apartment, the Wall Street banker, the ballet dancer, the Hebrew-speaking Seminary teacher. They were the women at my all-girls school: the English teacher who helped me find myself in Shakespeare, the history teacher who had taught for forty years. They were the women in my family: my single mother who handled her roles as an internationally admired opera singer and hostess to every missionary who came through our ward with equal finesse.

That night I lay awake, energized by the idea of sharing Mormon women's stories, I realized the magnitude of the gift I had been given:

women's voices had been the foundational paving stones of my spiritual, academic, familial, and professional paths. I could not imagine a world without female exemplars. I had also learned from painful experience with friends that this range and depth of female exemplars is uncommon for most Mormon women and that some women feel invisible or unappreciated at Church because they fall outside the norm. The next morning, I reached into my network of Mormon women, invited them to share their trials, professions, family lives, philosophies, and dreams, and the Mormon Women Project was born. We have since interviewed almost 250 Mormon women from around the world and added their voices to the continually growing digital library of interviews.

A world without women's voices has not always felt incomplete. For most of recorded time, most women have functioned in critical yet private spheres, away from the central stage of human civilizations' comings and goings. Women's voices, women exemplars, and female contributors to the public stage are a mere fraction of recorded history. Entire nations have been documented with only the most cursory mention of half of the population. We need go no further than our own scriptures for examples of nations rising and falling with women's voices barely registering. The men of God we trust to deliver truth to our age—editors such as Mormon, Moroni, and Nephi—considered their records complete with a mere handful of women making the cut. How could this be? How could respected theologian and philosopher Thomas Aquinas deem women not critical contributors in their own right but merely "misbegotten males"? For thousands of years, that's the way it was.

But it is not that way now. If we position the beginning of women's improved representation in the world to Mary Wollstonecraft's 1792 treatise *A Vindication of the Rights of Woman* (which may be considered generous since most strides really didn't take root until well into the nineteenth century), a mere 3.7 percent of the world's recorded six thousand-year history has been concerned with the development of women's full potential. With blinding speed, the lot of women in progressive nations has changed dramatically for the better: our voices are now heard at unprecedented levels of influence, our freedoms are unmatched in history, our ability and right to pursue our passions, talents, and potential are at their greatest height ever.

If we narrow that 3.7 percent of history even further, we can magnify the changes in the past fifty years alone. In 1962 in the United States, it was legal for a man to kill his wife if he discovered her cheating on him; it was legal to deny the most qualified candidate a job because she was a woman; women made 60 percent of what men earned; husbands were only arrested for domestic violence if the wife's injuries required more than a certain number of stitches; schools did not allow girls to raise or lower the American flag; women who exhibited "the housewife syndrome," or any degree of discontent with life as a homemaker, were given tranquilizers ("mother's little helper"), diagnosed as "paranoid," and, in extreme cases, committed to mental hospitals. Happily, significant progress has been made over the past fifty years in our recognition that women are people too.

There is tremendous work yet to do. For instance, the United Nations Population Fund shows that in 2005 more than 163 million women were missing from Asia's population, whether through sex-selective abortion, infanticide, or other means. And this is just the tip of an iceberg of disheartening statistics. Women who have enjoyed the fruits of 222 years of female advancements cannot yet feel at peace with the condition of women in our global community today.

The challenges of our age come not only from what there is left to do. Some of our challenges come from keeping up with this rapid pace of change: women's experiences are not only changing from century to century but from generation to generation, decade to decade. People and institutions who came of age with one cultural understanding of women find themselves rushed along to a more contemporary first-world vision, making them the subject of scorn or disillusion when they don't rise up unfettered to meet the current generation where it is.

As members of The Church of Jesus Christ of Latter-day Saints, we are part of an institution that treasures wisdom and practices from all six thousand years of our scriptural history, but we also believe that the Restoration of the gospel under Joseph Smith in 1830 ushered in the monumental achievements in society, technology, and culture that we enjoy today. Indeed, it seems no coincidence that Joseph Smith's turning of the key to the women of the first Relief Society coincides with the flood of improvements for women in the United States as well as many countries abroad. As one of many who have noted the correspondence of the Relief Society's founding with the improvement of women's lives globally, Apostle Orson F. Whitney said that the "lifting of the women of Zion . . . was the beginning of a work for the elevation of womankind throughout the world. . . . From what has since taken place we are justified in believing that the words were big with fate. . . . The spirit of women's work [is] . . . one of those sunbursts of light that proclaim the dawning of a new dispensation." And yet as Mormons today, we are still committed to a governmental structure that is exclusively male, while most mainline Protestant denominations at least in the United States have moved away from gender restrictions in their teachings and practices.

We are tasked, then, with holding in our hands seemingly contradictory truths at every turn: how do we respect the traditions, practices, and truths of our earliest progenitors, while holding sacred the rebel explosion of the Restoration? The coexistence of these kinds of paradoxes is at the very foundations of our religious experiences: How do we reconcile the eternal search for knowledge with the sincere claim that we "know" the Church is true? How do we acknowledge God's hand moving among scriptural peoples when so many of their actions hinged on violence we despise? We are today tasked with confronting similar tensions specifically in regard to women: How do we honor the prophets, writers, and editors of our scriptures while holding at the same time a concern that half of their populations are silent? How do we reconcile millennia of male-centric priesthood while also having faith in our doctrine of eternal gender equality and Restoration-born improvements for women?

I feel peace in the words of Joseph Smith: "By proving contraries, truth is made manifest." The truth is found not in sweeping these tensions under a rug or bundling them into tidy packages of platitudes; it is in wrestling with them outright. With regard to women, we have members and leaders in the Church right now who span a wide range of experiences, philosophies, and cultural expectations, because the experiences, philosophies, and cultural expectations of women over the past hundred years have been varied and continue to migrate. Our wrestle today is to honor the past, rejoice in our present, and prepare for the future of our women in a way that is "of one heart and one mind." We must hold sacred the legacy we have been handed by the prophets and apostles before us, all the while embracing fully the miraculous emancipation of women from millennia of silence. How we do this, how we wrestle this tension, is a true test of our spiritual maturity.

I am suspect of tidy history and squeaky clean people. I believe Jesus Christ was perfect—but not because He never got mad or always made everyone feel good. He didn't. He was perfect because He was the most grown up grown-up who has ever lived. His responses to people and situations were consistently mature, principled, and selfless. In this way, He is our best model for any conversation each of us might have about women in the Church.

Chapter Two

A Brief History of the Conversation about Women

"Tremendous changes . . . have taken place in the social, economic, industrial, and educational life of most countries in the world since Relief Society was founded. And I don't think any change in the world has been more significant than the change in the status of women. At the time the Relief Society was founded, a woman's world was her home, her family, and perhaps a little community service. Today a woman's world is as broad as the universe. There's scarcely an area of human endeavor that a woman cannot enter if she has the will and preparation to do so."

Belle Smith Spafford, Relief Society General President,
"Reaching Every Facet of a Woman's Life: A Conversation with
Belle S. Spafford, Relief Society General President,"
Ensign, June 1974

From the earliest days of the Church's history, relationships between men and women have provided the backdrop for some of our greatest doctrinal revelations as well as some of our most poignant growing pains. Discussions in this space are not new. And collaboration between men and women to do good has been a hallmark of our history from the beginning. For example, the organization of the Relief Society on March 17, 1842, was the result of collaborative revelation between Joseph Smith and women such as Margaret Cook, Sarah Kimball, Eliza R. Snow, and others who had been wrestling with how to meet the needs of the Nauvoo community. The constructive three-way collaboration between the women, the prophet, and the Lord resulted in a women's organization that was the first of its kind in the modern world and still thrives today. As part of the Relief Society's organization, the Prophet Joseph Smith offered divine instruction to the Relief Society in a series of sermons. That instruction has opened spiritual doors to women for over 150 years, giving them a vision of themselves as "elect" women, opportunities to serve and lead, and a call to minister to each other under divine mandate.

We also know from the minutes of those meetings that even at this early date there were already questions about whether or not "female laying on of hands" was a "sin." The Prophet answered this question on more than one occasion, saying at one point that "it is no sin for any body to do it that has faith," and yet the practice became a point of inquiry and sometimes contention for almost a hundred years. As late as 1884, Eliza R. Snow declared, "Any and all sisters who honor their holy endowments, not only have the right, but should feel it a duty, whenever called upon to administer to our sisters in these ordinances, which God has graciously committed to His daughters as well as to His sons." But in 1901, Louisa "Lula" Greene Richards wrote a terse letter to President Lorenzo Snow expressing the confusion of the women of her day regarding the mixed messages that were circulating regarding female laying on of hands: "[If laying on of hands is not permitted], then myself and thousands of other members of the Church have been misinstructed and are laboring under a very serious mistake, which certainly should be authoritatively corrected." Confusion around the practice continued until a 1936 letter from President Joseph Fielding Smith to Belle S. Spafford, then Relief Society general president, officially ended female blessings, saying, "While the authorities of the Church have ruled that it is permissible, under certain conditions and with the approval of the priesthood, for sisters to wash and anoint other sisters, yet they feel that it is far better for us to follow the plan the Lord has given us and send for the Elders of the Church to come and administer to the sick and afflicted." Interestingly, we know that documented cases of anointings and blessings before childbirth continued at least into the 1940s in some places.

I use female blessings as one small example of how gender responsibilities and rights have permeated discussions of Church governance and practice since our earliest days. Male and female Church leaders discussed and debated female blessings for almost one hundred years! Far weightier than the issue of female blessings, however, was that of polygamy. The doctrine and practice created ongoing tension between men and women and defined much of the Mormon experience in the nineteenth century. Gender relations are in the very soil the Church grew from.

At the beginning of the twentieth century, the world wars shaped the culture of the Church as they did most of American culture, romanticizing the image of a warm hearth for battle-weary soldiers to come home to and resulting in a robust domestic focus. In fact, in the 1950s the Church "had become closer to mainstream American life than probably any period in history, before or since." A famous photo of the Mormon Tabernacle Choir taken in July 1962 shows the choir positioned in front of Mount Rushmore, prepared to sing on an international satellite television program as the ideal representation of mainstream American culture. This was six months before Betty Friedan's *The Feminine Mystique* was published, turning that America upside down.

While adopting Correlation to accommodate a growing, worldwide Church, Latter-day Saints in the 1960s and '70s weathered cultural wars that forced us to leave behind the comfortable acceptance of the 1950s. The tensions of this era birthed rich and sometimes controversial outlets for gender scholarship and conversations. *Exponent II*, a literary journal patterned after the *Woman's Exponent* originally founded in 1872, was launched in 1974 by a group of women in Boston. Since the *Relief Society Magazine* had been shuttered four years earlier, there was no longer an official distribution medium for Mormon women's voices.

Vigorous debate surrounded the ratification of the Equal Rights Amendment (ERA) in the 1970s as well. Citing the heroic suffrage work of the physician grandmother who delivered her, Relief Society general president Barbara Smith stated in 1974, "My grandmother sought her right to be . . . a professional woman, a practicing physician, in a time when it was not only very unusual here, but almost impossible for a woman to be so educated. She was, at the time she received her medical degree, a mother of three children." However, after clarifying her support for equities in property rights, job benefits, inheritance laws, and other gender hot points, President Smith concluded by saying, "It is my considered judgment that the Equal Rights Amendment is not the way. . . . Once it is passed, the enforcement will demand an undeviating approach which will create endless problems for an already troubled society."

President Smith's considerations were overshadowed in the subsequent excommunication of Sonia Johnson, a Mormon woman who vocally supported the ERA; thus, any possibility for measured conversation about alternative solutions for women died in 1975 when the Utah convention of the International Women's Year commission became a battleground for political issues. Gender again came to the forefront of the Mormon cultural conversation (and drew national attention) in 1993 when several Church members were excommunicated or disfellowshipped for publishing scholarship exploring women's roles and identities both here on earth and in the eternities. More recently, national attention has again been drawn as the Ordain Women movement publicly requested that Church leaders seek a revelation allowing for the ordination of women to the priesthood; the group's founder, Kate Kelly, was excommunicated in June 2014.

I mention this brief history in an attempt to underscore the loaded backdrop against which any gender conversation takes place today. Discussions around how women should contribute to Church administration, how men and women should work together in the domestic sphere, and what role women should play in the public sphere are woven into every element of our history. And I have not even attempted to survey doctrines surrounding priesthood, Heavenly Mother, Eve and the Fall, or motherhood. It is naïve and unwise to come into this discussion today believing that the men and women before us have blindly followed an undeviating allegiance to a consistent ideal and that we are the first to ever draw attention to gender issues. We should not deny or disregard the impassioned and sometimes turbulent flow of gender discussions over the past two hundred years.

What does make the conversations today different from conversations of those that came before us, of course, is the reach and speed of communication facilitated by the Internet. Prior to its democratizing effects, the lay membership of the Church was not able to as easily or universally participate in discussions. A bridge now exists between geographical locations, allowing the ideas to flow across ward and stake boundaries more freely, as well as between hierarchical layers of leadership. The opening of both of those borders means that we all, as members of the Church community, have lived experiences that are not only valid but can be shared with others. And we bring those lived experiences to the Internet with a passion.

Unlike some other institutions that have also had to adapt to the mainstream adoption of the Internet over the past twenty years, a few characteristics set our people apart as particularly vigorous users of the tool. We are a lay ministry and thus trained from an early age to be particularly active in shaping our worship experience. Sunday's Church experience is only as good as we make it. We also interact daily with our faith—not that we necessarily have more of it than other people but that it is a practical, daily faith that requires us to be constantly gauging, questioning, affirming its presence. Also, we must include the fact that we have an open canon and a legacy of men and women just like us asking hard questions and getting revolutionary answers. We are a people who own not only our faith but also our practice of it and the doctrine supporting it. These are glorious characteristics, reflecting truths and divine structures that exist within Mormonism.

In addition to our natural cultural tendencies, our prophets and apostles have explicitly encouraged us to be active online. In a 2008 talk, Elder Ballard encouraged members of the Church to get online, and the result was a massive movement toward digital expressions of faith. "Today we have a modern equivalent of the printing press in the Internet," Elder Ballard said. "The Internet allows everyone to be a publisher, to have his or her voice heard, and it is revolutionizing society." Some credit this talk with the boom of the Mormon mommy blog phenomenon, as a small but important handful of our women began expressing their faith publicly without necessarily venturing out of the domestic sphere. As if providing proof of the institutional support around these online initiatives, the *Church News* featured an article in January 2014 with instructions on "How to Create Your Own LDS Blog." Earlier this year, *The Atlantic* magazine expressed surprise that our missionary force has been tasked with using Facebook so liberally. "Instead of second-hand nostalgia for the past," the author writes, "I found some rare faith in the future."

These same characteristics and practices that make us such prime participants in Internet dialogue also can be our deepest pitfalls. We feel so empowered by our lay ministerial responsibility that we err on overstepping our bounds. Our highly personal daily faith practices sometimes prompt us to feel overly protective of the way we practice. We feel an ownership and spiritual connection to the way we practice our faith, and we feel threatened when others practice differently, as if a different practice devalues what works for us individually. And since an open canon means our prophet can receive divine guidance to know what is right for the whole Church, we members sometimes think it also means the divine guidance we each receive through personal revelation should apply to the whole Church too. This balance between prophetic revelation and personal revelation is tricky. For part of the twentieth century, some sincerely believed that "when the prophet speaks, the thinking is done"—even though President George Albert Smith sought to dispel this belief after the phrase had become popular, writing, "Even to imply that members of the Church are not to do their own thinking is grossly to misrepresent the true ideal of the Church."

It feels that there has been a heightened pitch and urgency to the dialogue around gender that has been bubbling since our Church's earliest days. The major shift, I feel, is that the Internet is no longer used just to discuss ideas and experiences; it has become a tool for crowd-sourced action. The first crowd-sourced activity that I became aware of happened in February 2012, when bloggers at *By Common Consent* and *Feminist Mormon Housewives* brought attention to the fact that some temples were not allowing menstruating girls and women to participate in baptisms for the dead; this was a policy that had been phasing out since the late 1980s but was still being enforced sporadically in certain temples. Perhaps I noticed this effort in particular because a foundational memory in my own young faith was when I fasted and prayed that I would be able to perform baptisms at an upcoming temple trip, despite having my period at the time. I distinctly remember falling to the floor in gratitude to the Lord when I received a call from my bishop saying the restriction had been waived at my ward's petition, and I would be able to participate. While I did and still do see the experience as an answer to prayer, it frustrated me that in 2012, twenty-five years after my own experience, Mormon women were still being stigmatized for menstruating.

Describing their effort as "cheerful Mormon helpfulness to ensure that the temple experiences of young women, new female converts, or any woman who wishes to participate in the sacred ordinances—especially baptism for the dead—are smooth and positive," these bloggers confirmed that the decision to allow menstruating girls and women to participate was at the discretion of the individual temple presidents. They recruited readers to call individual temples, find out if the restriction was still in place, and fill out a public Google doc, documenting their findings. From the sixty-eight temples called and surveyed, fourteen (22.5%) had a complete ban on menstruating women and five others actively discouraged menstruating women, even if they were wearing tampons (a total of 30%). The remaining forty-three put no restrictions on menstruating women.

The surveyors concluded, "Even among the temples with official inclusionary policies it was still clear that someone could run into resistance or untrained temple workers etc. This helps explain why there is such a variation in people's experiences. Many women have never run into a problem while others' experiences have been in temples where exclusion was the norm. . . . Women and men . . . should know that if they run into resistance in their temple, they are in a strong position to politely push back. It would still be a good idea to call ahead if you are taking a youth group just so there are no unpleasant surprises."

Similar grassroots actions—meaning actions that gained momentum through the social media promotions of an online, lay member audience—have shaped much of the gender conversation since 2012. Rather than describing each, I will summarize the most significant markers in our recent history.

- A group of women organized online to wear pants to church on a designated day, December 16, 2012, in a show of individuality in the face of cultural expectations. Wear Pants to Church Day was repeated in December 2013.

- The Let Women Pray movement of early 2013 drew attention to the fact that a woman had never prayed in general conference. A Facebook page invited visitors "to join us in letter-writing, appealing to the leadership of The Church of Jesus Christ of Latter-day Saints to invite a woman to pray in the April 2013 General Conference." Over 1,600 letters were sent to selected general authorities and female leaders.

- An online gallery by photographer Katrina Barker Anderson featuring nude portraits of Mormon women, entitled *Mormon Women Bare*, received national media attention as part of a widespread conversation about the Church's definition of and emphasis on modesty.

- The Ordain Women movement launched a website featuring profiles of Church members advocating women's ordination to the priesthood. The group asked for tickets to attend the priesthood session of the October 2013 general conference "as a demonstration of our eagerness for the blessings and responsibilities of the priesthood." They were denied entrance to the meeting. The group repeated the action in April 2013 and were denied again. The group's founder, Kate Kelly, was excommunicated in June 2014.

The "Temple 'Issue' Report" and the Wear Pants to Church Day empowered individual women to privately push back on practices they felt limited their potential for spiritual expression. The Let Women Pray effort moved beyond the informative and individual and unabashedly moved into the realm of advocating for change at levels beyond the individual's control. All three, however, found common ground in targeting practices that were not grounded in doctrine or *Handbook* rules. (The goals and methods of Ordain Women moved beyond the *Handbook,* putting that effort into a distinct category.) The underlying assumption in these three efforts was that easily adapted practices can have an important impact on how listened to, respected, and comfortable women feel in communal Church settings.

But it is not just grassroots efforts that have gained momentum over the past couple of years. Changes on the general level around women's visibility and participation have progressed at unprecedented speed. The most significant change came in October 2012, when President Monson announced that girls could go on missions at age nineteen, instead of the traditional twenty-one. The Young Women received a new and improved curriculum better suited for contemporary teaching. A worldwide leadership training meeting modeled more inclusive collaboration between male and female leaders. Sister Jean A. Stevens, first counselor in the Primary general presidency, prayed in the Saturday morning session of April 2013 general conference, making her the first woman to pray at conference. Missions introduced the newly created role of sister training leaders. A new lineup of Young Women board members reflected dedication to ethnic, cultural, and career diversity. The annual general Relief Society meeting and general Young Women meeting were replaced with a combined semiannual Women's Meeting for all women age eight and older. And photographic portraits of the Church's female general leaders were hung alongside those of the First Presidency and the Quorum of Twelve Apostles in the Conference Center in Salt Lake City. This was followed by photos of the female general officers appearing in the center spread of the May 2014 general conference edition of the *Ensign*, which had previously only featured male leaders.

I have no doubt that by the time this book is published and read, more examples could be added to both of these lists. In contrast to the developments of the past fifty years, not to mention the past several hundred years, policies and practices in the Church today are evolving quickly. Florence Nightingale perhaps summed up the urgency of our age when she said, "Jesus Christ raised women above the condition of mere slaves, mere ministers to the passions of the man, raised them by His sympathy, to be Ministers of God. He gave them moral activity. But the Age, the World, Humanity, must give them the means to exercise this moral activity, must give them intellectual cultivation, spheres of action." As the conversations unfold, we as a lay ministry have the responsibility and opportunity to explore those spheres of action for women today. Some of us are thinking about what it means to be a Mormon woman for the very first time, either in a process of self-reflection or by putting ourselves in a Mormon woman's shoes. Our history—in the past, yes, but also as it unfolds in real time before our eyes—challenges us to engage in the conversation and remain tethered to each other through our dedication to our heavenly family.

Chapter Three

Why Should I Be Concerned about How Women Feel at Church?

"We are unified in building the kingdom of God and in the covenants which we have made, no matter what our circumstances. . . . If there are barriers, it is because we ourselves have created them. We must stop concentrating on our differences and look for what we have in common; then we can begin to realize our greatest potential and achieve the greatest good in this world."

Bonnie L. Oscarson, Young Women General President,
"Oh, How We Need Each Other,"
General Women's Meeting, April 2014

When I was in ninth grade, my class studied the Bible "as literature." The educational belief was that any well-rounded liberal arts education had to understand the foundational stories of our civilization, and because I attended a private school, we could study the Bible in this way. I have always remembered a pop quiz my teacher gave after our initial readings from Genesis: the top of the page read, "Are you your sister's keeper?" which was followed by blank space. (Since I went to an all-girls school, such license was intuitive.)

At the time, I remember hesitating. Cain is responding snidely when he answers the Lord's question "Where is Abel thy brother?" with the famous line, "Am I my brother's keeper?" He seems to be implying it is absurd for him to keep track of his brother's location at all times. To me, then, it seemed reasonable to suppose that we don't need to be (and can't be) responsible for our brothers' and sisters' whereabouts every moment of every day. Keeping tabs would be exhausting, fruitless, and plain weird. In addition to the practical limitations of being a "keeper," I understood the spiritual implications of the dialogue too, and I hesitated because I wanted to distance myself from any accountability I might have for others' mistakes. I did not want to acknowledge that I have responsibilities for others' pain.

Since that time, I have come to believe that our spiritual accountability for each other is much greater than I supposed in ninth grade. ("I would be my brother's keeper; I would learn the healer's art. . . . Lord, I would follow thee," comes to mind now.) Perhaps the weight of accountability for others has been magnified in my life because I am now the mother of small children. Or maybe I now feel the weight because I have developed many more close relationships than I had in ninth grade. Perhaps I just understand the gospel better; I now see us each working as God's hands, lifting each other up. In the end, the closest thing we can do to emulating Christ on this earth is to be there for each other. We have a scriptural obligation to "mourn with those who mourn, comfort those who stand in need of comfort" (Mosiah 18:8–10). We may go so far as to say accountability is a mandate from our Father in Heaven to be His hands in the lives of our spiritual brothers and sisters.

My children are now old enough for me to send my eight-year-old out with my eleven-year-old—into the store or to a summer camp—with instructions for the older sister to look out for the younger one. As an only child, I think I am particularly susceptible to the image of my daughters being there for each other. Few things bring me greater joy than when they display their loyalty to each other: holding hands while walking, comforting each other when hurt, and sticking up for each other with words on the playground. The power of sisterhood is palpable in my home. Of course they fight like crazy too, but we talk in our house about feeling "safe" around each other, "working as a team," and "being loyal to sisters" first and foremost.

In his snide response to the Lord, Cain was, in the style of Satan, manipulating a great truth into appearing as a lie. The truth is that we are responsible for each other. We are a spiritual family. We care for and "keep" each other in the same way family members do. But Cain twists this truth to appear ugly and unreasonable, grounded in physical impracticality rather than spiritual transcendence: "Are you really asking me," he seems to be challenging the Lord, "to be responsible for my brother like he is a pet dog I have on a leash, knowing at all times where he is?" Just as parents cannot always know where children are, and siblings must function independent of one another, Cain cannot know where his brother is at all times; thus he mocks the Lord, dismissing the greater truth implicit in the Lord's question.

Let us not, then, dismiss our accountability for our sisters as Cain dismissed his accountability for his brother. When their potential is not explored, we are all responsible. When their impact is not magnified, we are all responsible. When they feel marginalized or underutilized or unappreciated, we are all responsible. When they are not brought to Christ, we are all responsible.

Disunity vs. Diversity

As brothers and sisters accountable for each other, we should not confuse diversity with disunity. Disunity is a destructive factionalizing that occurs when pride is put before loyalty. The scriptures are replete with warnings against a house divided against itself: "Be one; and if ye are not one ye are not mine" (D&C 38:27). And Paul commands, "Be of one mind" (2 Cor. 13:11). "Only let your conversation be as it becometh the gospel of Christ . . . that ye stand fast in one spirit, with one mind striving together for the faith of the gospel" (Philip. 1:27). Our battle against disunity shows in our cultural and doctrinal dedication to obedience, a principle that provides cover against many forms of factionalizing and exhibits dedication to a single point of focus.

Diversity, however, is also a divine principle at work in the creation of the world, which was made beautiful through the variety of life that was placed here. Can we doubt our God's commitment to diversity when every person on earth has possessed unique genetic composition? Elder Dieter F. Uchtdorf recently alluded to the difference between diversity and disunity in the general priesthood meeting of the April 2013 general conference: "Sometimes we confuse differences in personality with sin. We can even make the mistake of thinking that because someone is different from us, it must mean they are not pleasing to God. This line of thinking leads some to believe that the Church wants to create every member from a single mold—that each one should look, feel, think, and behave like every other. This would contradict the genius of God, who created every man different from his brother, every son different from his father. Even identical twins are not identical in their personalities and spiritual identities."

Diversity means that difference does not have to breed disunity. In the spiritual realm, diversity is the glorious equation of difference coupled with loyalty and commitment. We can be accountable for someone without having to insist they be the same. Diversity is the freedom to answer another's needs in a way that is different from our own. It allows us to bring more of God's children under the umbrella of eternal truths.

Balancing unity and diversity is one of those "contraries" that we must prove as stewards of others. In this conversation about women in Church governance, our challenge is to balance the demands of unity with the opportunity to address diverse needs in unique ways. *Handbook 2* outlines those things that are needed to maintain unity. But beyond that, diverse applications of principles are not just tolerated, they are encouraged. In the 2012 edition of *Handbook 2*, section 17 is entitled "Uniformity and Adaptation" and prefaced with these words: "Members of the Church live in a wide variety of political, social, and economic conditions. Wards and branches also vary in size and leadership resources. These conditions may require local leaders to adapt some Church programs." A subsection on Uniformity outlines how to keep doctrine and programs pure; a subsection on Adaptations discusses leaders' "discretion" to consider changes. Sometimes in our commitment to unity, we don't stretch ourselves to see beyond traditional practices. But our accountability to our women demands that we think creatively and compassionately about their needs, even when they are different from our own.

Consider this plea from Elder M. Russell Ballard as he outlines the most effective methods of local Church administration: "It is increasingly imperative to empower leaders of stakes, wards, and homes to do whatever it takes, in harmony with gospel principles, to bring people to Christ. Every person and situation is unique in some way. While principles are universally applicable, practices are not. As every parent knows who has tried to rear the second child exactly like the first, what works in one situation may fail in another."

In my own home, I can relate to Elder Ballard's metaphor perfectly: I have one child who needs to be given more time to relax, more space to make mistakes, more encouragement to "let her hair down," and I have another daughter who must be prodded to do her homework, to be productive and focused. I feel like a schizophrenic parent sometimes when opposite statements, policies, and rules apply to different children. But parents know this kind of tailoring—this innovation, this creative adaptation to the needs of each child—is absolutely crucial to the healthy development of each child.

In his book *The Power of Everyday Missionaries*, Harvard business professor and former area seventy Clayton Christensen goes so far as to say we must all be "entrepreneurs in Zion." In speaking about a number of ward leaders who implemented innovative missionary tactics in their areas, Christensen concludes,

[The leaders] rightly assumed that the power was in *their* hands to bring to pass much righteousness. Here is their scriptural license: "For behold, it is not meet that I should command in all things; for he that is compelled in all things, the same is a slothful and not a wise servant; wherefore he receiveth no reward. Verily I say, men should be anxiously engaged in a good cause, and do many things of their own free will, and bring to pass much righteousness; For the power is in them, wherein they are agents unto themselves. And inasmuch as men do good they shall in nowise lose their reward. But he that doeth not anything until he is commanded, and receiveth a commandment with doubtful heart, and keepeth it with slothfulness, the same is damned." (D&C 58:26–29)

Christensen continues,

A sense among some in the Church is that obedient Saints are those who follow the programs of the Church assiduously, and that innovation is a symptom of rebellion if it hasn't been "approved." [The "entrepreneurs in Zion"] followed the Spirit in an unscripted way. The programs of the Church are designed to leave room for a great deal of individual initiative and personal guidance. Indeed, an expiration date has not yet been appended to the last clause in the ninth Article of Faith (italics mine): "We believe all that God has revealed, all that He does now reveal, and *we believe that He will yet reveal many great and important things* pertaining to the Kingdom of God."

Elder Ballard and Professor Christensen offer visions of bold thinking and creative application of principles. Brigham Young weighs in too with his customary bravado:

Intelligence, to a certain extent, was bestowed both upon Saint and sinner, to use independently, aside from whether they have the law of the Priesthood or not, or whether they have ever heard of it or not. "I put into you intelligence," saith the Lord, "that you may know how to govern and control yourselves, and make yourselves comfortable and happy on the earth; and give unto you certain privileges to act upon as independently in your sphere as I do in the government of heaven."

Addressing the Concerns

What is our responsibility, then, to our women? It is to be accountable for their spiritual needs, although diverse and perhaps different from our own, and to do so with imagination, innovation, and uniquely tailored approaches. But despite experiences like my ninth-grade Bible class, it was only quite recently that I truly internalized the specific challenge we have to understand and address the concerns of women in the Church today.

In the summer of 2012, I was preparing to give a one-hour presentation at a FairMormon conference, to be held in August of that year. (At the time, the organization was known as FAIR: The Foundation for Apologetic Information and Research but has since changed its name. It is an organization made up of self-proclaimed apologists who are committed to writing and speaking in defense of the Church.) The Church's Public Affairs department had recommended me to the FairMormon organizers after I participated in a workshop on women and the Church that had been organized and moderated by the Public Affairs department. Despite having written personal essays for LDS-themed publications, and despite being particularly comfortable standing before an audience because of decades of solo piano performances, I was terrified. The FairMormon presentation was going to be the longest and most formal talk I had ever given. I spent those summer months trying on thesis after thesis, but nothing felt quite right. I was aware that my audience—highly traditionally minded—might not be entirely sympathetic to hearing about how we can better serve our sisters in the gospel. Stating that we have a problem can be perceived as challenging the divine origin and leadership of our religious institution, and it was important for me to not come across as critical or dismissive of the leaders I admire and revere. How was I to say something meaningful and meaty while not coming off critical? That occupied my prayers, fasts, and temple visits for months.

During that time, I was running some errands and had just gotten out of my car in a parking lot. My phone buzzed: a friend, knowing of my assignment, texted me with the link to a well-known female blogger's latest post. I casually clicked on the link and skimmed. It was a reprimand of "progressive" women for just not understanding doctrine well enough. If these women understood doctrine, the blogger explained, they would fall in line and not experience any of the pain they were claiming. I had read half a dozen others like it over the summer from other sources. I was hit with a force that literally knocked me to the side of a building, where

I leaned to catch my breath as tears clouded my eyes. "The pain is real!" I felt a voice knock against my ears. "How can we dismiss others' pain simply because we do not feel it ourselves?"

That day, I realized that merely establishing the validity of the pain was the first thing I needed to do in my talk. After that, my mental block was lifted and the FairMormon presentation flowed almost seamlessly.

The most disheartening comments I received after the talk (aside from the ones saying I was an apostate, which always made for a sunshiny day) were those that tried to diminish the impact of women's issues on Church membership. Statistics I had cited—the only statistics publicly available at the time that even attempted to quantify the magnitude of the problem—were discredited as being poorly executed or too small a sampling. Questioning the magnitude of the problem was, in my mind, the same as saying, "We don't want those women anyway. Why should we care if they're leaving?"

My invitation to feel empathy for women in the Church who struggle was not an invitation to share in their critiques or draw the same conclusions from their experiences. It was not an invitation to start chewing on the complaints we might have about our humanly flawed Church community. It was merely an effort to remind us as a people that we leave the ninety and nine to go after the one. We do that. We mourn with those who mourn, comfort those who stand in need of comfort. And we have members of the body of Christ who feel cut off, as a hand is cut off from the body. It is our divine mandate to be one, or we are not His, to be a Zion people. Isn't this enough for us to stop and pay attention, even if we have not felt the same disconnect in our own lives?

In the two years since that day, I have sensed an increased tolerance and genuine concern for the feelings of women who are plagued by what they perceive to be gender inequities at church. If a loved one is depressed, do we tell him to just get over it because *we* think everything in his life is fine? Happily, our modern public health sensibilities have made us aware that such a reaction is not just inappropriate but useless and completely irrelevant to the patient's experience. Why then is it appropriate for us to tell a woman expressing pain and frustration that she should just get over it because we aren't experiencing pain and frustration too? It is neither appropriate nor useful nor relevant to that woman's experience.

Some of our leaders are modeling this increased tolerance and genuine concern in their own public statements. For example, at the 2013 Church History Symposium, President Dieter F. Uchtdorf cautioned against dismissing another's lived experience. In describing existence as a tree, he said, "One of the weaknesses we have as mortals is to assume that our leaf is all there is. And you find this often in *other* people. But I think if we look in the mirror, we find this even in our own perceptions. It is that our experience encompasses everyone else's—that our truth is complete and universal." And later, "One of the traits we share as human beings is that we assume that our own experience is a true and proper base from which to view the rest of the world. For example: when we're healthy, we presume that those we meet are healthy and judge them by that standard. When we're sick, we're more likely to wonder if others are sick as well. It goes even to very trivial areas: when you drive a Ford, you see Fords on the road. We assume that the leaf of our existence defines the rest of the world."

Oftentimes we learn to respond to and work with someone who is suffering unquantifiable pain only when that someone is a person we love. That seems to be true regarding feeling empathy for struggling women. In the wake of the FairMormon talk, I received dozens of emails from fathers and husbands whose personal experiences had brought them face to face with the pain I was attempting to bring to light.

After describing the trajectory of his beloved daughter out of the Church, a faithful father concluded with this heartrending plea: "Please if you can, provide me some insight from a . . . believing woman's perspective that I can present to my wonderful daughter for consideration. What I understand the least is why God would intervene so profoundly in my life and not my daughter's."

Other emails began with variations of "The most important thing in my life is the spiritual, emotional, mental, and physical well-being of my wife and daughters." Another concluded with, "My wife experiences a great amount of pain with this issue, and I have felt so lost as to how to help her. Your talk has given me hope for our family."

Since August 2012, I have read and collected a range of personal accounts from women who have struggled with their female identity in the Church. I share them throughout this book, and several of them here in this chapter. My purpose in doing so is not to depress any of us, although a little sobriety on this subject will hopefully translate to greater empathy. Neither is my intent to draw attention to the particular concerns of these women, although understanding specific pain points will help us address needs more directly. I do hope with these stories that each of us can put ourselves in the shoes of these women, or perhaps in the shoes of the husbands and fathers and sons who love them. I hope that "I've never felt that way" is no longer an acceptable excuse for not caring.

- "I grew up in Utah, and was always fully active—graduated from BYU, served a mission in Brazil, married in the temple. The whole time, I was 100% orthodox and obedient, but secretly I was plagued by doubts, mostly about gender. I felt persistently less-than as a woman in the church. When I went to the temple, I felt deep shame as a woman. I would read the scriptures and cry because I could not find myself there. On my mission, I often felt patronized and condescended to, knowing I was an effective missionary but always being subordinate to men who were younger than me and had not studied the gospel as rigorously as I had."

- "Ultimately my faith loss stems from the oppression of women in the church. Our practices do not match our rhetoric or our historical practices. Our teaching of 'eternal salvation through proper gender roles' makes me physically ill. In our home we teach true equality and the idea that my children are learning these outdated views makes it hard for me to let them attend church despite feeling that I need to be there to help end the problem. This is a problem I struggle with every single Sunday without exception."

- "When I was 26, married for 6 years and expecting my third child, I had a discussion with my husband about a topic I can no longer remember. I do remember it was church related and I was trying to make a point about women. I asked him, 'Which women in the Church do you see as your spiritual leaders?' When he paused, I realized that he didn't even see his mother as a spiritual example to him (and he admires his mother immensely). Suddenly I saw the conference *Ensign* and the centerfold filled with pictures of our male church leaders and I felt sick inside. Women in our church are not seen as spiritual leaders, we are hidden.

  "When I found [other Mormon women online], I was relieved to realize I wasn't the only one who felt that women were a shadow in the church. It was hard for me when I learned that Relief Society is now an empty shell compared to what it used to be—a strong independent organization of women who write their own lessons, manage their own money, and work creatively for the good of community: for the relief of society.

"The more I learned, the more disturbed I became and the more I began to question the church's truth claims and even the existence of God. I still struggle to understand the inequality between the sexes, and I question the patriarchal structure that claims its authority from God. The way I see it, either God does not support patriarchy and thus does not support Mormonism, or He does, and I don't want anything to do with that god.

"I've also struggled to find and connect with a divine feminine, which I want to believe in. It's not something I'm familiar with, so it's taken me a long time to be comfortable with Her as a being of power and authority."

- "Put simply, I just do not believe that patriarchy is divinely inspired. For a church that teaches the existence of a Heavenly Mother, we ironically do not teach that women are equal to men. I'm tired of all the fallacies. I'm tired of hearing people say that women are more naturally gifted at nurturing than men. (I believe the sexes are different in temperament, but I'm a firm believer that nurturing can be taught, just like assertiveness in the workplace can be taught.) I'm completely fed up with the obsessive emphasis on girls' modesty. I'm offended by the notion of church courts, particularly for offenses such as 'heresy,' and think they ought to be abolished. At the very least, women ought to serve on them. I'm tired of the excuses I hear for not ordaining women, such as, 'We already do all the work anyway. I don't want the added responsibility.' To me, that is simply learned subservience. I have disliked the temple ever since my first endowment—Eve has almost no lines and zero after leaving Eden."

- "I don't see how they can say men and women are equal in the Church. Men have all the power and authority. My twelve-year-old son gets the priesthood and all of a sudden he's got more power and authority than me! And how many women do you see on the stand in general conference? But you see row after row of men. God is all concerned about men, not about women. Just think about the scriptures: hardly any women show up. God is always talking about his sons. We're all supposed to be like the Father, like Jesus. But the Father and Jesus are men; I'm a woman! I can't be a son of God; I can't be a Father or an Elder Brother.

"They say we have a Mother in Heaven, but she's top secret. No one knows anything about her and it's subversive to even mention her.

So who's supposed to be my role model? How can I be like a person I know nothing about? I don't know. Maybe they don't tell us about her because there's nothing much to tell. You know, my son will be anointed to be a king and priest to the most high God. . . . I get to be a queen and priestess to my husband. So is my husband my God, then? I don't get to serve God; only his sons do? The patriarchal order—doesn't that just mean 'men rule forever'? Doesn't God love me, too? If I had a daughter, I wouldn't make her feel like such a second-class citizen. I wouldn't make her feel like I feel right now."

"If We Can't Fix It, It Ain't Broke"

While collecting these stories, I have also noted how many ways we can say "I've never felt that way so I don't care." In a 2013 *Deseret News* article about the possibility of a woman saying a prayer in the upcoming general conference, the comments reveal the range of ways we can discount a person's passion about female identity in the Church. Phrases include:

"Get a life."

"It doesn't matter."

"If these women don't like the way the church is run, they should just leave."

"A meaningless change."

"If it bothers you, it's your problem."

"People who have the 'issue' need to do some more soul searching."

"Who cares?"

"Much ado about nothing."

"PC garbage."

Some people claimed that being "gender blind" is what made them *not* care about the fact that a woman hasn't ever been seen leading the Church in prayer.

The dismissiveness of the comments suggests that if an imbalance in female representation is unnoticed, the imbalance doesn't matter. The mental conversation seems to be, "This is such a small issue that people who are bothered by it don't know what is really important, and the fault lies in them not being able to see the big picture." The small things are dispensable in the face of the larger priorities.

But for those who do notice imbalances and are affected by them, the mental conversation goes differently: "This is a small thing, and I am bothered by it because the big picture rests on the building blocks of small things. Rectifying small things creates a stronger foundation for the big things to rest on." One commenter described these small things as "easily correctible minutia": "I have no problem with women praying in general conference or anywhere. What does bother me is all the indifferent and often judgmental responses to those who are genuinely pained by the easily correctable minutia. Have these indifferent and judgmental people forgotten the core of the gospel, charity? Why are so many averse to resolving easily corrected issues that will result in a greater sense of self-worth and well-being for others, while doing absolutely no harm to anyone?" In gaining empathy for the efforts of crowdsourcing efforts or private struggles, I think this commenter's final question is the key for each of us: Why do we push against "resolving easily corrected issues that will result in a greater sense of self-worth and well-being for others while doing absolutely no harm to anyone?"

Scholar Melissa Inouye has commented on our proclivity to dismiss "easily corrected minutia" by referencing a sign she saw at a car repair shop in Hong Kong where she lives: "IF WE CAN'T FIX IT, IT AIN'T BROKE," the sign said. Inouye remarks:

> It is a peculiar feature of church culture that when someone proposes a practical change to how things are done within the Church, such as making church procedures more responsive to local cultural realities, or creating more opportunities for women to be involved in decision-making and pastoral care, such proposals for "reform" often run the risk of being called insubordinate, incompetent, or unfaithful.
>
> In other words, when a person uses common sense to identify problems in the Church and to propose practical solutions, he or she is often dismissed with an answer something like: "IF IT'S NOT ALREADY BEING FIXED, THEN IT AIN'T BROKE.". . . In many cases, the things that need to be fixed have less to do with human error than they have to do with the changing circumstances that arise from Mormonism's transformation from a small American religious movement into a global church. . . .
>
> Of course, the Church is not a democracy and the gospel is not a matter of majority rule. But anyone who knows even a little Church history knows that if anything's constant within the Church as an institution, it's change. (Not surprising for a church that believes in continuing revelation.) Past generations of Latter-day Saints, including not only prophets and apostles but also local leaders and members, have risen to real challenges and sought

practical solutions, exercising human initiative instead of sitting around waiting to be divinely compelled.

Change in the LDS Church is not a process of lobbying higher-ups, but of each person seeing what needs to be done and then doing it within his or her own sphere of influence. Day by day, our church institutions and communities can become better and better at perfecting the Saints, proclaiming the gospel, redeeming the dead, and helping the poor and needy. These are jobs for everyone, not just "the Brethren," "the Lord," or "someone else."

In conclusion, when we nail our wooden shingle over the church garage, let it read: IF IT AIN'T FIXED, WE CAN!

Anecdotal evidence suggests dismissing expressed pain is less and less acceptable. The online comments around Let Women Pray, for instance, were measurably milder than those surrounding Wear Pants to Church Day. (The initiator of that effort received death threats on her Facebook page and had to take the page down.) While Ordain Women members faced criticism both in 2013 and 2014, their April 2014 campaign to attend the general priesthood meeting provoked a strain of articles and blog posts online about the importance of "disagreeing agreeably." Although our public response may be improving, many still genuinely wonder: What is it about certain practices that cause some women so much pain that they walk away?

Chapter Four

Why Are Some Women in Pain?

"Every one of us has privileges and blessings, and every one of us has fears and trials. It seems bold to say, but common sense suggests that never before in the history of the world have women, including LDS women, been faced with greater complexity in their concerns."

Patricia T. Holland, Young Women General Presidency,
"One Thing Needful: Becoming Women of Greater Faith in Christ,"
Ensign, October 1987

To some of us, the answer to this chapter title's question might be obvious. To others, it might require a mental stretch to put ourselves in the shoes of someone who feels uncomfortable or even oppressed by her identity as a Mormon woman. Elder Dieter F. Uchtdorf rhetorically asked the difficult but important question in his October 2013 general conference address: "If the gospel is so wonderful, then why would anybody leave?"

To understand why some are struggling with their identity as Mormon women, we can look at six contributors:

1. Disconnect between lived experience and Church experience

2. The importance of diverse visual representation in modern culture

3. Misuse of counsels and Church structure

4. Rise of single sisters

5. Greater awareness of history

6. Disconnect between doctrine and practice of equality

Disconnect between Lived Experience and Church Experience

First, let's start with lived experience. As a woman in the United States today, I live with unprecedented opportunities to expand my knowledge, experiences, and contributions to my community. But even I remember firsts for women: I remember the excitement of watching Sally Ride and Christa McAuliffe, some of the first women in space when I was ten years old, and how exciting it was to me as a young girl to think women could penetrate even the world of space travel. My own daughter knows no such firsts. She has never encountered a situation before in her life where her gender limits her opportunities. My girls are growing up in a world that is telling them they can do anything, be anything. That they can dominate in school, in sports, in music, in business, in government. She cocks her head and gives me a puzzled look when I describe a time or an industry that was not welcoming to women.

Let's think about what the world was like for women in America not so very long ago. In 1962, the year the Tabernacle Choir was photographed in front of Mount Rushmore and represented America to the world, a wife had "no legal rights to any part of her husband's earnings or property during the existence of the marriage, aside from a right to be properly supported." The bar for being "properly supported" was low: in a Kansas Supreme Court case, a wife was denied the right to have running water despite her husband being deemed financially capable of installing it. Forty-two states considered earnings acquired during the marriage to be owned solely by the earner, meaning that if a couple divorced and the wife had been a homemaker, she walked away from the marriage with nothing.

Flight attendants in 1962 were still routinely fired if they married or reached age thirty-two. Newspapers still divided employment ads into two separate gendered sections, with sexually explicit stipulations rampant in the female notices. Supreme Court Justice Sandra Day O'Connor described her job search after Stanford Law School: "I called every phone number [on the job bulletin board]. They said, 'We didn't mean women. We don't hire women.'" Racially segregated job ads were legally abolished four years *before* gender segregated ads.

My own alma mater, Yale University, didn't accept women into its college until seven years later. (The a cappella singing group I joined on campus was founded in 1969 as one of the first women's on-campus institutions. It was called The New Blue, to contrast with the "old blue" of Yale men. Thus I was reminded of my college's gender history daily.) Academic expectations for women were almost nonexistent. The National Press Club in Washington, DC, was entirely male, and only 2.6% of lawyers were women. In 1962, the *Washington Post* admiringly published a letter from a reader who claimed she could perform a "tricky chore combination": "this homemaker claims she can iron and telephone at the same time."

The world has changed, and it has changed fast. By 1962, President Thomas S. Monson had already been a bishop, a stake president's counselor, and a mission president. He became a member of the Quorum of the Twelve Apostles a year later. Elder Jeffery R. Holland was already twenty-two years old. Considering how many men and women in our Church grew up in the gender culture described above can help us empathize with just how fast the world has changed for those who lead us today. On the other hand, the Church is now largely made up of people who have no living memory of gender dynamics pre-1962. The Church is the only place many members have ever experienced institutional gender divisions. They have little context or understanding for where gender divisions came from or what their benefits might be. This doesn't make the Church structure wrong; it makes it hard for some people to embrace unquestioningly.

It is not just the media or "the world" that has adopted an entirely new paradigm for viewing women, their potential, and their contributions. The rhetoric of the institutional Church has shifted dramatically in the way male and female relationships are depicted in our official publications. For example, a February 1973 article in the *Ensign* magazine entitled "Strengthening the Patriarchal Order in the Home" cites statistics from that time that demonstrate "male-dominated" marriages were in decline. The author warns, "The recent transition in the United States from a patriarchal to a democratic or even a matriarchal type of family organization has had its consequences." And he doesn't mean good consequences. The author predicts that chaos and spiritual bankruptcy will occur if male-dominated marriages are no longer the norm.

> Imagine, for example, the confusion that would result if two bishops were appointed over your particular ward and the first one got up in sacrament meeting and announced that the following Sunday the sacrament meeting would be held one hour earlier. While he was making his announcement, suppose the second bishop stood up and expressed his desire that the sacrament meeting be held at the original time. With two people presiding, would democratic principles work? Suppose you had two stake presidents, two elders quorum presidents, two Sunday School presidents, two Primary and Relief Society presidents presiding over each of the priesthood quorums, groups, and auxiliaries. How would the Church function?

The author also declares that a democratic (as opposed to patriarchal) "family government is also a departure from biblical teachings. The Apostle

Paul admonished, 'Wives, submit yourselves unto your own husbands . . .' (Eph. 5:22; see also Col. 3:18). He also taught that 'the husband is the head of the wife . . .' (Eph. 5:23). In addition, the Lord instructed Eve in the Garden of Eden that 'thy desire shall be to thy husband, and he shall rule over thee' (Gen. 3:16)."

In contrast, a 2013 *Ensign* article entitled "Equal Partnership in Marriage" contradicted almost point for point the warnings of the article forty years earlier. In summary, the author debunks the belief that "male-dominant" marriages are in fact favorable and divinely mandated:

> Latter-day Saint theology teaches that gender difference does not superimpose a hierarchy between men and women. . . . Social science research supports the prophetic instruction that couples who have an equal partnership have happier relationships, more effective parenting practices, and better-functioning children. Scholars have consistently found that equal partners are more satisfied and have better overall marital quality than couples where one spouse dominates. Equal-partner relationships have less negative interaction and more positive interaction. Moreover, there is evidence that equal partners are more satisfied with the quality of the physical intimacy in their relationship.

The difference between the two approaches could not be starker. The image of two bishops battling over who gets the podium seems farcical to many today. Rare is the man today who could go to ward basketball boasting of his wife's submission to him and not be confronted with a cry of "foul play."

Some of the social science research supporting equal marriage partnerships comes from our own Mormon scholars who are providing empirical evidence that the shift in gender relations benefits women (and men!) in almost every walk of life. In their 2012 book *Sex and World Peace*, authors Valerie Hudson and Bonnie Ballif-Spanvill (both have taught at BYU), argue that "the very best predictor of a state's peacefulness is not its level of wealth, its level of democracy, or its ethno-religious identity; the best predictor of a state's peacefulness is how well its women are treated. What's more, democracies with higher levels of violence against women are as insecure and unstable as nondemocracies."

"Gender inequality," Hudson and Ballif-Spanvill say, "in all of its many manifestations, is a form of violence—no matter how invisible or normalized that violence may be. This gender-based violence not only destroys home but, we argue, also significantly affects politics and security at both the national and international level." Hudson and Ballif-Spanvill's work has received widespread attention from academics and heads of state: Secretary of State Hillary Clinton publicly referenced research from this book about women by Mormon women.

Additionally, BYU family life professor E. Jeffrey Hill presented a study at 2011's Women in Business conference at the BYU Marriott School of Business, demonstrating that the greatest happiness in marriage is achieved when the couple is together working 160%, or one and two-thirds of a full-time job, even when the couple has children. This statistic was supported by a 2013 study published in the *American Sociological Review,* which demonstrated that the lowest levels of divorce in America today are found when the husband does 40 percent of the housework and the wife earns 40 percent of the income. These statistical and historical insights—coupled with very real support from lived experience, certainly in my own case and in the cases of many women I know—suggest there is real value in our current gender practices in America.

In contrast to this understanding from her educational and cultural experience in the twenty-first century world, my daughter's experience at church is very different. At church, she never sees her Primary leaders or her mother's Relief Society leaders sit on the stand during ward or stake conference. She has asked me in tears why only boys pass the sacrament and why the Church paintings and photographs in her Primary room are of all men. She wonders why the Cub Scout boys in Primary get a blue and gold banquet; what, she asks, do the Activity Day girls do to celebrate their accomplishments? My daughter and other young girls find themselves wondering, "What is my role here? Why am I limited in my aspirations here when no such limitations are put on me anywhere else?"

When a woman asks these questions as an adult, the results can be devastating. The pain is real when a woman starts to wonder why the freedoms that benefit her life so greatly outside the Church are not present in the organization to which she has devoted her heart and soul. As women functioning in the Church's gendered organization where structural parity cannot be claimed to currently exist, we as members are asked to suspend our understanding of and trust in structures that our own people—as well as many other trusted scholars—say make communities more functional, prosperous, and happy. Each woman searches for peace in reconciling external world experiences with the structure of gospel administration. For some, this can be hard.

The Importance of Diverse Visual Representations
in Modern Culture

In 1960, John F. Kennedy and Richard Nixon famously faced each other in the first televised presidential debates in American history. Nixon appeared sickly and sweaty; Kennedy handsome and strong. Not only did the debates have a major impact on the outcome of the presidential campaign, but they also heralded a new era for American media: we wanted to see ourselves represented in the images of our leaders.

The need to see ourselves reflected in our role models and leaders serves several fundamental human needs in our modern age. Today, even more than in 1960, we are challenged in finding meaningful communities. We are told to be ourselves, to express ourselves, and not to care what other people think about us, but at our cores we yearn for tribes where we feel safe and where the boundaries have been drawn for what is and is not acceptable. We celebrate diversity of peoples, races, cultures, and genders for the beauty and variety they bring to our earthly experiences, but we also treasure the feeling of identifying with someone just like us. As our culture becomes more and more ethnically and culturally fractured, we each feel the need to find ourselves reflected in public role models. We are no longer accustomed to one kind of person—historically, a white male—representing or speaking for the needs and feelings of each of us individually. In his October 2013 conference talk, Elder Uchtdorf declared, "The diversity of persons and peoples all around the globe is a strength of this Church." This need for diversity is not merely self-gratifying superficiality; it satisfies a deep spiritual need for our individual worth to be honored in a cacophony of voices.

With more information available than ever before in history, connecting with people who we feel can empathize with our life experiences provides a filter by which we can evaluate information more effectively. We trust people who are like us. Bonding with them alleviates the feeling of isolation that can come from living such disparate lives, full of choices and pitfalls.

Speaking from her perspective in Hong Kong, scholar Melissa Inouye has written eloquently about the need for representation in Church leadership that looks and thinks like the global Church population. Her observations about the need for female leaders on global Church populations also apply, I feel, to those of us working on a local level. Inouye tells of her branch in Hong Kong:

> In my branch in Hong Kong, in which the majority of members are single, middle-aged women converts from mainland China, the General Conference

meeting is not as well-attended as a normal meeting. I suspect that this is because these Chinese women converts have a hard time identifying with the global church organization, especially when Conference messages come through a translator and are usually delivered by North American men who all look about the same to them and whose names are very difficult to remember.

At one large church meeting in Hong Kong (not a General Conference, but a District Conference at which General Authorities spoke) I noticed that a group of branch women sitting together in front of me were having a hard time giving their undivided attention to the talks, which were being delivered by various visiting General Authorities. Then "Sister Dai"—a woman who is universally admired within the branch as a Primary President, visiting teacher, and Supermom—stepped up to the podium. The women broke out in exclamations of "Hey! It's our Sister Dai!" and snapped to attention. I am not trying to argue that people should not learn how to pay attention in church, or that church members will only pay attention to talks given by people they know personally. But observing the difference that the messenger—not just the message—makes in people's ability to be engaged was instructive. When my fellow branch members saw someone with whom they identified (with whom they had something significant in common and who was also known to them through long acquaintance), they were more receptive to the message that was being taught and more engaged in the conference itself. The same is true for the young women and single women that the Church is struggling to retain. To help women within the Church deepen their connection and commitment to the kingdom of God, the kingdom of God needs more women leaders.

While some may scoff at contemporary diversity efforts as tokenism or just filling quotas, there is no turning back on our need to answer the fundamental questions, "Where am I? Where do I fit in? Who is speaking for me?" In a media-driven culture such as our own, where 57% of Internet traffic in 2015 will be video consumption and 1 minute of video is estimated to be "worth" 1.8 million words (in the words of a prominent LDS media analyst), the answers come from how we see ourselves represented in video and other visual media.

Let's imagine a teenage girl, being raised in the United States in 2014, with Instagram and Facebook and Twitter accounts. Daily, she scrolls through a stream of messages from friends and family, photos and articles and conversations from celebrities she admires and causes she believes in. She posts, responds, "favorites," and "likes," building her voice and her influence through the most democratic medium ever invented. She speaks for herself, and she surrounds herself with others who speak with her. She feels a connection with celebrities or public figures she admires; she reads their tweets and feels heard by them. She builds an online community—a tribe—around herself of people she knows and those she merely admires from afar who she feels hear her, represent her. Let's also imagine this teen-age girl opening the general conference issue of the *Ensign* magazine to the center spread of general authorities' photos. Until the April 2014 general conference issue, it was a page full of photographs of men. The general Relief Society presidency was not represented on the page of leaders, nor were the Young Women or Primary general presidents. On the local level, her Sunday pulpit is almost exclusively occupied by men, with the exception of a female speaker or two. She likely can name her stake president but may not know the name or face of the stake Young Women president. Her ward Relief Society president is barely on her radar. The contrast is jarring: she doesn't see her tribe represented in those who speak for her. This may not be wrong, but it is hard.

This lack of visual representation is not because we don't have stellar women to highlight. We have women who are better than just figure-heads: they are role models. In February 2014, nine new Young Women general board members were selected from around the world, heralding an enormous step of progress for our quest to represent our membership accurately and speak to their experiences and needs. Here in the Young Women general board is a model for a global Church. Out of nine representatives, four live in Utah, which is still an overrepresentation since only 14 percent of the Church's membership lives in Utah. However, if we consider New York City representative Janet Nelson as one of five American representatives, then American representation on the board is much closer to the Church's own domestic/international division. It gets exciting when we look at the remaining four: women from Peru, South Africa, Japan, and Brazil are in those ranks.

But I am not only heartened by the countries of origin and the colors of these women's faces, as beautiful as they are. There are two PhDs on the list, a judge, and a BYU faculty member. The story a woman tearfully shared with me about being released as Young Women president in her ward because she went back to work and was considered a poor example to the girls will, hopefully, be ancient history to the next generation be-cause of the example of our general leaders. And, if I'm reading the biog-raphies right, two of the women are not married and do not have children. What a gift to our girls to have admirable role models who might not fall within our preached ideal, as many of them will not either. "It has been a long time in coming and it's been a long process for us to figure out what it needs to look like," said Young Women general president Bonnie L. Oscarson of her board's composition. "This is no longer a Wasatch Front church or even a church in the United States. [This board] helps make the Church smaller. It helps us address the needs throughout the world, and I think the message that it sends to everyone is important."

I see awareness, appreciation, and action on the part of our male and female leaders regarding the impact of gender and cultural representation on the general level. Are we doing this well ourselves on the local level? Are we stretching ourselves, as Young Women general president Bonnie Oscarson did, to reach the same standard of visual representation on the local level as she did in her board? Could we imagine our stake centers displaying photos of the stake Relief Society presidents alongside the traditional images of the stake presidents, as is now done in the Conference Center? If it is done on the general level, is it not a practice that we could confidently adopt on the local level? Similarly, if our female leadership is placed front and center on the stand, as they now are, at every general session of our worldwide conference, could we not confidently adopt a similar practice on the local level during stake and ward conferences?

On a personal note, I feel particularly grateful to see the face of Janet Nelson among the nine new Young Women board members. Sister Nelson raised four kids in a townhouse in Brooklyn, when Brooklyn wasn't the hipster haven it is today. She's lived in New York City for thirty years; I lived there for twenty-three. There are only a handful of Mormons who understand my personal identity as a Mormon New Yorker, and by virtue of our shared experience, she is one of them. While we were in her ward in Brooklyn, it was impossible to miss Sister Nelson's influence, which extended until the very night we moved out of the city: it was Sister Nelson who gave us sleeping bags and blankets to sleep on after the movers had taken away all our furniture. She is my tribe, my people.

But my mind quickly moves from celebrating Sister Nelson's new opportunity to wondering how her influence will be felt by young women around the world. How will these women be used? How will their voices be heard? Increased transparency into the activities and responsibilities of the women's general boards would help increase my confidence that these women are truly being used as role models and not just figureheads. My hope now is that, when these women complete their terms, I will be able to say with confidence that their voices were heard and that they played an active role in lifting and encouraging young women everywhere. We on the local level don't have to wait to see how this board's next few years play out; we can take the initiative in our own spheres to visually represent and use women conspicuously, and not in token titles only. We can be bold in showing half of our congregations that we value them, not just by saying it but by seeing it.

At the Mormon Women Project, we repeat the mantra I cited earlier: you can't be what you can't see. Latter-day Saint women today live in a world of limitless possibilities and choices, the freedom of which, in some ways, makes role models and a guiding hand more important than ever. The examples of other women—from the Mormon Women Project, from the lives of our female spiritual leaders or from other admirable women—offer a template for the spiritual creation of a life path, before we individually go and create those paths physically for ourselves. The Lord described this process of creation in Moses 3:5 when He said, "For I, the Lord God, created all things, of which I have spoken, spiritually, before they were naturally upon the face of the earth." Role models very literally allow us to see potential paths played out in others' lives before enacting them in our own. We can create life choices spiritually before creating them "naturally."

When women do not see themselves reflected in the images that represent us as a people, there is for some women a sense of invisibility and thus unimportance. Perhaps the effect could be described as a visual famine. After a *Deseret News* article about the possibility of a woman praying in general conference for the first time, a reader addressed previous comments that such a change would be meaningless. The commenter said, "The reason [a woman praying in conference] is important is because organizations (like the church) sometimes inadvertently send messages about what they believe through their actions. For example, imagine that half of the church membership was of Asian ancestry and over a period of 150+ years we never asked an Asian person to pray at general conference. Would there be a message there? What would you think if you were of Asian ancestry? . . . We have to be thoughtful about our actions as a church because sometimes traditions (perhaps false traditions) send wrong messages. Women not praying at General Conference is probably a good example of this."

If our global leaders recognize we can do better in making representation a priority, we can too. I received an email from a Mormon Women Project reader that I felt beautifully stated the longing each woman has to draw strength from the representation of those like herself, satiating the visual famine:

> There is a huge void in society today when it comes to showing us strong accomplished women. We are bombarded with misleading media about women where they are portrayed as objects, petty, and foolish. We are largely left out of history books and when we go to church, a place where we should see strong female role models . . . stories of women in the scriptures and in our lesson manuals are also scarce. They often fall into two categories: the saintly mother or the temptress devil. Where are the real women? Complex women who strive to do their best in all they do? Who are spiritual, powerful and accomplished and also have weaknesses? With no clear image of Heavenly Mother and very little in regards to women everywhere else in our lives, I am hungry, no ravenous, for the stories of my fellow sisters. When I read these stories, I am buoyed up and gain a clearer image of what I can accomplish. I find strength in others. I can be more like what I see.

Similarly, when Relief Society general president Julie B. Beck announced the publication of *Daughters in My Kingdom,* an official history of the Relief Society, she praised it by saying, "We've had stories [about women] written for the historians. We've had stories written for the scholars. We've had stories written for the press. But we've never had the story written for the women themselves."

I believe our general authorities have been called of God. I draw comfort from knowing that we are mirroring a pattern of apostleship established by the Savior Himself. I have drawn enormous strength from exemplary women in my private life who have helped me see what I can be. But I also sympathize with those women who struggle to put aside the comfort and assurance we find in the diversity of modern representations. For generations, we've sought for ourselves in the scriptures and in the history books, longing to see ourselves reflected back in an image we can emulate. Today, we seek for ourselves and the world reflects back. It is difficult to find that reflection at Church.

Misuse of Councils and Church Structures

When Elder David A. Bednar recently visited the Kampala Stake Center in Uganda, he prefaced his remarks by saying, "We are not here to teach you Western culture. We are here to teach you about the gospel culture. Gospel culture takes precedence over any other influence." As part of his discussion on gospel culture, members were also asked to counsel together. Men were cautioned not to exercise "unrighteous dominion."

What is the gospel culture? If culture is defined as the attitudes and behaviors characteristic of a particular social group, then the way we interact with each other is the best indicator of our integrity. Do we really believe what we preach? Look at our behavior. That is our culture as much as our art, music, Jell-O, or roadshows. The way we interact with each other in local Church government is one of those indicators of integrity, as are our interactions in our homes and in our workplaces. Elder M. Russell Ballard has made it his mission over the past twenty years or so to improve our interactions in local Church leadership so that they are more in line with our beliefs. His book *Counseling with Our Councils* was first published in 1997 and again in 2012. The book was preceded by two general conference talks (in October 1993 and April 1994) about ministering to the needs of members through Church councils. Elder Ballard also took the lead in the 2010 and 2012 Worldwide Leadership Trainings.

I will be talking more about Elder Ballard's vision for ideal Church councils and the power they have for good later in this book, but for these purposes here I must address how these councils contribute to some women's feeling of disuse and neglect. Elder Ballard is not naïve to how councils can contribute to gender tensions. In the early pages of his book, he relates a conversation he had with a stake Relief Society president:

> "Elder Ballard," she said, her voice edged with exasperation, "will the brethren in leadership positions ever understand that the sisters want to make a contribution to the real issues facing the Church and its members? . . . I feel like I'm the hired help at the council table. I'm there to serve, but not to contribute. When they talk about ways to accomplish the mission of the Church, my opinion is never sought. And when they refer to the decisions of stake leaders, they never acknowledge me as a leader who can make a contribution to the spiritual growth and development of stake members. Sometimes they even talk about ways to meet the needs of the sisters in our stake without even inviting me to participate. I'm given assignments, and I do what I'm told. But I never feel that I am asked to *counsel*."

In charitable dismay, Elder Ballard comments,

> To be perfectly candid, I sometimes have a difficult time understanding why so many of our leaders fail to see the vision of how working through councils can enhance their ability to accomplish all that the Lord expects of them in their respective stewardships. . . . It is a shortsighted priesthood leader who doesn't see the value in calling upon the sisters to share the understanding and inspiration they possess. . . . It is easy to understand why many sisters

are frustrated when they sit in council with priesthood leaders and are not invited to make substantive contributions to the council.

Being a bishop or a stake president or a mission president is an incredibly hard job. Elder Ballard and anyone who has seen one of these leaders at work know that it is an overwhelming and thankless job. But too many women have experienced the frustrations Elder Ballard describes, and one of the reasons he is determined to fix it is because including women could greatly ease the burdens on those men. When female voices are not included in the counseling process, the council is working at half capacity. Women bring insights and networks and experiences that are foreign to men, but when our ideas are not heard or acted on, a little part of us shuts down.

Life in the Church is like life with a spouse. Faith, like love in a marriage, may be the thing that keeps us together, but the Church is the structure in which that faith is played out, as marriage is the structure in which love is played out. Like marriage, the structure of the Church must serve to strengthen the faith of participants, or else it becomes difficult to continue. Similarly, individuals must strengthen the structure, or else they are not acting on their beliefs.

As in a marriage, contributions and efforts to improve the experiences at Church are an important way we each show our dedication to the institution. If we don't care, we don't work to contribute. If we care, we contribute. Contributions are the manifestations of our love for the gospel and the Church that supports it. When those ideas go unappreciated and unanswered, it can feel like offering a gift to a spouse with outstretched arms and having the recipient push it aside. What sense would it make for the recipient of our affection to say, "It's not your gift I love. It's you I love"? That kind of behavior is as utterly baffling for a spouse offering a gift as it would be for a woman offering her time and talents. For men and for women, the process of offering ourselves makes us feel vulnerable because our contributions are reflections of ourselves. Male leaders can tell women they love them and they're important, but if at the end of the day they push aside the women's gifts, the words will have no meaning.

For some, even the ideal counseling situations do not make up for the fact that women's voices are not built into the council structure to the same degree as men's. Specifically, a ward council meeting officially includes ten men: the bishop, his two counselors, the executive secretary, ward clerk, high priests group leader, elders quorum president, ward mission leader, Young Men's president, and the Sunday School president. Three women are included: the presidents of Relief Society, Young Women, and Primary. Priesthood executive committee (PEC) consists of all ten men from the ward council, with a potential invitation to the Relief Society president. The Young Men president is a permanent member of the priesthood executive committee, but the Young Women president is not even on the list of potential invitees. Why the disparity? In the best situations, the presence of twenty male voices in the two meetings is counterbalanced by the voice of three female voices (maybe four if the Relief Society president attends PEC). That is a tremendous amount of weight put on the shoulders of those three women to understand and speak for half of the ward's population. And it is a tremendous responsibility on the bishop to give as much weight to those three women's ideas as he does the nine men he works with.

Unfortunately, the "unrighteous dominion" Elder Bednar referenced in Uganda is felt too often in the United States today. Because of our local Church governmental structure and priesthood responsibilities, men are in the position of evaluating a woman's behavior, to deem her worthy of either a temple recommend or a particular calling. This power is sometimes abused, rarely maliciously but more often out of ignorance. For example, I remember the sacred feeling in our home when the restriction on women getting their endowments without the accompaniment of a husband was lifted and my mom could attend the temple. (My father was inactive.) But when she later turned to a local leader for help in her marriage, she was told she might be able to patch things up if she just took off her garments more often. I have an image of my mom standing in our little galley kitchen, shaking a dishtowel not only to emphasize her point but because she herself was shaking: "Do not ever confuse the gospel with the Church," she told me. "The first is free of human error; the second is not. Don't ever forget that."

My mother's example is a relatively innocuous example of well-meaning counsel gone awry. People have personally written to me with more egregious examples, and a common theme seems to be men siding with a man in disciplinary or evaluative settings, regardless of the man's faithfulness. The women have no one to speak for them in these settings. Their experiences, feelings, intuitions, and motivations may seem foreign to their male judges. Women who struggle with not having greater responsibility at the local Church level often cite misuses of power as a major driver of their discomfort.

Not having a woman's voice properly heard and respected can result in more mundane conflicts as well. A stake Young Women's presidency member described a flyer she had made to advertise that year's girls' camp. The flyer used the phrases "flushing toilets," "running water," "basic electricity," and other phrases in order to encourage a wide range of inner city young women to feel comfortable attending camp. The stake president refused to publish the flyer with the phrase "flushing toilets" on it, saying it was inappropriate language for a Church flyer. The Young Women presidency informed the stake president that some of the young women had been menstruating during camp the previous year and were uncomfortable with the lack of hygiene in the tents and the lack of bathrooms, so the phrase was added specifically to make them feel comfortable attending. The flyer was eventually printed without the offending phrase. The Young Women presidency was flustered and discouraged by the outcome. One member of the presidency said, "Our inability for us to show the girls that we had heard their concerns from the previous year is just plain wrong. I also suspect that the stake president was extremely uncomfortable with the discussion of menstruation and reacted to that more than to the situation at hand. I think he felt on the spot with all the stake Young Women leaders and himself alone. It might have been better to address the subject over email so he had some space in which to rebalance himself."

In Part II, I will discuss some wonderfully respectful and innovative practices I have learned about that specifically address this kind of sidelining of women's voices, but it is necessary here to underscore how painful these kinds of silencing experiences can be for women and girls.

Rise of Single Sisters

While I was conducting my research for this book, an unanticipated theme emerged quite clearly: seeing, hearing, and including single women requires its own particular awareness and efforts. While we may all cringe at the vintage quip, "I hold the priesthood every night in bed," there seems to still be a tacit understanding that being married to a man who is involved in Church administration gives a woman a window into that world, even a voice in that world through her support and influence. Those I interviewed seemed to recognize that single women in the Church do not have the same loose tether to Church administration that married women do, and so they are at an even greater risk of feeling overlooked and unneeded.

The disconnect single women may feel from Church administration is of utmost importance to us now because we have more single women in church membership than ever before. The breakdown of unmarried

Mormons in Utah results in eight unmarried men for every ten unmarried women between the ages of thirty-one and forty-five, five unmarried men for every ten unmarried women between the ages of forty-six and sixty-five, and two unmarried men for every ten unmarried women over sixty-six. Presumably, the male-to-female ratio is even starker outside of Utah where more women tend to join the Church than men. Although the Church doesn't release demographic statistics publicly, independent scholars estimate that up to one-third of the Church's American population is single.

Single women can feel their identity in the Church is defined by what they are *not*: they are not wives, they are often not mothers. Even maintaining virtue—a revered spiritual characteristic—as a single woman can be perceived as merely an absence of sexual experience. They are what they lack. Is it any wonder single women in particular struggle with feeling a part of our community?

Interviews with single women revealed to me how deeply they also feel a lack of identity as trusted ecclesiastical and administrative leaders at church. Unless they are part of the small cadre of women who serve in the presidencies of their single wards, single women feel like they are less likely to be considered for local callings because they are unfit in some way to teach and preach to those having traditional family experiences. A lack of emphasis on women's career choices in the Church also serves to underappreciate the very things that might be of most worth and pride in a single woman's life: her career or academic achievements or her involvement in a broader community.

The hard truth is that we don't have structural or doctrinal mechanisms in place for single women to make concrete and specific contributions to the Church institution. If a single woman feels heard and appreciated at church, it is usually because a local leader is particularly attuned to her and others like her. But this kind of attunement and initiative can be uneven from ward to ward: some leaders, male and female, may be more committed to embracing single sisters than others. The lack of institutional identity for single women puts the responsibility on the local leaders to create belonging and fulfillment for those single women in wards and stakes.

Greater Awareness of History

Despite the fact that they were published for mainstream consumption only in 2012, I already take for granted the fact that I can reach to my private bookshelf to access the minutes from Joseph Smith's instructions at the founding of the Relief Society in 1842, either in Deseret Book's *Beginning of Better Days: Divine Instruction to Women from the Prophet Joseph Smith* or else in the Joseph Smith Papers' online version of the meeting minutes. I love that I can put myself in the shoes of the women who listened to the prophet for those hours he spent with them: the remarkable Emma Smith, Sarah M. Cleveland, Elizabeth Ann Whitney, and so many others. It makes me lift my chin a little higher to read how Joseph declared, "I now turn the key to you in the name of God and this Society shall rejoice and knowledge and intelligence shall flow down from this time—this is the beginning of better days." I am not the only one to draw confidence and comfort from access to the minutes: I've interviewed several women who had no awareness of the minutes' content prior to their publication but whose confidence in themselves as Mormon women skyrocketed when they learned for the first time that their foremothers gave healing blessings with the encouragement of the Prophet. Such is the effect of having our women's history sold in Deseret Book and easily accessible online.

Until very recently, the minutes and other documents regarding our women's history were a treasure sought out by writers and historians, who had to go to the Church History Library to access them under watchful eyes of librarians. Books such as the seminal *Women of Covenant: The Story of Relief Society*, written by Jill Mulvay Derr, Janath Russell Cannon, and Maureen Ursenbach Beecher for the 150th anniversary of the founding of the Relief Society, and others such as Maureen Ursenbach Beecher and Lavina Anderson's *Sisters in Spirit* and Claudia Bushman's *Mormon Sisters* represented the extent of accessible insight into the workings of the women of the early Church. As historian Claudia Bushman writes in the introduction of her book *Mormon Women Have Their Say*, the histories of Mormon women have traditionally been considered tools for teaching faith and inspiring religious foundations in the rising generations. Rarely have Mormon women's stories been culled for sociological or anthropological insights into how they interacted with men, how their organizations function and worked in harmony or in conflict with men's, and to what extent their organizations served to grow and strengthen the Church as a whole.

All of that is now changed. As easily as I can reach for the Relief Society minutes, I can reach for Joseph Smith's own words in my copy of *The Joseph Smith Papers*. I can pull up on my laptop the original copies of the *Woman's Exponent* magazine, the Mormon women's periodical published from 1872 to 1914, from the Harold B. Lee Library Digital

Collection at Brigham Young University. The first three existing volumes of a seven-volume series from Deseret Book, Richard E. Turley and Brittany A. Chapman's *Women of Faith in the Latter Days*, give me hundreds of pages of details from the daily lives and struggles and joys of our foremothers from which I glean their most raw feelings about polygamy, physical deprivation, childbearing in the wilderness, and death. Mormon women's history, like all Mormon history, has been blown wide open both due to an explosion of academic interest in Mormon studies and also an institutional commitment to honestly and openly telling our story.

This historical transparency signals huge steps forward in the way the institution models authenticity and honesty, and it will, in the long term I believe, result in stronger faith. However, the outpouring of historical information and analysis has resulted in some short-term growing pains as those who previously were unfamiliar with some of the episodes or contradictions in our past have had to face their faith with opened eyes. It seems that it is a rare member, in the United States at least, who has not been affected—either personally or through a friend or family member—by the sense of disillusionment and betrayal some experience when learning elements of our history previously unknown. Perhaps the most publicized example of these growing pains was the story of Hans Mattsson, a former area authority seventy from Sweden, whose faith crisis was chronicled in the *New York Times* in 2013. Some of the stories to which we are now privy show political strivings that cloud the vision of Zion; they reveal power struggles and human frailties we may have previously thought exempt.

Similarly, increased access and exposure to Mormon women's history over the past five to ten years has revealed some behaviors and practices we didn't expect. I've already mentioned the example of the Prophet's sanctioning and encouraging the women's healing blessings, which does not happen today. We also read in the Relief Society minutes about how the women leaders were elected by their peers and chose their own counselors, which would be very unusual if it happened today. Joseph Smith told these early Relief Society leaders that he would "ordain them to preside over the Society . . . just as the Presidency preside over the church." The questions raised by these statements—What did the Prophet really mean? How did he see the women functioning "just as" the First Presidency?—provided part of the motivation behind the Ordain Women movement. This same method of organization was reiterated by Brigham Young when he reorganized the Relief Society in Salt Lake City in 1867: "that the Sisters elect a presiding officer to preside over them, and let that presiding officer choose two Councellors to assist in the duties of her Office—that [the prophet] would ordain them to preside over the Society—and let them preside just as the Presidency preside over the church."

Writer Fiona Givens describes more about what we learn about the organizing of women from the minutes:

> Joseph did not presume to dictate to the sisters how they should run their organization or how they should preside: *"if"* the sisters needed the prophet's instruction—"ask him [and] he will give it." Joseph expected the sisters to be fully capable of running their own organization with no help from the male branch of the priesthood unless they asked for it. He also did not presume to organize the Relief Society according to male priesthood rankings. He suggested that if the sisters wished to pattern their organization after the male priesthood they were at liberty to do so: *"If* (emphasis mine) any Officers are wanted to carry out the designs of the Institution, let them be appointed and set apart, as *Deacons Teachers* &c. are among us." Again, Joseph is reiterating the power and authority of the women to organize as the Spirit moves upon them rather than in obedience to male priesthood, emphasizing the equality of the women's organization to that of the men's. It is significant that Emma Smith, the first Relief Society President, chose not to model her organization on the hierarchical structure of the male priesthood.
>
> The historical and spiritual record show that Emma (Presidentess) and Joseph (President) were to preside over their respective branches of the priesthood as the High Priestess, Eve, and the High Priest, Adam, were called to preside in the ancient church. . . . Joseph clearly saw the Relief Society organization as an institution destined for the creation of "priests"— a kingdom of them, in fact. The Relief Society and its male equivalent are to co-operate in their respective responsibilities to build a society of mutual respect, love, unity and understanding in which the King of Kings may take up His residence.

Why don't things still work this same way? In the most egalitarian of wards, the bishop and Relief Society president council and cooperate with each other effectively, but we would be hard pressed to describe the Relief Society presidency as having "just as" much responsibility in presiding over the ward as the bishop. The bishop, by *Handbook* mandate, always has the final administrative word. And our current model of having the general Relief Society president report to a member of the Quorum of the Seventy does not echo the original model of Emma Smith working independent of male oversight.

From the issues of the *Woman's Exponent*, every lay member of the Church can learn about Mormon women's engagement in the suffrage movement and their establishment of cooperative stores, silk manufacturing, grain storage, and a network of hospitals staffed by female doctors. We can all read our foremothers' empowering words to young women in the *Young Woman's Journal*: "To women there belongs a right which lies deeper than suffrage, higher than education, and sweeter than enforced virtue. It is the right of choice; the right to choose what she shall be." In Turley and Chapman's *Women of Faith in the Latter Days*, we read a bold letter sent by Abigail Smith Abbot to Brigham Young, asking why the women who had made sacrifices at home couldn't have a parade of their own since returning male soldiers of the Mormon Battalion were being honored in this way. These organizational practices, accomplishments, and attitudes—now so easily studied and compared to our own day—seem to put the women and their divine organization in a place of greater reach and ability than we enjoy today.

A Utah stake Relief Society president told me about when she first became familiar with the Relief Society minutes. It was in 2007 when she was working as a docent at the Church History Museum and the original minutes came to the museum as part of an exhibit. Despite having served as ward Relief Society president three times and in stake Relief Societies twice before her own calling as president, she described reading the minutes as "an epiphany." "I was blown away," she recalled, "It was a whole new vision for Relief Society."

But women in my mother's generation of women have been quick to remind me that we do not even need to stretch back to the nineteenth century for a model of greater female participation. Several women I've talked to who are now in their 70s and 80s have mourned the spirit of "complementarity" and productivity that they felt defined their mid-century years in Relief Society. Helen Claire Sievers was a Relief Society president first in 1978 and then again each decade until 2000, serving as a ward, branch, and district Relief Society president in places as diverse as the Marshall Islands and Boston. Helen says she "would trade giving prayers in General Conference in a heartbeat for a return to the real control over the Church auxiliary organizations that women traditionally ran: the Relief Society, the YWMIA [Young Women's Mutual Improvement Association], and Primary, as well as renewed access to the people of the Church and to the Priesthood leadership." Helen details what she mourns: manuals written by the Relief Society general board, by women, for women; "Notes to the Field," which were direct communications from the general board to the local leadership; the *Relief Society Magazine* (discontinued in 1970); regular visits and trainings by the members of the general board to stake conferences, as board members accompanied general authorities as guest speakers; control over money, assets, and travel; and direct access by the Relief Society general presidency to the First Presidency. She concludes her survey in this nostalgic vein:

> It felt like real teamwork in the Church. We each did important things—different, but important, things that enriched and enlivened the members. I never wanted the priesthood then, because what women were doing in the Church mattered in very profound ways. What we do at the ward level still matters because a teacher, a friend, a class member always matters. Helping people who are sick, or otherwise in need, always matters. But at the macro level, we as women have pretty much lost it all.

Laurel Thatcher Ulrich says it was a Relief Society fundraising project, a guidebook to Boston titled *A Beginner's Boston*, which eventually sold 20,000 copies, that "emboldened" her to take the first steps toward a part-time master's program at Simmons College. Ulrich went on to become our one and only Mormon female Pulitzer Prize winner and the 300th Anniversary University Professor of History at Harvard University. All because of a Relief Society fundraiser. Are women finding the confidence and curiosity to follow life-changing pursuits in Relief Society gatherings today?

Fiona Givens speaks also about the vision of returning to mid-twentieth century practices:

> We might hope to one day see returned the Temple priesthood powers to offer healing blessings and other blessings in behalf of family members. . . . Perhaps someday we might see the stewardship returned to the Relief Society Presidency for the disbursement of funds for its own organization and that of her auxiliaries. With luck, so too will the Relief Society and auxiliaries once again have the oversight for the writing and distribution of Relief Society, Young Women, and Primary manuals.

Such statements, such visions for how women can participate, are now possible because we are familiar with what came before us. Relief Society general president Julie B. Beck left her presidency in 2012 having paved the way for greater awareness and understanding of the history of the Relief Society by overseeing the publication and encouraging the use of the Relief Society history book *Daughters in My Kingdom* and by speaking forcefully about the potential of Relief Society. Perhaps President Beck considered the risks of expounding on this rich and sometimes contro-versial history. She, and the Lord, decided it was worth the risks and, presumably, the rewards in the long run.

Knowing the Relief Society history does prompt some to look back wistfully and with some confusion over why things may be different today. I'm not saying the way Relief Society functions today is wrong; I'm saying the comparison can be hard. But our history, as President Julie Beck un-doubtedly believes, also offers men and women alike a vision for our glo-rious restored gospel that amplifies women's contributions. Accessibility to our history allows us today to take the best of our past into the future and feel greater connection and admiration for those who came before us. Our challenge today is to embrace the hope and comfort that comes from knowing our past, rather than being confused by it.

Disconnect between Doctrine and Practice of Equality

In my August 2012 FairMormon conference talk, one of the most challenging points that I made is that I feel we do ourselves a disservice as Mormons—when communicating both to external audiences and in-ternal audiences—when we continually assert that men and women are "equal" in our Church. While this may have made some listeners and readers squirm, almost all of the personal responses I received on this point expressed relief. It seems that while we feel confident in our *doctrinal* belief that men and women have the same worth in the sight of God, we feel uncomfortable doing the cognitive leaps required to claim that men and women are equal in our *practice*.

The questions seem to be: If we believe in equality, do we have an obligation to practice equality? And if we practice equality, what does that look like? These questions arise in our cultural consciousness because they are the same questions that American society has been wrestling with since the day we declared independence from Great Britain. It was literally "self-evident" to the founders of our country that all people are created equal. How that belief in equality actually translated into a practice of equal-ity was a discussion that shaped the very foundation of our country: for our founders, practicing equality initially demanded that white settlers in America should have the same taxation and representation as their broth-ers in England. And from the first moments of the country's founding, debate also raged over whether the equality the new Americans had fought to achieve extended to people of all races. Throughout the nineteenth and twentieth centuries, Americans asked themselves questions similar to those we had at our founding: What does equality look like? How do we practice it? What terms do we draw as a society to determine what opportunities, resources, and experiences are equal? How do our institutions support those terms?

And then there is gender equality. The American twentieth century was shaped to a large degree by how we answered these same questions regarding women: Did practicing equality mean that women could vote? Did practicing equality mean that they could apply for the same jobs as men? Did practicing equality mean that they could control how many children they had? That they could be paid the same as men?

Slowly but surely, the course of American history has determined that practicing the "self-evident" belief that people are equal to each other means that institutions (e.g., governments, employers, and schools) must treat people the same. American society has a doctrine of equality, but it also strives to practice equality in ways that are visible manifestations of that doctrine. The changes in women's lived experiences since 1962, as I described earlier, are examples of those manifestations, and they all suggest a determined march toward American society's ruling ideal: if men and women are believed to be equal, then institutions will ideally facilitate the same opportunities, resources, and experiences for people of both sexes.

Mormon women, who have been beneficiaries of this determined march over the past hundred years, are taught our gospel has a similar if not more glorious doctrine of equality than the one being played out in the world around them. But they are not seeing the institution of the Church practicing that equality doctrine in the same way as the world around them. They are not seeing the institution facilitate the equal opportunities that have resulted in so many open doors for our grandmothers, our mothers, and now us. We are challenged instead to separate the equation and believe in equality without practicing it in the same way to which we are accustomed. I'm not saying this is wrong; I'm saying it is hard.

There is no doubt that we Mormons claim some of the most exciting and affirming doctrine on the value of womanhood of any faith or denomination. For example, "glorious" Mother Eve is described in the *Encyclopedia of Mormonism* as "honored by Latter-day Saints as one of the most important, righteous, and heroic of all the human family. Eve's supreme gift to mankind, the opportunity of life on this earth, resulted from her choice to become mortal." Although we know little about her, we affirm a belief in Heavenly Mother. A BYU Studies Symposium paper by David L. Paulsen and Martin Pulido collected and organized hundreds of references to Heavenly Mother by prophets, apostles, and other leaders, sharing "important historical accounts that cast serious doubt on the specific claims that, first, a sacred silence has always surrounded this treasured Mormon doctrine and that, second, Heavenly Mother's ascribed roles have been marginalized or trivialized." We have scripture that tells us God is no respecter of persons, and our official document on the family confirms that "all human beings—male and female—are created in the image of God. Each is a beloved spirit son or daughter of heavenly parents." It seems that what we Mormons mean when we say men and women are "equal" in the Church is that the worth of female spirits is measured to be of the same value as male spirits. What is poured into the vessel of our earthly experience is intended to have parity: the same amount of love from our heavenly parents who created us, the same amount of attention, the same amount of guidance, and the same opportunity of returning to live with Them.

But we live in a world of visual representation and of scientific measurements, and we attempt to overlay an absolute mathematical proof onto spiritual constructs. This is part of what it means to live in twenty-first century America. And in doing so, we recognize that if practicing the doctrine of equality means making sure opportunities are the same, we don't measure up. Our contemporary American minds go to a place where the seats behind the pulpit become a free weight scale and a man on one side requires the counterbalance of a woman on the other to become mathematically equal. This same mathematical application is applied subconsciously every day of our lives to evaluate ideal situations in the contemporary world we inhabit as we consider how few women serve in Congress, how few women are CEOs, or we evaluate whether a family's sons and daughters are ideally balanced (or whether that poor lone boy will survive with all those sisters). We worry about girls in classrooms outnumbered by boys, or vice versa. We worry about men without wives and women without husbands. Our minds teeter back and forth, searching for that ideal place where things are 50 percent men and 50 percent women.

That search for equilibrium is not to be requited in Church leadership. This can be a difficult mathematical conundrum for us to wrap our brains around. How can "equal" not mean fifty-fifty?

Some people do not think there is any other way to represent "equal" than through mathematical absolutism. A blog series called "Equality is Not A Feeling" rose out of a statement by Ordain Women movement founder Kate Kelly during that group's October 2013 effort to attend the general priesthood meeting: "I have heard from many women, 'I see nothing wrong with the status quo. I feel equal.' To them I say: 'You can feel respected, supported and validated in the church, but equality can be measured. Equality is not a feeling. In our church men and women are not equal.'"

In each post of this series, found at the blog *Doves and Serpents*, the author tries "to illustrate, visually, numerous ways in which (in)equality in the Mormon church can be measured." Thus, she offers graphs and charts depicting every possible literal imbalance. For example:

- In the 2014 Primary Sharing Time outline, 100 percent of quotes or stories by latter-day church leaders are from men; 87 percent of the stories used to illustrate principles in the outline are about boys.

- Since 1974, 2,708 general conference talks have been given by men. Only 269 (9 percent of the total) have been given by women.

- *Handbook 1*, the administrative instruction guide that is only available to leaders and not general membership, can be accessed by 118,000 men (bishops, stake presidents, general authorities, etc.) and only nine women.

And so forth. As background to her efforts, the author explains her drive toward quantifiable "bean counting":

I'm in teacher education, so "equality" is something my students and I talk about a lot. They have assignments in which they have to go into a school and be observers of school culture. They are directed to take note of all sorts of things, some of which include depictions of different races and genders in things like bulletin boards and textbooks. They are directed to observe a class and use tally marks to indicate both the quantity and quality of teacher-student interaction, based on race as well as gender. . . .

As part of my dissertation work, I spent eighteen months in an elementary school as a keen observer of the power dynamics at play that had to do with mostly race, class, and language, so I've done more than my fair share of bean-counting. It's something I do. Once you start doing it, it's hard to just no longer do it. At least, that's been my experience. Quantifying things like this is just something I do.

The author's professional responsibilities are to look for parity in the representation of race and gender, with the assumption that that parity will contribute to richer learning opportunities for the students. Understanding this can make us more sympathetic to her frustration at not seeing those same beneficial principles at work in Church governance in the same way as they are in her school environments.

Several recent, well-placed statements by our general authorities make it evident to me that our Church leaders are recognizing the challenges of using the word "equal" to describe our gender practices to the world. There seems to be a deliberate effort to distance our definition of equality from the world's, which leaders believe to be potentially erasing or negating any inherent gender differences. Our leaders are carefully and frequently clarifying that while we believe in equal worth, equal power, equal value in the eyes of the Lord, and equal opportunity to return to live with Him, our practice of equality does not demand the same opportunities to serve and lead.

In his trip to Uganda earlier this year, for example, Elder David A. Bednar was cited as saying that when women become more equal partners, the Lord will hasten His work, but that *equal* does not mean *identical*. Priesthood is not "male," he said. The effort now seems to be on stressing the nonmathematical definition of "equal" as a measurement of intangibles, a measurement of worth rather than identical responsibility. Elder M. Russell Ballard dedicated his April 2013 conference talk to stressing that "men and women have different but equally valued roles." Talks in October 2013 by Elder D. Todd Christofferson, Sister Carole M. Stephens, and Elder Neil L. Anderson also seemed intent on separating equality from its mathematical roots to propose that equality *can* actually be a feeling. Men and women can contribute differently, but their offerings are received by the Lord with the same degree of acceptance, approval, and love. Elder Ballard has suggested an analogy to help us understand this principle. In his book, *Counseling with our Councils*, he says:

> Perhaps we might look at the respective contributions of men and women in this way: You have no doubt visited the ophthalmologist for an eye exam. In the process of determining a patient's correct vision, the doctor will typically test the patient's eyesight by asking him or her to look through a variety of settings on a machine, some of which are blurry. . . . Only when he can determine the exact prescription for both eyes can a patient's vision be corrected precisely.
>
> In much the same way, men and women express themselves differently and tend to have different skills, talents, and points of view. When either viewpoint is taken in isolation, the resulting image may be blurry, one-di-

mensional, or otherwise distorted. It is only when both perspectives come together that the picture is balanced and complete. Men and women are equally valuable in the ongoing work of the gospel kingdom.

Elder Ballard restated this message in his talk at BYU Education Week in 2013: "Our Church doctrine places women equal to and yet different from men. God does not regard either gender as better or more important than the other."

Although this definition of equality seems to be stressed more recently than we may remember in the past, it is not a new definition. In 1980, in the wake of the ERA discussions and a time not unlike our own, Sister Patricia T. Holland reached back to statements by President Spencer W. Kimball and to the Doctrine and Covenants to support her own thoughts about equality:

> President Spencer W. Kimball stated in a fireside address to the women of the Church, "We had full equality as his spirit children." He then went on to say that "within those great assurances, however, our roles and assignments differ."
>
> I believe that every one of us has a specific mission to fulfill on this earth and with some literary license I quote from Doctrine and Covenants 121:25: "For there is a time appointed for every man [and woman], according as [their] works shall be" (D&C 121:25).
>
> And Doctrine and Covenants 46:11–12: "For all have not every gift given unto them; for there are many gifts, and to every man [and woman] is given a gift by the Spirit of God.
>
> "To some is given one, and to some is given another, that all may be profited thereby" (D&C 46:11–12).
>
> I believe that we made sacred promises in premortal councils regarding our role in building the kingdom of God on earth. In turn we were promised the gifts and powers necessary to fulfill those very special tasks. . . . I also believe that those assignments and roles differ as much from woman to woman as they do from man to woman.

The *Encyclopedia of Mormonism* further explains this idea that equality in a spiritual realm does not mean always satisfying the demands of mathematical absolutism:

> All persons are of equal value in the sight of God. Each person (of every nation and every race) is as precious to him as another. From God all people will receive equivalent opportunities through Jesus Christ to attain eternal life, his greatest blessing. . . . They have equal chances to develop their abilities and equal opportunity to realize them in the work of Zion, all contributing according to their individual strengths and talents. A Zion people labor

together as equals by organizing themselves according to the principle of "equal power. . . ." But equality of power also defines the relations between members so that each is the center of decision and action in performing an individual stewardship within the community.

The definition here seems to take pains to clarify that "equality" does not connote identical opportunity and responsibility. This is consistent with the language of the Doctrine and Covenants and the rhetoric of our contemporary leaders: the word "equal" is always qualified, as in "equal value," "equivalent opportunities," "equal chances," "equal power," with an additional emphasis on "individual strengths and talents," and "individual stewardship."

If, however, we believe that "equal" does not mean that opportunities and responsibilities have to be the same, as our leaders are teaching us, where do we look for an example of how to put this principle into practice? We do not seem to have a secular paradigm we can reference to see separate spheres for men and women—or blacks and whites, or straight and gay, or any other division for that matter—truly flourishing. In secular paradigms, greater worth almost invariably means greater access to visible responsibilities: think promotions in the work environment where greater skill and value to the company means managerial, public responsibilities. Those with public visibility are perceived to have greater worth (which of course is intricately connected to the previous discussion about the impact of visibility). This is the model we know. This does not mean the alternate model our leaders are advocating is wrong. It means it is hard to understand and implement, and there is going to be pain and misunderstanding and sacrifice in the process. And the Savior told us we would be uncomfortable. In fact, one of the most searing parables Jesus shared during his life in Judea addresses the basic human drive for fairness: the parable of the laborers in the vineyard.

The parable is often cited to support the idea that God saves by grace, not by worthiness. We don't rack up tally points that get us into heaven. We are, instead, all granted the absolution of the Atonement no matter when and how we come to accept it. But the parable also challenges the paradigm of absolute measurements, pointing us instead to what we could call *divine math*. God does not apparently work in zero-sum games, where there are only a certain number of pie pieces to go around, and if one person gets one piece then someone else misses out. Neither salvation nor opportunities for growth or love are pieces of a pie.

The Savior recognized that this exponential multiplicity of reward challenges our natural drive for fairness and mathematical rightness when He shared the parable with His followers.

> For the kingdom of heaven is like unto a man that is an householder, which went out early in the morning to hire laborers into his vineyard. And when he had agreed with the laborers for a penny a day, he sent them into his vineyard.
>
> And he went out about the third hour, and saw others standing idle in the marketplace, And said unto them; Go ye also into the vineyard, and whatsoever is right I will give you. And they went their way.
>
> Again he went out about the sixth and ninth hour, and did likewise. And about the eleventh hour he went out, and found others standing idle, and saith unto them, Why stand ye here all the day idle?
>
> They say unto him, Because no man hath hired us.
>
> He saith unto them, Go ye also into the vineyard; and whatsoever is right, that shall ye receive.
>
> So when even was come, the lord of the vineyard saith unto his steward, Call the laborers, and give them their hire, beginning from the last unto the first.
>
> And when they came that were hired about the eleventh hour, they received every man a penny. But when the first came, they supposed that they should have received more; and they likewise received every man a penny. And when they had received it, they murmured against the goodman of the house, Saying, These last have wrought but one hour, and thou hast made them equal unto us, which have borne the burden and heat of the day.
>
> But he answered one of them, and said, Friend, I do thee no wrong: didst not thou agree with me for a penny? Take that thine is, and go thy way: I will give unto this last, even as unto thee. Is it not lawful for me to do what I will with mine own? Is thine eye evil, because I am good?
>
> So the last shall be first, and the first last: for many be called, but few chosen. (Matt. 20:1–16)

"Is thine eye evil, because I am good?" Does my possession of something deny you of that same thing? In our earthly paradigms, the answer is often yes. We learn at early ages to defend what is ours—that fairness is paramount to a sense of rightness in young lives. It *doesn't* seem fair, based on our earthly understanding of mathematical rightness, that a worker who labored only an hour receives the same pay as the worker who labored all day. Increased work and increased worthiness are so often rewarded with public recognition, through money or increased visibility or added responsibility. But Clayton Christensen, the Harvard Business School professor, reminds us, "Many of the Savior's most profound teachings are counterintuitive. . . . The solutions that our minds are prone to develop are often different from those the Lord would have us pursue." Christensen concludes, "For my thoughts are not your thoughts, neither are your ways my ways, saith the Lord" (Isa. 55:8).

Challenging the mathematical concept of equality is not the only way the Savior asks us to "prove contraries," but it may be one of the hardest.

Chapter Five

Are We Practicing What We Preach?

"No marriage or family, no ward or stake is likely to reach its full potential until husbands and wives, mothers and fathers, men and women work together in unity of purpose, respecting and relying upon each other's strengths."

Sheri L. Dew, Relief Society General Presidency,
"It Is Not Good for Man or Woman to Be Alone,"
General Conference, October 2001

If apostles today teach a different definition of equality than does the world around us, then what does our practice of equality look like? Are our practices in the Church currently meeting our definition of equality? Are our leaders telling us to walk away completely from the world's way of practicing equality?

The answer to each of those questions lies in where we draw our boundaries. There is presumably a certain degree of sameness and difference that fulfills the divine vision for how men and women relate to each other. There is presumably a horizon at which sameness needs to end so that divine difference has room to rise. We are working out where that boundary lies. Some secular voices push that boundary almost to nonexistence: many today would say it is ideal to have no boundary at all but a complete eclipse of male and female identities. Our Church leaders instead teach that the Lord doesn't endorse a complete eclipse. But we are still left with the question: Where does our commonality end and our difference begin?

As I have expressed earlier, the tension between these differing boundaries—one espoused by our external institutions and ideals and one espoused by church doctrine and practice—breeds a conundrum for many women. Why are the beneficial structures and opportunities they enjoy in parity with men not similarly reflected in their church experience? I am convinced, however, that the tension does not need to be as pronounced as it is for two reasons: first of all, we are a pragmatic people who use willing servants where we find them, and that means using our women more effectively; and second, despite a firm doctrinal belief in different responsibilities for men and women, our leaders have stressed not only how men and women are different, but how much they are the same.

First, our pragmatism. We are a pragmatic people who put our shoulders to the wheel and let no one shirk. We are a working people. And it will take considerable work to continue to grow the Church globally in the twenty-first century. We cannot thrive in the coming decades if we do not include the female workforce of the Church. Our leaders know that: the missionary age change and the introduction of sister training leaders shows our institutional dedication to increasing the visibility of women and the training of women to lead and make decisions. If we don't explore the full potential of women, we will be growing the Church with one hand tied behind our backs. A pragmatic approach to seeing, hearing, and including women wherever possible will increase our capacity to grow the Church in the coming decades.

The future of the Church as a global community might be represented in microcosm by the current Church in Hong Kong. Returning to Melissa Inouye's experience discussed in Chapter Three, she describes the local practical approach to Church leadership:

> Mormon domestic workers whose days off do not fall on Sunday attend the Sabbath services on Tuesday, Wednesday, Thursday, Friday, or Saturday. Two senior missionary couples from North America are assigned to superintend these full three-hour-block weekday meetings. They get Sundays off. Most Mormons are shocked to learn that these missionaries have official Church sanction to go to Disneyland on Sunday, but so it must be: Sunday is their Sabbath from the Sabbath.
>
> Another way in which the Hong Kong domestic worker units are unusual is in their leadership structure. . . . In the overwhelmingly female domestic worker branches of Hong Kong, . . . the Relief Society President exercises stewardship over nearly everyone in the congregation, and the executive secretaries and branch mission leaders are women. (When I asked a sister in the Island 1 Branch if the branch mission leader was really a woman, she gave me a blank look, as if I had asked whether President Monson, the Prophet, was really a man.)

Is this a vision of Brazil or perhaps even India or mainland China in the future? Will the growth of the Church necessitate expanded female participation as we use and train and develop the local populations? Relief Society general president Linda K. Burton recognized the practical importance of engaging women fully when she said the Church will benefit as "men's vision of the capacity of women becomes more complete." We do not let inflexibility stunt the growth of the kingdom.

Focusing on our Commonalities

Second, a rhetorical clarification of men and women's similarities. We have, over the past decades, built up a library of authoritative statements and cultural understandings around how the roles of men and women are different: women are mothers, men are priesthood holders; women are nurturers, men are breadwinners; men are public representatives, women act in supporting roles. Accurate or inaccurate, these identifiers have permeated so deeply that some women cannot see their own identities beyond what they think they're supposed to be.

Lost in the conversation, I believe, are the significant instances where the scriptures and our leaders talk about our similarities, our commonalities, even our sameness. In 1990, for instance, when BYU president Rex E. Lee addressed attendees at Women's Conference, he looked beyond the gender labels: "I look over the topics for this conference—relationships with aging parents, self-esteem for children, providing aid for abuse victims, and dimensions of service. . . . These are not women's issues. These are people's issues. Women are making gigantic efforts to find solutions to these concerns, but they should not be expected to do it alone." Elders M. Russell Ballard and Dallin H. Oaks, most recently and notably, have encouraged us to pay particular attention to the vast scope of identity, purpose, and pursuit that men and women have in common.

In an April 2013 General Conference address, Elder Ballard said, "Just as a woman cannot conceive a child without a man, so a man cannot fully exercise the power of the priesthood to establish an eternal family without a woman. . . . In the eternal perspective, both the procreative power and the priesthood power are shared by husband and wife." Later that year at BYU, Elder Ballard followed up with this statement: "Our Father in Heaven is generous with His power. All men and all women have access to this power for help in their lives. All who have made sacred covenants with the Lord and who honor those covenants are eligible to receive personal revelation, to be blessed by the ministering of angels, to commune with

God, to receive the fulness of the gospel, and, ultimately, to become heirs alongside Jesus Christ of all our Father has."

In statements like these, Elder Ballard is echoing the Lord's scriptural claim that He is "no respecter of persons" (Acts 10:34, D&C 1:35, 38:16) and that all people—rich and poor, bond and free, male and female—can be "partakers of the heavenly gift" (4 Ne. 1:3). He specifically indicates that "all" who have been endowed in the temple "have access" to priesthood power, underscoring commonality—not difference—between the genders.

In his talk in the April 2014 General Conference, Elder Dallin H. Oaks made the following statement:

> We are not accustomed to speaking of women having the authority of the priesthood in their Church callings, but what other authority can it be? When a woman—young or old—is set apart to preach the gospel as a full-time missionary, she is given priesthood authority to perform a priesthood function. The same is true when a woman is set apart to function as an officer or teacher in a Church organization under the direction of one who holds the keys of the priesthood. Whoever functions in an office or calling received from one who holds priesthood keys exercises priesthood authority in performing her or his assigned duties.

Elder Oaks's statement starts with unusual self-reflection on the rhetorical patterns that have built up around discussions of priesthood over generations: we are "not accustomed" to attributing priesthood authority to women, but "what else can it be?" he asks. It is as though Elder Oaks is astonished anyone thinks men and women *don't* share this commonality. Have we been overlooking the vast horizon of commonality that unifies us as brothers and sisters and concentrating instead on a narrower range of responsibilities and opportunities that divide us?

In light of Elder Ballard and Elder Oaks's statements, it seems evident that our practice of equality in the local Church experience is, in many cases, falling short of the vision being put forward by our Church leaders. If we were ideally practicing what we preach, I do not believe our leaders would dedicate so much effort to reiterating our beliefs. In Part II, we will take a tour of various local Church practices and attitudes that offer a glimpse into some ways equality can be practiced in the way leaders are currently preaching it. This tour might help us expand our spiritual imaginations to what is possible in Church governance. As we see models for effectively practicing equality in a gospel context, our desire and our ability to see, hear, and include women at the local Church level will bring us closer to truly practicing what we preach.

PART II
EXPLORING SOLUTIONS

Chapter Six

Getting Down to Work

"If the Lord is hastening His work we cannot keep doing things the same way we have always done them."

Elder David A. Bednar, Quorum of the Twelve Apostles,
Address at the Uganda Kampala Stake Center, January 22, 2014

In Part I of this book, I looked at why some women feel uncomfortable, underutilized, or even antagonistic toward their Church experiences. We probably all feel a little down right about now. The good news is it's time to move on to figuring out what we can do about it.

As I stated early on, I am working off the assumption that men and women will still be working in our current Church administrative structure for quite some time but that there are a range of ways we can improve the current experience within that structure. This is probably a good time also to say that I have deep gratitude for any person, man or woman, who accepts a calling in a local Church setting. Most of the time, these are thankless jobs, fraught with complicated interpersonal relationships and deep-seated feelings. I don't know anyone who has been close to local leaders who does not appreciate what difficult jobs they have. No matter how seemingly insignificant, our callings put us in the work of redemption, of salvation, of making this life truly reflective of our divine natures and potentials. And we do this in cinderblock church buildings with little training, while still having our own earthly work commitments to maintain. It is amazing that we do as well as we do, and a sign, I believe, that we are working under a divine mandate.

Because we are working in the art of redemption, we all care very deeply. If we were simply trying to offer an amusing social outlet or after-school youth program, we might not care quite so much, and we might not feel triumphs strengthening our very souls and failures chipping away at them so acutely. But our relationship with the Church is a reflection of our relationship to our faith; although we might cognitively separate the two when it is convenient or needful, the reality is that the way we feel at church impacts the way we feel about our faith. Faith, at least the way Mormons approach it, is neither practiced nor cultivated in isolation, and the communal relationships and interactions are the road on which faith finds its way. Despite the fact that we already have dedicated and good-hearted leaders, don't we want to make the Church experience even better if it is in our power to do so?

In Part II of this book, we do the work of figuring out how we can make the Church experience even better. There is no silver bullet here for addressing all of the concerns and contradictions I laid out in Part I; many of the concerns I outlined can only be addressed through a private wrestle with the Lord or perhaps some day from changes facilitated by prophetic instruction. But I hope by this point no reader is comfortable declaring that women (and men) who struggle with gender relations at church just need to pray and get with the program because everything is exactly the way it should be. There is so much we can do to aid our brothers and sisters in their wrestles and to make the path of church attendance smooth beneath our feet so that church becomes a place where struggles are supported, not compounded. The *Handbook* explicitly states that local leaders are free to "adapt some Church programs," and that the "guidelines [in the *Handbook*] are intended to help priesthood leaders determine which adaptations may be appropriate and which are not." In Part II, I hope to show how we can make church a haven, not a hindrance, for those who seek greater gender cooperation in their Church experiences. So let's get to it.

Chapter Seven

Identify the Audience and Walk in their Shoes

"We must cherish one another, watch over one another, comfort one another and gain instruction that we may all sit down in heaven together."

Lucy Mack Smith,
Relief Society Minutes, March 24, 1842

Now that we've established that some women crave greater inclusion, visibility, acceptance, and voice within the Church, what can we do to reimagine our current church culture to bridge the gaps women experience? A strategic approach to magnifying the impact of women at church must begin with establishing who in our wards, branches, and stakes need to be seen, heard, and included more effectively. In my professional life I work in advertising, and these are the women and men who, in the advertising world, we would call our "target audience."

For our purposes in this book, the target audience is not just any member of the Church but specifically members—men and women—who are struggling with the involvement and visibility of women in the Church's administrative structure. If we want to help those who are struggling spiritually and emotionally over the place of women in the Church, we first need to identify who they are.

Throughout Part I of this book, I've tried to present a clear picture of some of the struggles these fellow saints experience and some of the messages the Church or its members send that cause unnecessary tension. As an advertising professional, I know personally how hard advertisers work to put themselves in the shoes of their target audience so as to better understand how to make a connection with them in a thirty-second television commercial or single-page print ad. How much more, then, should we put ourselves in the shoes of concerned Church members if we are really committed to delivering the warm embrace of the gospel?

How can male and female leaders better understand and have greater compassion for this particular audience of Church members? How can they expand their empathetic stance? Consider the efforts my colleagues and I undertake in advertising to put ourselves in the audience's shoes: we carry out online and in-person surveys, we do focus groups, and we intercept people on the street, in stores, and in their places of work. Case studies abound in advertising of planners taking creative and heroic measures to answer questions about the target audience and understand them better. What does the target audience need? What are they lacking? Only when advertisers understand the answers to these questions can they really understand how to serve their audience.

A well-known example of this immersive approach is the "got milk?" campaign. When a San Francisco agency, Goodby, Silverstein & Partners, was hired by the California Fluid Milk Processors' Advisory Board to sell more milk, they were handed reams of research about milk's dietary benefits. "Milk is good for you" had been the primary message of previous communication attempts. This was an understandable message because it is a reasonable answer to a relevant question: "Why do people drink milk?" Seems logical enough. But through additional ethnographic and tracking research, in which they actually tracked potential customers' milk consumption, Goodby, Silverstein & Partners recognized that a healthy beverage wasn't something that any potential customer was actually looking for. The target audience wasn't asking for a finger-wagging mother figure to look over them and tell them to drain their cup because it's good for them. They put themselves in the customer's shoes so thoroughly that they were finally able to ask the right question: The question that provided the insightful breakthrough wasn't "Why do people drink milk?"—the question was, "*When* do people drink milk?"

By putting themselves in the shoes of milk consumers, the agency planners realized that people rarely drink milk in public, and they rarely if ever drink it independent of food. "Milk, it seemed, could not create its own desire. On the other hand, these appetizing, sometimes naughty companion foods [cereal, cookies, brownies] . . . seemed capable of creating a powerful craving that could only be satisfied with milk as part of the equation." The researchers only came to this understanding by recreating the lived experience of their target audience, which opened their eyes to entirely new truths. People have an emotional response to milk that was difficult to capture in the statistics and surveys that had previously been completed. That emotional response could only be understood by walking in the shoes of the target audience.

We can apply this approach of immersive understanding to those we interact with at church. In his April 2014 General Conference address, Elder W. Craig Zwick pleaded with us to put ourselves into the place of others so that we can more easily adopt the empathetic stance that is so crucial to nurturing others' spiritual health. He suggested that we can "transform hazardous situations into holy places" by evaluating another's viewpoint from their own perspective. He counseled,

> There exists today a great need for men and women to cultivate respect for each other across wide distances of belief and behavior and across deep canyons of conflicting agendas. It is impossible to know all that informs our minds and hearts or even to fully understand the context for the trials and choices we each face.
>
> Nevertheless, what would happen to the "corrupt communication" Paul spoke about if our own position included empathy for another's experience first? Fully owning the limits of my own imperfections and rough edges, I plead with you to practice asking this question, with tender regard for another's experience: "What are you thinking?"

Poet Carol Lynn Pearson famously invoked the American Indian proverb, "Never criticize a man until you've walked a mile in his moccasins," when she invited her readers to "walk in pink moccasins" and consider how our traditional Church rhetoric might change if a female leader were speaking to male members as their ecclesiastical authority. Such thought experiments may be theoretical, but they play an important part in helping us see things from the perspective of the people we wish to reach. Next time you find your mind wandering at church, read the scriptures replacing all male references to female ones. Can you imagine the Book of Mormon with a Nephia and Moronia? Imagine what it might feel like to see all women on the stand instead of all men. Imagine reading only the words of women in our Relief Society and priesthood manuals. While discussing women of the Bible at work recently, a good-hearted male colleague happened to mention that he hadn't really paid much attention to any of the women in the Bible because he couldn't relate to them. The moment he said this, his hand flew to his shocked mouth and he apologized profusely to me. We had a good laugh about his response because it was such a textbook moment of realization for him: women are constantly engaged in a process of likening male role models unto themselves, while men rarely have to go through the same process of disassociating their own gender to find inspiration in female characters.

This principle is humorously but poignantly illustrated in the observations of a male Primary chorister in Provo, Utah:

> One Sunday I asked for volunteers to play Helaman and his warriors so that we could sing the song ["We'll Bring the World His Truth"]. I called upon each of the boys, but none of them would do it. So, I asked Jane if she could help me. She stood up, snarled her 11-year-old snarl, and said: "I will, but I am tired of all of the songs and the stories being about boys. The boys around here don't even take the songs and scriptures seriously. I will help you, but I'm not Helaman, I'm Shelaman!" In no time the girls of the Primary had crowded around her as the stripling warriors, and they all broke into the chorus: "We are as the armies of Shelaman/we have been taught in our youth." Jane knew that this was a safe space, and she needed to express something to me as a tie-wearing authority figure. Believe me, I listened.

Challenge yourself to find parity in practices, activities, and traditions: Why do Boy Scouts have a Blue & Gold Banquet and the Activity Days girls do not have an event of their own? Why do boys go home teaching with their fathers but girls do not go visiting teaching with their mothers? Why are boys honored in front of the congregation when they turn twelve and receive the priesthood, and girls are not required to receive the same recognition when they enter Young Women? Why are individual priesthood leaders introduced and sustained at ward conferences when female leaders are not? If there is a father-and-son campout, is there also a father-and-daughter or mother-and-daughter campout? (My ward recently announced from the pulpit that our annual "father-and-son campout" was now a "father-and-child campout." There were audible cheers from the congregation, and not just from my three daughters.)

These questions might make us uncomfortable, they might even feel wrong. But there's a lesson there, an opportunity to stretch our empathetic stance by seeing the Church experience through the eyes of a woman who may feel invisible or underappreciated. As one woman wrote to me, women have "vastly different experiences" in their Church membership than men. By walking in women's shoes, we can make sure we are asking the right questions about what we can do to improve the impact of women at church.

Chapter Eight

Are We Asking the Right Questions?

"I believe that the moment we learn to unleash the full influence of converted, covenant-keeping women, the kingdom of God will change overnight."
Sheri L. Dew, *Women and the Priesthood*

With an understanding and appreciation of those sisters with concerns, we are prepared to ask what those women's needs are and how the Church is best equipped to answer those needs.

Perhaps not surprisingly, the most revolutionary concept in understanding an audience to emerge in recent years was pioneered by a Mormon who has likely spent his fair share of time trying to put himself in others' shoes spiritually as well as commercially. Harvard Business School professor Clayton Christensen has adapted this practice of immersive customer understanding into something called the "job-to-be-done" framework. "Looking at the market from the function of a product really originates from your competitors or your own employees deciding what you need," Christensen writes, "Whereas the jobs-to-be-done point of view causes you to crawl into the skin of your customer and go with her as she goes about her day, always asking the question as she does something: Why did she do it that way?"

The "got milk?" research efforts were an excellent example of Christensen's thesis: asking the right question revealed the effective, emotionally driven answer that might not be evident in traditional approaches. If we adapt the job-to-be-done model to our experiences at church, we might ask different questions. For instance, a common question we ask ourselves might be, "Why are some women unhappy at church?" With this question, we start from the defensive position of assuming that women are unhappy (thus labeling them irrevocably) and that their experience at church is less than ideal (which can feel emotionally threatening to those who are not unhappy). We immediately set up an us versus them stance: "Something I am doing or something about the Church I love is perceived to be at fault (or not good enough, or offensive, etc.), so therefore I am at fault."

It can be hard for those who love the Church experience to empathize because they perceive the women's unhappiness to be a personal indictment of their own comfort. And so a typical, defensive answer to this question might be, "Some women are unhappy at church because they just don't understand the doctrine well enough." The drawback of this answer is that it doesn't allow any room for the lived experience to diverge from the spiritual ideal. There seems to be an assumption that spiritual confirmation of a truth necessitates being totally okay with the way that truth is translated into human practice. This may not always be the case. In reality, doctrine carries no guarantees of its principles being practiced ideally.

If, however, we reframe the question in the job-to-be-done model, we might get to this: "What job do women need their Church experience to perform in their lives?" This is a foundational shift in the way we evaluate women's needs. This alternative question not only relieves us of our defensive stance, but it allows us to assess individual needs with empathy. An answer to this second question might be something like, "Women come to church to feel part of a community of Saints who are working to improve each other's lives." If a woman is unhappy at church, we can draw our own conclusion that there is something that is prohibiting her from having that need filled in her life. Such a question clears a path to a more productive solution because what one woman needs to feel a part of a community of Saints may be different than what another needs, and so no one's personal comfort is indicted.

In his book, *The Power of Everyday Missionaries*, Clayton Christensen applies his insights about asking the right questions to a Church setting. Opening a chapter about reaching out to less-active members, Christensen says:

> One of the most important skills that a leader needs to master is to ask the right question, because asking the right question is critical to knowing the thoughts and the ways of God. One example where we might be asking the wrong question, and consequently missing the thoughts and the ways of God, occurs every Sunday in every ward and branch in the church, when the question is asked: "How many people attended sacrament meeting today?"... Attendance numbers are important, but I can't help wondering if we are sometimes collecting the right answer to the wrong question as it relates to building the kingdom of God. . . . The Savior suggested that the right question is, "Who *didn't* come today?"

Reframing questions and asking new questions can help us understand our specific audience so that we can arrive at less self-reflective, more empathetic answers. For instance, I am convinced good-hearted male leaders are constantly asking themselves, "Am I *telling* women enough how much we love and appreciate them?" Many times the answer is yes. This is a question that can, to some degree, have a quantifiable answer on paper. From general conference talks to Mother's Day flowers, women at church are *told* regularly how much we are loved. And yet we still are having problems with women feeling sufficiently heard, respected, and involved. If we adjust the question just slightly, we might get closer to the heart of the problem: "Are we *showing* women how much we love and appreciate them?" Better yet, "Are we *seeing, hearing, and including* women at church in a way that shows them we love and appreciate them?" And I will take it one step further: "Are we *seeing, hearing, and including* women at church in a way that allows them to know we respect them and their ideas?"

And there, I believe, is where we have finally asked the right question. I will talk more about the rhetoric we use to speak about women later, but my point here is that when women are unhappy at church, it is our responsibility to ask ourselves what job these women are expecting the Church to do for them and then do everything in our power and with the tools we have to work with to fulfill that job. If we merely tell them that they are loved, but don't do anything to acknowledge or adopt their offered contributions to the Church community, we are no better than the spouse who disregards the wife's gift because the wife is the object of affection, not the gift. To the woman, to any participant in a community, the job to be done is to have expressions of the self be recognized as valued contributions to the community.

Is the Church organization equipped to meet this need? Can it use women in a way that both converts them to God's love for them and the Church's regard for their ideas and experiences?

I answer a resounding yes. In the 2012 worldwide leadership training, Elder Ballard asked Young Women president Elaine S. Dalton about the main purpose of the Church:

> *Elder Ballard:* What is the main purpose of the Church, Sister Dalton? What is this work we're trying to do?
>
> *Sister Dalton:* It's to bring families, to seal families so that they can be eternal in our Heavenly Father's kingdom.
>
> *Elder Ballard:* Absolutely. And we could use His words, "This is my work."

Sister Dalton: "And my glory."

Elder Ballard: What? "To bring to pass the immortality and eternal life of man" (Moses 1:39). And so in a lot of the efforts we do in the Church, we've got to also always keep in mind that we're trying to help each other make that wonderful goal of being able to go back to Heavenly Father when life is over.

The Church facilitates a fabulously focused and defined offering that is well established in the hearts and minds of its members and reaffirmed continually by our leaders, such as in the example above. When we really internalize the promise of that offering—to bring to pass the immortality and eternal life of each one of us—we are prompted to change our behavior in positive ways. We are strengthened by the sustaining fruits of gospel activity. We interact with the gospel in ways that allow it to fulfill its promise to us.

Our leaders have encouraged us repeatedly to see the Church as a flexible support for the work of salvation. Elder Ballard has reminded us, "Sometimes we get so focused on bringing people to the meetinghouse that we forget we are supposed to be bringing them to Christ." Harold B. Lee similarly observed, "Much of what we do organizationally . . . is scaffolding, as we seek to build the individual, and we must not mistake the scaffolding for the soul." The sooner we accept the Church as the institution supporting the work of faith, the more eager we will be to use its tools to the fullest. Conversely, the sooner we recognize the job the Church is designed to do, the sooner we will stop expecting it to be all things to all people and recognize that much of the work of salvation is not up to leaders or institutions or manuals. It's up to us.

So in the spirit of asking the right questions, I suggest the following three for focusing our efforts toward magnifying women's impact:

- What job are members of my congregation asking the Church to do for them?
- Does that job fall under the mission of fostering immortality and eternal life?
- Does the Church have the structure in place to deliver on that request?

Finding Flexibility in the Scaffolding

In the stories I've collected, it has occurred to me that for us as members and leaders, the last of the above questions is the most difficult for us to answer. This is not because we don't trust the Church to deliver on the job to be done. It is more often than not because we hesitate to see the Church as a flexible, living organism that is built for the members. Instead we make the mistake of thinking that it is the members that are built for the Church. We lose sight of the Church as the support system, and, in President Lee's words, we "mistake the scaffolding for the soul." We think that because we have always done things a certain way, that it is the only way that a need can be met—when, in fact, individual members' needs usually require some spiritual and organizational imagination to comprehend and address.

Let's look at an example of a common ward practice to see how these questions might lead us to creative and appropriate answers to specific needs: the baby blessing. For a baby blessing, the job that the target audience needs done is to feel acknowledged, appreciated, and involved in her child's official launch into Church membership. Remember that we are talking about a target audience that isn't happy just sitting on the sidelines; a woman in the target audience sees her inability to stand in the circle as a divine slight to the hard work she put into growing and birthing a child of God. Does having a woman, a new mother, feel acknowledged, appreciated, and involved put her more solidly on a path to immortality and eternal life? It would seem so. Does the Church have the structure in place to deliver on the job she is asking it to do? Can the Church make her feel acknowledged, appreciated, and involved in this instance?

To answer this, we must go to the *Handbook of Instructions*, which offers every member and leader the opportunity to learn how the scaffolding is intended to work. Today, no member is denied the opportunity to answer the last question for him or herself, and a quick search of the *Handbook* online or in print will bring us to the structure for performing baby blessings:

> "Every member of the church of Christ having children is to bring them unto the elders before the church, who are to lay their hands upon them in the name of Jesus Christ, and bless them in his name" (D&C 20:70). In conformity with this revelation, only Melchizedek Priesthood holders may participate in naming and blessing children. Priesthood leaders should inform members of this instruction before their children are named and blessed. While preserving the sacred nature of the blessing, leaders should make every reasonable effort to avoid embarrassment or offense to individuals or families.
>
> Children are normally named and blessed during fast and testimony meeting in the ward where the parents are members of record.

In studying this passage, we can all see that "only" Melchizedek Priesthood holders may lay their hands on the child to give the blessing, although the "only" is not found in the scripture from which the practice is drawn. (In my own case many decades ago, my dad stood in the circle to bless me, although he only held the Aaronic Priesthood, while my uncle, a Melchizedek Priesthood holder, said the blessing; my father was always grateful for this opportunity. The *Handbook* now states, however, that only men ordained to the Melchizedek Priesthood are allowed to participate—though they need not be temple worthy. The practice of welcoming non-recommend holding men into the circle while still excluding worthy women gives angst to some recommend-holding women.) For our purposes, though, let us assume the bishop and the family are committed to following the *Handbook* exactly. The question becomes: Are there *other* ways the mother can feel acknowledged, appreciated, and involved?

This is where our spiritual and organizational imaginations can motivate us to see the flexibility in the scaffolding, the opportunity to say, "What new practice could accomplish our goals without overstepping our administrative bounds?" I've received feedback on what a number of members and leaders are doing:

- "My ward has the mother come sit on the stand for her child's baby blessing, where she is thus honored before the congregation and has a better view of the ordinance. Short of joining the circle, I think that's a brilliant adaptation."

- "The bishop told me before the sacrament meeting, as the mother of the baby getting blessed, that he would like me to bear my testimony right after the blessing. As the men were sitting down, I was able to share my thoughts about the moment immediately after it happened. I felt like an honorary participant. With the blessings of my other babies, I felt like nobody would have noticed I was even there unless I had forced myself to bear my testimony with the rest of the congregation."

- "We've blessed all of our babies at home, surrounded by family where everyone could write down one or two things about the blessing directly after it was over. My baby daughter's older sister, who was 4 at the time, even stood under the circle where her father and uncles and grandfathers were holding the baby, looking up through their arms. Later, she told me she felt the Holy Ghost for the first time at that moment, looking up from the center of the circle."

- "Today I watched a mother hold her new baby as the men circled to give the baby a name and a blessing. It's the first time I've ever seen that, but it was beautiful and right and lovely."

- "When my first two children were born, we did the baby blessings at home (with our bishops' assent) because I strongly felt that I should be involved. I knew that Mormon women had a rich history of blessing each other and their children, and I thought it would be beautifully symbolic of our mutual love and commitment if my husband and I held our baby together during the blessing. We composed the blessing together, and then he read it as we held our baby with all our friends and family gathered. Those were beautiful blessings.

  "But by the time I had my third child, I knew I wanted something a little different. I felt that it was time to bless my child in the presence of my ward community. I didn't want to hide who I was and what I wanted anymore. I knew it was a risk, and that people might feel threatened by my participation, but I also knew that this was a good desire and that there is precedent for women holding their babies during baby blessings in Sacrament Meeting.

  "So my husband and I approached our bishop. He was initially uncomfortable with the idea of me holding the baby inside the circle while it was blessed by my husband. I said that if I wasn't able to hold the baby, I'd like to hold the microphone. I knew that didn't require priesthood. The bishop was even more uncomfortable with that idea, and began to rethink his stance on me holding the baby, which he thought was a more dignified role than microphone holder.

  "Our bishop thought and prayed about this for a couple of months and spoke to the stake president. From what I understand, he told the bishop that this was his decision. The bishop came to no clear answer, so he ultimately told us that he was willing to let us decide and that he would fully support the decision, though personally he was uncomfortable with my participation. This bishop later expressed appreciation for the process by which this decision—to let me and my husband determine our course—was made.

  "While I was impressed that he was willing to leave this decision up to us, I was disappointed that he didn't feel good about the proposed baby blessing. I was sad that he didn't seem to see the vision behind this desire, that he didn't see the symbolic beauty of such an action. So I then had to decide if it was worth it to pursue. I finally decided that this opening the bishop gave us was God-given, and that I would regret it for the rest of my life if I didn't do what I knew was right for us.

"So we proceeded forward with it, and it came together perfectly. When it was time, I carried the baby to the front, sat in the folding chair they had waiting for me, held the baby out, and the circle of men (which included three current or former bishops) put their hands under the baby to help support him. It was so fluid that I doubt half the ward even noticed I was there.

"Afterwards, about three women approached me and told me that it was a beautiful way to do it, and that they wished every baby blessing was like that. I heard no negative feedback at all.

"I am happy with our decision. I won't lie—it was a difficult thing to do, and I had to gather up all my courage to do it. But for more inclusive practices to take hold, someone has to be willing to pursue it and carry it out, even in the face of disapproval. In the end, it meant a lot to me to know that even though this was a difficult process, there was space for me within my ward and church to follow my conscience and proceed forward with this blessing in a way that was personally important to me. It also felt good to be honest with my ward family about who I am. I hope it was good for them in turn to realize that people within their own congregation may have desires and perspectives that are different from theirs, and that that's just fine. There is and should be room for that within our church."

We can see that in none of these examples did anyone but Melchizedek Priesthood holders stand in the circle, lay their hands on the child's head, and evoke priesthood power. Some may be uncomfortable with the way the mothers holding the baby "participated" in these blessings, since they could be seen as participating on a technicality: she didn't stand in the circle per se, but she was clearly involved. If it makes us uncomfortable, we could ask ourselves why are we uncomfortable. Is it because we have never seen it done that way? Is it because the blessing is ineffectual if a woman holds the baby? Is it because, although not a saving ordinance, we want to see our baby blessings reflect the exactness required by ordinances? These responses are understandable, but we also must again ask ourselves what is accomplished by alienating a woman for whom such participation is important. Telling her to just get in line isn't only uncharitable, it's unnecessary.

New cultural practices don't just spring out of the ground. The way we shift culture is to create culture, to offer another version of a practice, another way to show obedience to the word of God. And any other version starts with a vision of how things could be. We encourage positive innovation by deliberately approaching practices and habits with an eye to restoring faith where it might otherwise be weak.

Offering a New Vision

As men and women fulfilling Church callings at the ward or stake level, we have the opportunity every week to shape and craft the experiences of others and to strengthen or weaken the scaffolding that is protecting the development of individual souls. Regardless of whether we are in the nursery or in the bishop's office, the way we plan and carry out our tasks can reflect our level to commitment to our own faith and to the nurturing of others' faith. When we see something amiss—either in an area of our stewardship or under another's stewardship—how do we go about offering a new vision of how things could be?

Dave Blanchard, one of the founders of Praxis Labs, a business accelerator for faith-motivated entrepreneurs who have committed their lives to cultural and social impact, has suggested the following approach for evaluating opportunities to improve practices. I adopt it here as a framework to approach adaptive thinking about women's contributions, useful to each one of us serving in a local setting. So, in other words, all of us. The principles of Blanchard's approach are Prayer, People, Process, and Perseverance.

Chapter Nine

Prayer

"We find ourselves here—one of the ones Moses saw—part of a great pan-orama, and yet struggling as individuals to find the identity we once knew, as well as the sense of purpose and belonging we once had. As we gain our gospel knowledge here on earth, where we have to learn it all over again, we see this precious truth—that in our premortal life we exercised our agency when we chose Christ as our leader. He does his part and each of us can do ours to make covenants and build a partnership with him."

Aileen H. Clyde, Relief Society General Presidency,
"Confidence Through Conversion,"
Ensign, November 1992

Ward and stake leaders who take their callings seriously are often en-gaged in a process of reflection about how things are going or what they could be doing better. It is a rare Relief Society president or elders quorum president who goes Monday through Saturday without thinking about or reaching out to others about his or her calling. Internal conversations, with oneself or with the specific intent of conversing with God, often bring us to the point of evaluating what more we can do. We ask questions such as: What could I do to make the experience more meaningful for those I teach, serve, or minister to? Where am I weak? What do I do well? Where could I find more time to prepare? How could I be better in tune with what my class or congregation needs?

I suggest that this process of introspection and prayer is where we identify where there might be opportunities for proactive thinking about increasing the visibility and involvement of women. The questions we ask ourselves throughout the week—consciously or subconsciously, through prayer or personal reflection—are simply ways to work out what those who are struggling need and how the Church is best equipped to answer those needs. I include in this Prayer phase all of the introspection that comes when approaching a challenge or working through it; it's the element of self-awareness and spiritual in-tuneness that must accompany any effort. The authors of the national best-selling book, *Crucial Confrontations*, call this the "Work on Me First" phase: when we're preparing to confront either something we believe can be improved or someone who's bothering us, this is the phase in which we make sure we are confronting the right problems and that our strong emotions don't get the best of us.

This process of prayer will have different goals for different people, depending on where they are in their understanding of and compassion for those who wrestle with gendered practices. There are some who are oblivious to the tension around gender interactions. For these, perhaps the purpose of prayer is simply to ask to have a real conviction that gender interactions are important to care about. For others who have already come to this conclusion, prayer can help identify the specific tensions. Some might have already identified the tensions and are seeking inspiration on how to relieve them. Some may be seeking to prioritize, evaluating the individual or communal impact of a particular practice. Wherever we are in the process of empathizing with, identifying, or solving gender tensions, prayer is the critical first step in which we should all be constantly and meaningfully engaged.

Not only is prayer important in helping us open our spiritual imaginations and seeing the options the Lord might suggest to us, as decision makers and implementers, it is also important in establishing a conviction within ourselves that an adaption of a practice is in fact of God. Unfortunately, few policy evolutions will be met with unanimous approbation, even if a ward council or auxiliary presidency has been brought on board. A blogger recently put a comic spin on the damned-if-you-do-damned-if-you-don't response so many Church decisions receive in this age of instant idea sharing: "You can't please everybody. I can't, you can't, the church can't—and that shouldn't be our goal anyway. Doing X will infuriate some people, but if you change course and do Y instead, a whole 'nother faction will be enraged. Build unique, elaborate, sophisticated temples? So worldly! Build humble, cookie-cutter, cost-effective chapels? So boring!" In the face of criticism or pushback, a leader who is confident that his or her recommendation has come from a place of inspiration and pure desires is better prepared to weather the criticisms.

For example, I read online about a bishop who invited his ward's young women to provide the bread for the sacrament in an effort to involve them in an ordinance that so obviously puts the young men front and center, visually and spiritually, in the ward's perception. It was his way of trying to address a gender concern, to involve the young women more completely in serving the whole ward as the boys do, and I think it's safe to assume he prayed about this particular solution and perhaps consulted his ward council and the Young Women president specifically. In fact, this bishop's seemingly innovative solution is not in fact innovative at all, but was rather a way of connecting contemporary young women with their spiritual foremothers: making the sacrament bread was a sacred domestic ritual cherished by early Mormon women. For example, Frances Ann Adams' 1903 obituary in the *Woman's Exponent* included the detail that she had made the sacrament bread for her ward for twenty-five years.

Despite this historical significance, which undoubtedly was lost on most of this bishop's congregation but was precious nonetheless, the bishop has been criticized in various online conversations for patronizing the girls and merely playing into chauvinistic attitudes: asking the girls to be responsible for the bread merely tethered them to their role of keepers of the kitchen, only exacerbating the fact that they are in the background while the boys do the real work. While it may be impossible to find a comprehensive solution satisfactory to all, I hope that the bishop can find peace in the face of criticism knowing that his solution came from sincere concern, creative thinking, and inspiration through meditation on the matter. I also hope critics can appreciate this bishop making the effort to implement an adaptive practice that is tied to our foremothers. (The example at the end of this chapter offers an example of the introspection and self-awareness that can accompany this particular adapted practice.)

Those who struggle with gendered division of labor are not always in a position to take public action or even influence those in decision-making roles at the local Church level. Even women who are in leadership roles are curtailed in the scope of their decision-making abilities, since almost without exception they report to higher male leaders. The next chapter will discuss the channels of communication that might be available to those who would like to make constructive suggestions or engage in a dialogue with a decision maker, but prayer can also be a safe place in which we figure out the best way to express our concern or suggestion. It can be an opportunity to privately consider the opportunity and approach, to study and reflect in our minds and in our hearts before we take on any communication or behavioral change. It is, most importantly, an opportunity to educate ourselves about God's will, rather than seek a way to impose our own.

If we are feeling uncertain how to proceed, how to express our ideas, how to get anybody to listen, or even if our idea is a right or good one, starting with prayer is an essential step for answering critical questions, such as the following:

- Which specific practice am I struggling with? Or alternatively, which practices are people under my stewardship struggling with?
- Am I the only one in my local congregation who is struggling? How could I go about finding out if others are struggling too? Who might those others be? Or, are there women or men in my congregation struggling with gender division?
  - What is it about this practice that makes me/them uncomfortable?
  - What job am I asking the Church experience to do for me?
  - Why do I feel it is falling short?
  - What is the principle behind this practice? Am I at peace with the principle?
  - Is the job I am asking the Church experience to do for me something that it is actually designed and equipped to do, or are my needs outside of what it offers?
  - What is it about this practice that is affecting others adversely?
- How much flexibility is there within the particular area of practice?
  - Am I familiar with what the *Handbook* says about policies related to this practice?
  - Is our practice inextricably linked to a principle? Can we divide principle from practice in this case?
  - Do we engage in this practice because it is found in scripture, in the *Handbook* or in the specific writings of prophets, or is it a reflection of traditions, customs, or the personality of a specific leader?
  - What practice modification is entirely off the table?
  - Is there historical precedence for this practice being done differently? When and where?
  - Are there scriptural examples or justifications that are appropriate to cite?
- What solutions are available that honor the principle and any official direction but take advantage of organizational flexibility?

Prayer in the Real World: Baking a Sacrament Prayer

The process of Prayer as discussed here involves more than simply talking to God. It's the process of coming to know ourselves and coming to know the mind and will of God. It's feeling connected to the rightness of what we're doing. This doesn't necessarily always happen while we are on our knees. Prayer, as we are fond of noting, is a form of work.

Being rooted to our foremothers holds particular significance for historian Kristine Wright, who wrote about the personal impact of her own efforts to participate in "the sacramental meal." In this excerpt from an essay, "Baking a Sacrament Prayer," Wright offers an example of the kinds of insights that prayer and reflection can bring when we magnify the avenues of Church participation.

It is early on Saturday morning when I begin the process of making the bread. After working with whole grains for many years, I can't bring myself to use white flour but think there could be a possible rebellion if I present a dense, 100 percent whole wheat loaf to my ward. I settle on spelt, which will still yield a loaf light in color and texture. I grind the spelt berries—embracing the teachings of a whole history of Homemaking classes. Yet this is no superficial exercise in Molly Mormonism—I find great pleasure and meaning in my task. I measure out water, yeast, olive oil, honey, and salt and begin to mix the ingredients. I watch the transformation of these simple yet symbolic elements.

This time I am not using my bread mixer. I want this to be the work of my own hands—and I realize at this moment that, by separating myself from the task through technology, in some ways, I haven't really made bread in several years. Bread is a living process, and kneading the dough brings its own rewards. The repetition and rhythm free the mind for contemplation. My hands are sticky, but I feel the familiar sensation of the dough beginning to spring to life beneath my fingers—the leaven in the lump. It is here that the transcendent nature of this holy food begins—the symbol of the body of Christ.

As I rhythmically knead the floury mass, I feel the power of this newly born, embodied ritual. The familiar words spring to my mind: "O God, the Eternal Father, we ask thee in the name of thy Son, Jesus Christ, to bless and sanctify this bread to the souls of all those who partake of it, that they may eat in remembrance of the body of thy Son . . ."

My little daughter pulls up a chair beside me. "What are you doing?"

"Making the sacrament bread," I reply.

"Oooh, nice," she sighs, slipping her arm through mine. . . .

The dough has been transformed into a smooth ball, and set in a protected place, then sheltered with a red tea towel. Covering the sacrament bread with colored cloth doesn't resonate with my Mormon sensibilities. I search for a large white napkin. Mirroring the ritual preparation of thousands of sacrament meetings, I gently drape the bread in white. I go through the typical bread-baking process—punching down the dough and allowing for a second rise, shaping the loaf, waiting for a third rise, and then into the oven. Once it has cooled, I cover the bread again with the white cloth.

I take the bread to church the next morning, and I'm completely unprepared for my own reaction. We sing, "O God, th' Eternal Father" and all of sudden I am too emotional to sing as I watch two priests, both of whom I have known since they were three, carefully breaking up my bread. I know that my sacrifice is a broken heart and a contrite spirit, but it feels very meaningful to lay something tangible on the altar as well. There is "a difference between doing something yourself and observing someone else doing it. [It is] a matter of great significance."

In a small way, I am a partner in feeding my ward this sacramental meal. The deacons approach our row. Gandhi's words spring to my mind, "There are people in the world so hungry, that God cannot appear to them except in the form of bread." I approach my God through bread—the morsel of bread that I eat now, the bread that I have fed His sheep today, the bread I have baked.

The author here has found a practice in which she can have particular, personal investment. This might not be the answer for every person seeking how to adapt and magnify current practices, but Wright has clearly found something that allows her to meditate on the significance of her covenants and feel like she is contributing to her community's worship. She has come closer to understanding God and His will through her highly personal, contemplative work. That is, after all, the greatest reward of any prayer.

Chapter Ten

People

"Truly, we may each be an instrument in the hands of God. Happily, we need not all be the same kind of instrument. Just as the instruments in an orchestra differ in size, shape, and sound, we too are different from one another. We have different talents and inclinations, but just as the French horn cannot duplicate the sound of the piccolo, neither is it necessary for us to all serve the Lord in the same way."

Mary Ellen Smoot, Relief Society General President,
"We Are Instruments in the Hands of God,"
Ensign, November 2000

For both those who are in positions of leadership and those who are not, knowing who to talk to and how to talk to them might be the most important step in the whole process. The People step is about evaluating who best to approach in a dialogue and how to approach them to ensure the most cooperative, mutually beneficial outcome.

As we've already discovered from several of the anecdotes included so far, emotions can run hot when men and women are feeling their way through situations at church. This is partly because we care so very much: as lay clergy for our church, it is our own responsibility to build the kingdom of God on the earth. We don't participate to win a nicest neighborhood contest or even so that our kids will have some moral standards. We participate because we believe that we are preparing the world for the Second Coming of Jesus Christ. That's heady stuff, and because we believe it's so important and because we care so deeply, conflict's sting can feel even sharper than it perhaps would in another setting.

Turning again to his April 2014 General Conference talk, Elder W. Craig Zwick discussed the intense feelings that can arise when we must cooperate with other people on things that are important to us, and he used a personal example to illustrate how misunderstandings might arise when working with others in high stakes situations. He described his and his wife's differing reactions when the cab of the semi truck they were driving filled with smoke. As he tried to slow the truck and steer it to safety, his wife jumped out of the still-moving truck with their infant son in her arms, prompting Elder Zwick to cry, "What in the world were you thinking?" They took different approaches in the face of a tense situation, but both had the common goal of protecting their family. Elder Zwick expands on the principle of his story: "When our truck cab filled with smoke, my wife acted in the bravest manner she could imagine to protect our son. I too acted as a protector when I questioned her choice. Shockingly, it did not matter who was more right. What mattered was listening to each other and understanding the other's perspective."

Finding the Right Approach

The women I spoke with are universally aware of how strategic they need to be when approaching male leaders. Many expressed to me a desire to be respectful but also bold and confident, and they described a process of education as they learned how to best work with male leaders. One stake Relief Society president told me, "I served under two stake presidents. The first played Make-A-Deal at our every meeting. 'If you do this for me, I'll do that. . . . If you want that for the women, then do this for me.' Once I figured out that was the way he worked, we got a lot done. When the next stake president came along, I tried the same tactic with him. He looked at me as if I had two heads!"

The woman went on:

> When I was a more recent convert in the church, I tried to go in and exert my authority and I started to see the doors slamming in my face. I learned that if you create a reputation that you're easy to work with, you get more opportunities to serve. I now know when to back off. I pick my battles. You have to have a platform before you have a battle. You have to show them you're easy to work with, you're dedicated, you're a hard worker.

The desire to be a trusted voice exerting influence from the inside was a theme that was repeated to me by men and women alike. "I want to be a voice for women in my stake," one stake presidency member told me. "The stake president knows he can trust me on these issues. He lets me run with my ideas on this front. But I couldn't accomplish anything if I was an angry outsider. Trusted voices will prevail." One stake Relief Society president likened herself to Glinda from the musical *Wicked*, working from the inside instead of blasting out of bounds like her best-friend-turned-nemesis, Elphaba.

Humor is another theme that rose again and again in my interviews. As we shared a quarter hour of belly laughs, one elderly woman sketched entire scenes for me: They started with the chauvinistic neighbor man who repeatedly told her to clean up her flowerbeds and sweep her front walk. Then her husband, the high priest group leader at the time, assigned the disagreeable neighbor to home teach them so no one else in the ward would have to put up with him. And then when the neighbor came to home teach and tried to advise the woman on additional womanly duties, the woman would simply reply, "Really? Really! *Really?*" to everything he said. A cheerful woman anyway, she giggled and sparkled as she recalled her clever tactic.

In my own experience, graciousness has no end of benefits. Sincerely acknowledging the goodness and value of another person as a starting point allows a conversation to blossom into a discussion of improvements. Assuming the person I am talking to has good intentions at heart allows me to more effectively point out why a tactic or approach may not be having the impact the other person is hoping for. Because of the breadth and depth of interviews I've participated in over the past several years, I'm convinced that people rarely introduce policies or practices to be malicious or to exercise dominance. More often than not, Church leaders sincerely implement policies and practices to fill holes and answer problems. Those may not be the holes or problems that are a priority to me, I may disagree with the approach, or I may think there are harmful repercussions to the approach, but rarely have I seen a leader propose an initiative that doesn't offer some sort of real, communal benefit in that leader's mind.

In Proverbs we read, "A soft answer turneth away wrath: but grievous words stir up anger" (Prov. 15:1). I feel like a "soft answer" is one that fully acknowledges, to the best of my ability, where the other person is coming from. It doesn't mean the answer is devoid of reason or intellectual rigor. In fact, reason and rigor are paramount to a soft answer; it is the hardness of absolutism and pride that are absent. Elder Zwick defines a "soft answer" as "disciplined words from a humble heart. It does not mean we never speak directly or that we compromise doctrinal truth. Words that may be firm in information can be soft in spirit."

It's true that strategies and negotiations are no replacement for sincere prayer, softened hearts, and the whisperings of the Spirit. But despite the essential role of the Spirit, the fact is that the Lord's kingdom on earth can only benefit from the wisdom of human psychology. In fact, many of the approaches outlined to me in my interviews parallel the approach advocated by the authors of the wildly popular books *Crucial Conversations* and *Crucial Confrontations*. And it might not be a coincidence that the authors of these books include a couple of Mormons.

In *Crucial Conversations: Tools for Talking When Stakes Are High*, authors Kerry Patterson, Joseph Grenny, Ron McMillan, and Al Switzler advise readers on how to work through differences with others. "Disagreements, poorly handled," the authors say, "lead to poor decisions, strained relationships, and eventually to disastrous results." Even though the authors mostly use workplace or family anecdotes to illustrate their points, their methods of resolution are equally apt in the Church settings we're discussing. And many men and women alike are already using their techniques without even knowing it.

When we put out an idea or extend ourselves into a dialogue that has the potential to stir up strong emotions, as conversations at Church sometimes do, we feel vulnerable. The authors encourage problem solvers to focus on "confronting with safety." "When there is enough safety," they say, "you can talk to almost anyone about almost anything." In order to establish a safe atmosphere in which to have a weighty conversation, the authors suggest:

- Don't rely on nonverbal hints and subtle innuendo. Rather than sulking or feeling like the other person should read your mind, come right out and talk about a problem.
- Build common ground before mentioning the problem. Start establishing mutual goals by describing what's important to you and the other person.
- Describe the gap. Describing what you expected or hoped would happen versus what was observed is clear and simple.
- Be committed to mutual respect. This isn't just about acknowledging the other person as a human being, but also acknowledging the other person's goals.
- Ask for permission. If the topic you want to address is not something usually openly discussed, be sensitive to the other person's hesitancies. Be gracious.
- Speak in private. Violations of this abound in parenting and workplace scenarios, and few infractions can be as damaging to a person's self image.

Creating safety is, then, perhaps one of the most important mindsets we can adopt when approaching a man or a woman about a practice at church. When the stakes are high in the stakes of Zion, the way we get to the resolution may be just as important as reaching the resolution.

Once we have committed to an atmosphere of safety and are prepared to use humor and graciousness where needed, we are ready to ask ourselves the following questions to help us continue down a path of productive dialogue.

- Whom could I talk to about my ideas and my struggles?
- Do I need someone else to speak for me to decision makers, or are the channels open to me to speak for myself?
- Am I known as a reliable contributor to the local congregation?
- Have I worked with leaders in the past who trust me?
- Am I meeting other people where they are in their own spiritual lives, or am I pressuring them beyond where they are comfortable?
- Do I have a reputation as a hard worker and a cheerful participant?
- Do I feel more comfortable talking to female leaders or male leaders about my ideas?
- How do I build on common bonds I have with those I need to communicate to?
- What tone do I want to use in bringing up my ideas?
- Is there a place for humor? Historical precedent? Scriptural justifications?
- Who will feel threatened if I bring up my ideas? How can I mitigate that feeling in them?
- Who will feel closer to God if my ideas are implemented?

Opening the Line of Communication

Those who have an idea and are looking for an ally are usually women reaching out to men. In my interviews, I heard numerous examples of women going directly to male leaders and being welcomed and heard. One stake Relief Society president expressed a desire to her stake president to be able to communicate with the local bishops directly. She did so in direct emails to them about stake Relief Society affairs, but continued to cc the stake president so he would always feel invited to chime in.

I also heard stories of women who felt they had reached a dead end and didn't know where else to turn when their male leader didn't acknowledge their suggestions. When an urban stake didn't have any returned missionaries to accompany the high councilor on his routine monthly visits to the wards, a stake Relief Society president suggested to the stake president that Relief Society, Young Women, and Primary presidency members should accompany the high councilor instead. The stake president didn't bite, saying that's not the way it's done. But the stake Relief Society president didn't give up: several months later, she went to a particular high councilor, talked with him about her idea, and he then brought the same idea back to the stake president. That time, he bit, and a new tradition was born in that stake of having female leaders travel to the various wards with the high councilors. Although saddened that her suggestion wasn't embraced the first time she mentioned it, the stake Relief Society president understood the need to have the right messenger for the right message. This strategy of working through a variety of people, even when it means recognizing that men sometimes respond to men's ideas differently than women's, was a theme I heard repeated over and over in my interviews.

A real frustration for many women is not having a guaranteed or built-in channel of communication for when things go wrong. The Relief Society president of a small inner-city ward in New Jersey expressed the frustration she felt when she had exhausted the range of allies and communication tools that were open to her.

> We had a wonderful practice of the men handling the nursery class during "Enrichment" meeting each month for Relief Society. This way, all the women could participate in the activity without having to worry about childcare. The men filled this role gladly and consistently. We then received instruction from the stake to have the men stop this role and have the women take turns filling this responsibility. I was dumbfounded. I asked others in the stake Relief Society presidencies how they were going to handle the change and how they felt about it. I called Salt Lake to get clarity on what the *Handbook* stated about men assisting with Relief Society activities, and discovered it was just a matter of an ambiguous word choice that made the policy confusing. I gathered all the information I could. I thought that if the stake presidency's reason for disallowing men to serve in the Enrichment nursery was because of the *Handbook*, surely they would listen to me.
>
> I wrote a long letter to the stake president. It was very kind and diplomatic. I offered the information I had gathered from the *Handbook* and other Relief Society leaders. I allowed perhaps there was another reason for the change in childcare that I wasn't aware of. I let him know I respected his decision and I appreciated the hard work he put into his church service. I received no response. I was ignored.

While there is, as always, another side to this story that we don't have here, this account points to some challenges we might face when trying to figure out whom to reach out to with a concern. For one thing, this

Relief Society president didn't feel she was privy to a full disclosure from the stake presidency regarding the change in policy. Why had he made the decision to have men stop participating? She didn't know. Second, she put together her own ad hoc process for collecting and presenting feedback from the other Relief Society presidents, rather than following any prescribed chain for registering conflicts. There's no mention of her bishop; perhaps she didn't feel she had the relationship with her bishop to use him as an ally or get his impressions of the situation. She wrote a letter to the stake president. Did she attempt to meet with him in person, so they could have a conversation about her concerns? Would he not see her? Was she too nervous to approach him in person? Did she think a letter was more respectful because it wouldn't put him on the spot like an in-person meeting would have?

Is there a right way to escalate a concern like hers? What if communication breaks down at some point up the line, and there is no response? Who then can we turn to? Many women I spoke with expressed concern about these seemingly unanswered questions. Not everyone can call or write Salt Lake City and receive a personalized response, like the woman in the example above. In fact, the *Handbook* states, "Members of the Church are discouraged from making telephone calls or writing letters to General Authorities about doctrinal issues or personal matters." (Personal letters General Authorities sometimes read aloud and cite in General Conference make this request understandably confusing.) In one of my own wards, the bishopric felt the local advisors were not paying attention to the needs of our building: leaks in the roof had made large stains on the chapel walls, and, strangely, we had no garbage cans in the building outside the bathrooms. A letter the ward council sent to the Church's central building department was forwarded unopened to our stake president, who was none too happy to see the bishopric circumventing official channels—even though he hadn't responded to our requests himself. Even though the *Handbook* stresses keeping questions within the jurisdiction of local Church administration, examples like this suggest that not having an alternative strategy can force members to rely more heavily on their own resources, inspiration, personal relationships, and ingenuity to get things done on the local level.

Another stake Relief Society president described her calculated process of sending her stake president an email each week with articles and blog posts about women in the Church that she suggests he read. She collects the articles each week, writes a brief summary of why the stake president should reach each, and then sends him one email a week. As an older woman serving with a young stake president, she feels a maternal appropriateness in educating him about the landscape of women in the Church. After four years of working together, she says it has been a journey and a learning process for both of them, but her weekly emails have ensured they never have a shortage of things to talk about.

Several men I spoke with described their personal evolutions as leaders as they have worked with confident and innovative women in their councils. One stake president told me:

> My stake's Relief Society president is passionate about the Relief Society and the potential of women. She's introduced me to ideas and articles and observations about things she's read. We go back and forth discussing them. My alertness to the Relief Society organization has uniquely come from her.
>
> Her observations are part of what is so valuable to me. My perspective on women is limited to my wife and the bishops' wives. But I meet with her every month to get a feel for what she is observing and feeling. She's made me aware of when a ward Relief Society president isn't being heard or included in discussions. Because of her, we've polled ward council members to see how well they're being included in ward council discussions. We surveyed how often bishops are meeting with their Relief Society president one on one. The results were revealing: in many cases there were no regular meetings. She has made me aware of challenges and opportunities I would have never known were there.

In some cases, learning about the history of Relief Society either from a Relief Society president or from the book *Daughters in My Kingdom* has prompted a transformation in a male leader. "What I got from *Daughters in My Kingdom*," said one stake president, "is the doctrinal purpose for which Relief Society was organized. I understood that there are close ties between the priesthood organization and the Relief Society. That was new for me. I don't need to distance myself from the Relief Society. As a leader, I can feel confident that we're all in this together." Understanding the history and purpose of Relief Society transformed this male leader into a true advocate for the women's organization.

Although such a role is not built into the organizational hierarchy, women can act as advocates for the men when the men might not even realize they need one. One woman wrote of her retrospective desire to act as an advocate and ally of a bishop:

As the Young Women president in a Utah ward, I was surprised by how aloof and disconnected our bishop could be regarding the struggles the young women and their often single mothers were facing. One mother and daughter stopped coming to church because they shared with me their feeling of discomfort around the male leaders. In retrospect, I wish I would have frankly expressed these concerns with our bishop so that he could have been more gentle and aware of these women. He had an abrasive personality, but I think a bit of coaching from members and leaders like myself could have gone a long way.

Men are learning too that they can go directly to the women of the wards and stakes to gain insight, and not just work through the limited female representation in leadership. In one ward, a bishop asked for feedback from the entire Relief Society on the church building's friendliness to mothers. Through this exercise, he realized that there were changing tables only in the women's bathrooms, the mother's lounge had a tattered rocking chair, and the nursery rooms were tiny and poorly heated. By going to the women directly, he became aware of needs that would only be revealed through their partnership.

One woman described another instance of men going to women directly and not simply working through their female leadership, in this case, an initiative taken by a new elders quorum president:

> Within a few Sundays of receiving his call, the new elders quorum president in our ward asked if he could speak to the sisters during the regular Relief Society time on Sunday. He wanted the entire lesson time. We, as attending sisters, had no idea what was on his agenda. I'm assuming the Relief Society president knew what was planned. He, along with his counselors, joined us after their priesthood opening exercises. The elders quorum president thanked us for allowing him there and then asked us to advise him on how the elders quorum could better serve the sisters in the ward. He wanted to know what our concerns were, and what they could do better to serve and support us as women, as sisters in the gospel, as mothers and as wives. He had his counselors write everything down so as to be shared and reviewed regularly (and anonymously). As soon as trust was established in that meeting, I remember the sisters shared their thoughts freely and openly. Surprisingly, it didn't turn into a gripe session with the airing of petty grievances, but it stayed within the spirit the elders quorum president established. I think if there are gender issues prevalent in a ward, perhaps based on traditions and practices of the past, this is an admirable way to bridge the gap and form a new level of cooperation and understanding. Fortunately, the elders quorum president was nothing but sincere in his efforts to do just that.

In my own ward, the elders quorum president invited a woman to teach his class one week, specifically asking her to share a female perspective of priesthood and effective use of priesthood power. To this president's credit, he understood that learning about priesthood from an exclusively male perspective is only learning about half of its influence. One ward took it even further, having the stake Relief Society presidency teach the priesthood quorums during ward conference, while the stake presidency taught the Relief Society lesson. Yet another ward took a different approach to incorporating female influence by assigning a single woman to be the sacrament meeting coordinator. The woman called to this position in her ward described her experience:

> My calling was to coordinate sacrament meeting—the entire thing, every week. I was given full access to choose the topic, the speakers, coordinate with the music person the hymns/musical numbers, etc. I wasn't told how to do this or micro managed. I came up with my own system.
>
> I put everyone in the ward in a spreadsheet. I asked the Bishop and others who had spoken in the past three months and I marked them off. Then I made sure to ask people who were new to the ward to speak within the first month they attended. Then I just started filling in each Sunday with people in the ward.
>
> Because I not only chose the speakers but also the topics, I could get a feel of the temperature of the ward and pick topics that were relevant at that time and then choose speakers that I felt could personally deliver a heartfelt talk on that topic. Every once in a while the Bishop would let me know he felt strongly a person should speak or a certain topic should be addressed, and almost every time that person was on the docket to speak very soon and the topic was also coming up.
>
> I LOVED that I had the autonomy to help sacrament meetings become more personalized. I loved that I was nervous for and whole-heartedly invested in every speaker. I loved how empowered I felt as a true contributor to my ward. I loved that I think people felt the Spirit every week.

Strong male leaders recognize the need to see all of the women in their wards as allies and partners, not just the small handful who attend ward council meetings. This is partly because it is difficult for three women in ward council to carry the voices and representation of half the ward, but also because of the professional and volunteer expertise all female ward members bring to the table. Several of the women I interviewed who felt well-utilized and appreciated and stretched at church have been called out by male leadership for their professional expertise and asked to contribute at church in that particular capacity. The recognition of their lives outside of the domestic sphere doubles the ward's skill set and creates a bridge for these women between their church lives and their professional lives, which most of the time exist in entirely separate bubbles.

A financial professional in New York describes her feelings about putting her professional skills to use in a Church setting:

> In my New York stake I was called to be a stake auditor. I was surprised because that was traditionally a calling for men, particularly because Ward Financial Clerk is a priesthood calling. But I felt valued because it was as if the Lord was saying your financial expertise matters, and the course you've taken professionally is the path I wanted you to take. I suppose though it was more difficult for me because I had never been a financial clerk—and didn't necessarily know what to look for, but perhaps that was good too and made me a more diligent auditor.

A bishop tells how he leaned on female allies and supporters throughout the ward, and in particular on the professional expertise of a woman in his ward in the sensitive area of welfare:

> One of the things I tried to do during my years as bishop was to help people to activate the power of God and heavenly inspiration in their callings. My hypothesis was that if people were asked to participate more (and if I had higher expectations of them in their callings) then this would help to ignite that. I had to think creatively and outside the box and often felt prompted to do certain things. I made it a personal goal never to do something as a bishop that I could ask someone else to do, and that included passing out the hymnals on Sunday, and including the Relief Society president in every temporal welfare case I ever handled, even if it didn't involve a sister. I certainly didn't do this perfectly, but I tried to.
>
> The best example I can think of is when I was working on a particularly tough welfare case with a single mom. After a lot of personal counseling with the sister, I one day felt prompted to invite our Ward Welfare Specialist (a sister) to our next interview. It's not something I would normally think of doing in an interview setting since I think of them as confidential, but I asked the sister's permission and she gave it. So her next interview was with the Ward Welfare Specialist and me. Our Ward Welfare Specialist was a trained social worker and had (obviously) also been called of God, so having her experience and inspiration was extremely helpful. After that, the two of them met one-on-one several times. I really believe this is what Church leaders are trying to get us to do. So much leadership training is focused on activating the ward council and delegating these kinds of responsibilities.

Even though we believe male-specific callings come through inspiration and not necessarily because of a man's professional expertise—when my stepfather, an English professor, was called as a financial clerk, we were all a little afraid for our money!—tapping into women's professional expertise gives a welcome excuse for considering their potential contributions to the ward or stake more thoroughly and making room for them even in areas women might not have fit traditionally. I admit I was a bit hurt when I was not invited to participate in a fifth-Sunday presentation my bishopric prepared about the Church's media tools, since I am professionally involved in creating those tools and their content. It would have been a natural and appreciated way to include me in an otherwise all-male presentation. Stretching ourselves to learn about our women's professional and volunteer experience and seeking for ways to recognize those skills can go a long way in fostering strong partnerships and lines of communication between men and women.

Strengthening Ward Council Relationships

The most essential people connections in any ward are those of the ward council. Elder Ballard has observed that congregations tend to reflect the attitudes and relationships of the ward council, and he has spent much of his ecclesiastical focus on empowering ward councils to be places of positive growth and innovation. He has also repeatedly stressed the importance of women in ward councils. He has warned,

> It is easy to understand why many sisters are frustrated when they sit in council with priesthood leaders and are not invited to make substantive contributions to the council. . . . Perhaps the Lord had in mind the arrogant priesthood leaders who would ignore or dismiss the wisdom of any council member when He gave this warning to the Prophet Joseph Smith: "When we undertake to cover our sins, or to gratify our pride, our vain ambition, or to exercise control or dominion or compulsion upon the souls of the children of men, in any degree of unrighteousness, behold, the heavens withdraw themselves; the Spirit of the Lord is grieved; and when it is withdrawn, Amen to the priesthood or the authority of that man." (D&C 121:37)

As much as we hope every person attends to that warning, there are factors at play in ward councils that challenge even the most humble men and women among us. Becoming aware of those factors will help us overcome them and allow ward councils to be the hubs of "empowerment" and "innovation" Elder Ballard hopes they will be.

As I discussed in Part I, parity in the representation of voices is simply not found in the central counseling bodies of local Church governance. Though ten men attend both ward council and priesthood executive committee meeting (PEC), only three women attend ward council, and no women are required participants in PEC (the Relief Society president may be invited at the bishop's discretion).

The sparseness of their numbers puts great responsibility on the female leaders to represent their large stewardship while considerably outnumbered by men with smaller quantitative stewardships. There is also great responsibility on the bishopric to spend as much focus and time on the three women's stewardships as they do on the other six men's. Even in the best of circumstances, the numerical disparity means those three women's voices must carry outsized weight and be particularly magnified. One bishop I interviewed has addressed the disparity of numbers by inviting the female auxiliary presidents' councilors also to join ward council meetings so that the gender ratio is more balanced. A practice mentioned to me by several bishops is to form a "women's council" of the Relief Society, Young Women, and Primary presidents, who meet monthly with a member of the bishopric to discuss the needs of the women in the ward in more depth than they in ward council meetings. One stake president meets with his bishops' wives every six months to expand his vision of what's happening with the women in the stake and to gauge the spiritual well-being of the women from other sources. Other bishops made a point of telling me that they tried to "avoid" rooms full of male leaders, trying to avoid the "awkwardness" of exclusively male voices. A stake presidency in Northern California counsels every bishop to treat his Relief Society president as an additional counselor, not as the assistant or peripheral contributor that the "auxiliary" designation might connote. As part of this vision, the Relief Society presidents in this stake attend bishopric meetings, and each meets individually with her bishop as well. In these ways, this stake presidency is attempting to balance out what one member of the presidency called the "mathematical decree" of male-to-female ratio that determines the makeup of a ward council.

In a 2006 study in the wake of the Enron and WorldCom scandals, researchers set out to answer new questions about corporate governance: Does it matter to corporate governance whether women serve on a board? If so, does it make a difference how many women serve? Is there a critical mass that can bring significant change to the boardroom and improve corporate governance?

The researchers concluded that having a critical mass of three or more women on corporate boards enhances governance. The report states,

> Women bring a collaborative leadership style that benefits boardroom dynamics by increasing the amount of listening, social support, and win-win problem-solving. Although women are often collaborative leaders, they do not shy away from controversial issues. Many of our informants believe that women are more likely than men to ask tough questions and demand direct and detailed answers. Women also bring new issues and perspectives to the table, broadening the content of boardroom discussions to include the perspectives of multiple stakeholders.

Their findings have resonance for our ward council settings, where we happily have three women regularly participating. If we dig deeper into the report, we can gain a greater appreciation for why this critical mass of female representation is crucial for a productive meeting culture.

How Many Women Constitute a Critical Mass on a Corporate Board?

The number of women on a board makes a difference. While a lone woman can and often does make substantial contributions, and two women are generally more powerful than one, increasing the number of women to three or more enhances the likelihood that women's voices and ideas are heard and that boardroom dynamics change substantially. Women who have served alone and those who have observed the situation report experiences of lone women not being listened to, being excluded from socializing and even from some decision-making discussions, being made to feel their views represent a "woman's point of view," and being subject to inappropriate behaviors that indicate male directors notice their gender more than their individual contributions.

Adding a second woman clearly helps. When two women sit on a board, they tend to feel more comfortable than one does alone. Each woman can assure that the other is heard, not always by agreeing with her, but rather, by picking up on the topics she raises and encouraging the group to process them fully. Two women together can develop strategies for raising difficult and controversial issues in a way that makes other board members pay attention. But with two women, women and men are still aware of gender in ways that can keep the women from working together as effectively as they might, and the men from benefiting from their contributions.

The magic seems to occur when three or more women serve on a board together. Suddenly having women in the room becomes a normal state of affairs. No longer does any one woman represent the "woman's point of view," because the women express different views and often disagree with each other. Women start being treated as individuals with different person-alities, styles, and interests. Women's tendencies to be more collaborative but also to be more active in asking questions and raising different issues start to become the boardroom norm. We find that having three or more women on a board can create a critical mass where women are no longer seen as outsid-ers and are able to influence the content and process of board discussions more substantially.

Impact on Corporate Governance

Having a critical mass of women directors is good for corporate governance in at least three ways.

- The content of boardroom discussion is more likely to include the perspec-tives of the multiple stakeholders who affect and are affected by company performance, not only shareholders but also employees, customers, suppli-ers, and the community at large.
- Difficult issues and problems are considerably less likely to be ignored or brushed aside, which results in better decision-making.
- The boardroom dynamic is more open and collaborative, which helps manage-ment hear the board's concerns and take them to heart without defensiveness.

If we replace "corporate board" with "ward council" in the conclusions above, we can appreciate the ward council structure even more and be especially attuned to gender imbalances when a Church decision-making body does not include such ideal representation. We can also take comfort in the fact that we in the Church are not the only ones discussing female institutional representation!

In appreciating the presence of women in councils, one stake president went even farther and explained that the greatest efficacy of the women came when they weren't sitting together. "I actively ask the women in my councils to sit apart from each other," he told me. "I think the women in my meetings all sit together for a feeling of comfort and security, but I need them spread around. They are like a sugar cube. I need them to dis-solve among all of us so that their influence can be felt among the whole group, and not just in a clump amongst themselves."

Another hurdle to the functioning of the ward council is the intrinsic difference in the communication styles of men and women. Men and women can come away from the same conversation with entirely different interpretations of what happened, entirely different analyses of the power plays at work, and entirely different conclusions about their emotional connection. The groundbreaking work of linguistics professor Deborah Tannen has illuminated what many of us already know: men and women generally communicate differently. Tannen goes so far as to characterize cross-gender conversations as "cross-cultural" interactions, requiring the same sensitivity and navigation as a conversation with someone whose culture and traditions may feel alien. Analyzing the verbal communication differences between men and women has made Tannen's work immensely popular and helpful to those struggling to understand why communication with the opposite sex might be hitting a wall. Among other insights in her best-selling book *You Just Don't Understand*, Tannen uncovers the contrasts between men's "report-talk" and women's "rapport-talk."

> For most women, the language of conversation is primarily a language of rapport: a way of establishing connections and negotiating relationships. Emphasis is placed on displaying similarities and matching experiences. From childhood, girls criticize peers who try to stand out or appear better than others.
>
> From childhood, men learn to use talking as a way to get and keep attention. So they are more comfortable speaking in larger groups made up of people they know less well—in the broadest sense, "public speaking." But even the most private situations can be approached like public speaking, more like giving a report than establishing rapport.

Tannen notably recalls a conversation that took place between a couple in their car. The woman asked, "Would you like to stop for a drink?" The husband answered, truthfully, "No," and they didn't stop. Tannen explains:

> [The husband] was later frustrated to learn that his wife was annoyed because she had wanted to stop for a drink. He wondered, "Why didn't she just say what she wanted? Why did she play games with me?" The wife, I explained, was annoyed not because she had not gotten her way, but because her preference had not been considered. From her point of view, she had shown concern for her husband's wishes [rapport-talk], but he had shown no concern for hers [report-talk]. . . . The husband and wife in this example had different but equally valid styles.

Tannen has thus generally found that women focus on relationships, often setting aside their own direct requests in sensitivity to others. Men focus on delivering the facts, sometimes with indifference to interpersonal effects. Differences in gendered styles of communicating such as the one described here can be exacerbated in a church setting where a woman may not have extensive experience communicating with men in a professional, non-familial way. Additionally, the men's priesthood authority gives their voices the perception of added weight.

Having a "good relationship" with a male or female leader does not necessarily mean that ideas are being heard, respected, and acted upon in a way that both parties feel accomplish their goals. Men and women may "get along", but simply being free of conflict doesn't guarantee that communication is thorough, productive, and consensus building. Some of these communication barriers may become of less concern as more and more Mormon women gain professional or volunteer experience working alongside men and thus become comfortable with and adapt to men's communication style. The fact that we, as a people, are still to some degree embedded in a mid-century culture where men and women don't interact outside of familial ties was brought home to me recently when a young newly married friend of mine deleted all of her male contacts out of her phone. While she might have perceived it as a romantic gesture of commitment to her new husband, and it's probably not wise to have old boyfriends on speed dial, for me, as a woman who works overwhelmingly with men and enjoys many male friends, the action was completely foreign and extreme.

Similarly, men are becoming more comfortable with and adapting to women's communication styles as they work side by side with them in professional settings. As modern American workplaces approach gendered balance, there will be fewer men likely to patronize a woman's input and fewer women likely to cower at a working partnership with a man or accept a token or silent partner role without question. As one bishop told me, "I try to interact with women at church in a way roughly similar to how I interact with them at work. I assume them to be equally as capable/incapable, outspoken/reserved, intelligent/notsomuch as their male counterparts. I suspect that some women (and men) are disappointed with this evenhanded treatment, but that's mere conjecture." Although this bishop apologized to me for not being "more sensitive" to gender issues in his ward, I actually think his attitude reflects a healthy modernism in the way professional men are viewing their female partners at church. (There are still opportunities for improvement, though: as one professional woman wrote to me, "If the men at church treated me the way the men at work do, I would weep for joy.") It also demands that the women who work with this bishop rise up to his professional expectations of women as real collaborators and contributors.

Despite these challenges, ward councils still provide the richest opportunity for men and women to work cooperatively at the ward level to benefit those under their stewardship. Even though numerical representation might not achieve parity, Elder Ballard has made the point both in his book and in the 2012 worldwide leadership training that every member of the council is entitled to inspiration and revelation, not just in their own sphere but for all matters relating to ward members. One former bishop shared with me his impressions of this insight. "Taking the training to its logical end, it would be perfectly normal and acceptable for a Primary president to opine on the most effective use of Home Teaching resources, for example, or how to help a struggling brother who is out of work. On the rare occasions where this manifested itself in practice [when I was bishop], it was pretty glorious."

Thus even though representation may be gendered, stewardships are not. The commitment to this principle is being modeled by our general leadership, most recently at the April 2014 General Conference, where women's auxiliary leaders talked about issues like pornography that affect a gender-neutral, age-neutral audience. Understanding the commitment to this principle may help us expand our understanding of how women can most effectively impact the ward council experience.

I personally have appreciated the opportunity to learn, through interviews and by studying the *Handbook*, about how ward councils should ideally function. I have served in presidencies, but never as a Relief Society, Primary, or Young Women's president, and so I have never personally sat in a ward council and participated in the cooperative ministry so many described to me. I've lived my whole life in the church, and yet I have learned a tremendous amount in this process about the inner workings of wards. I am not unusual: it is statistically more likely that a woman in the Church will never sit in a ward council and thus will be unfamiliar with how these relationships work and what they achieve. This is a critical point when we are considering how well women of the ward feel represented and heard: if they do not know who their leaders are, if they do not understand how those leaders are representing them, if they do not understand the time and concern leaders spend thinking about them, and if they have no insight into what those leaders are accomplishing, they will inevitably feel disenfranchised. Because so many more men participate in ward leadership throughout the course of their lives, starting very young when they join older brethren for priesthood meetings, there is a subculture among Mormon men that tacitly understands why we have meetings and what good they do. But women do not magically understand or appreciate the work that takes place in a ward council unless it is communicated to them. I believe that some feelings of detachment and voicelessness could be relieved if more women in our wards know who their leaders are and understand the extent of the work those leaders do on their behalf.

A Primary president expressed her own surprise when she started participating in ward councils: "I've realized that ward councils are where the rubber meets the road. Until I served as a president, I didn't see many of the complementary workings of men and women in the ward because they weren't overtly spoken of or visible. Now it's like being privy to the inner workings of a clock. One of my efforts is to share these examples in my presidency meetings and in regular conversations with members so good examples are known and hopefully perpetuated." I was surprised myself recently when I had to think hard about who the Relief Society president is in my own ward. I've been in the Primary for several years and I honestly have little awareness of how my female leaders might be working toward the greater good of the women in my ward in a council situation.

Women Working with Women: Claiming Influence

There is good news and there is bad news on the subject of women working with women. The bad news is that almost every woman I interviewed voluntarily brought up experiences in which adaptations and innovations to magnify women's impact at church had encountered roadblocks *from women*. While the idea that women sometimes fail to support other women didn't come as a surprise to me, I was surprised by the prevalence and passion of my interviewees' experiences. I was also surprised when I was told about women not wanting to claim influence that was rightly theirs. But I choose to look on the bright side: the good news is that *women,* as much or perhaps more than men, have the opportunity and the obligation to initiate and embrace opportunities to increase their impact at church.

I first became aware of the obligation and opportunity for women to claim their own influence in 2012, after I had publicly challenged bishops always to include the Relief Society presidents in their PEC meetings. I received an email from a former bishop, who said, "All three of the Relief Society presidents I worked with were resistant to attending Ward Council every week. I am sure that speaks volumes to the quality of meetings we were having. However, I also sensed a desire: first, not to attend meetings (understandable, I have shared that feeling throughout my life in the Church) and second, to operate 'apart' from the hierarchical structure. It took some coaxing to convince my Relief Society presidents that we needed them there."

This email took me by surprise, but since then I have noted this theme in the way some women approach church involvement: some women distance themselves from the Church government structure altogether, as the Relief Society presidents described above did, perhaps in an effort to "get more done" on their own terms or because they don't want to play the "game," as one woman described it to me, of male leadership hierarchy. Bishops who told me about establishing women's councils in their wards all quickly followed with an aside about how the women were the ones to push back when the idea was first presented. The theme of women not attending ward or stake meetings to which they are invited has resurfaced in my research time and time again.

This perhaps is a coping mechanism for women who feel more comfortable working with women instead of men or an effort to avoid any bureaucratic hindrances that might slow down a female leader's vision. In her analysis of the Claremont Mormon Women Oral History Project in the book *Mormon Women Have Their Say*, scholar Caroline Kline suggests that one of the ways women navigate gender structure in church governance is that they work behind the scenes to enact their own sense of how things ought to be. It can certainly be more comfortable and more effective to work in our own spheres without having to collaborate on a broader platform. There also is the sense that women can own more decisions and not have to run things by male leaders if they operate "under the radar."

Another diagnosis could rest in the fact that women are steeped in thousands of years of cultural conditioning to work behind the scenes, lest by stepping out and asserting their opinions they be deemed "bossy" or "aggressive." One former Relief Society president told me she knew more about the families in the ward than any of the men in PEC meetings because she was home with children and shared playdates and activities with the other women, but she hesitated to share these insights for fear of being perceived as a gossiper or "clucking hen."

I talk more about the roots of this hurdle in the next chapter, but here it will suffice to cite a few statistics: a study from the Girl Scouts Research Institute shows that girls are twice as likely as boys to worry that leadership roles will make them seem "bossy." By middle school, girls are 25 percent less likely than boys to say they like taking the lead. Between elementary school and high school, girls' self-esteem drops 3.5 times more than boys'. These kinds of statistics were second nature to me as a student at an all-girls' school for twelve years, and they were continuously reinforced by my parents' and teachers' constant reminders that I should be grateful not to have to compete with boys for a teacher's attention, since boys are statistically more likely to be called on in class than girls. These cultural factors understandably lead to women negotiating organizations and environments in different ways than men do.

There is likely another reason for women's hesitancy to embrace participation in meetings: no person on earth wants to attend more meetings. They wake us from Sunday morning slumbers or make us late for Sunday afternoon family dinners. They take us away from children's soccer games midweek or make us miss putting our kids to bed or put us behind on work. They fall at the times when mothers are the busiest: in the hours before church on a Sunday morning when children need to be fed and dressed, or right around dinner time. For many men, their experience as youth in the Church prepares them for the need to attend meetings when they are older: they see fathers, brothers, or other male mentors meeting, leading, and dedicating considerable time to their church responsibilities. Women have different experiences: with no offices in the church building and no requirement to meet at the church, much of our church work is done at home. We don't have the same cultural expectation that much of our church service will be fulfilled in meetings at the church. In fact, women may resent the amount of time husbands, sons, and brothers spend at church in meetings because it takes them away from time at home. Sensitivity to how much time we are spending in meetings is critical to making sure our work in the Church is balanced, fruitful, and fulfilling.

However, we still must recognize that, while women may get more done on their own, we all lose in the broader culture and operational framework of the ward or stake if women don't fully participate in the cooperative opportunities with men. Elder Ballard emphasizes the eternal and critical nature of working all together: "One of the key lessons Heavenly Father taught us in that 'world of spirits' was the important role of councils and counseling together in gospel governance. From the very beginning God has done His work through a system of organized councils." When we don't participate fully in this system, we shortchange the long-term health of our gender cooperation for the short-term rewards of a narrower focus. One Primary president put her feelings this way, regarding the need for women to be involved in the established structure: "I feel communication and visibility is a two-way street. We've recently had some very strong women in leadership positions in our ward who were rather vocal about how women really run the ward, but were not vocal in ward councils. My husband and I felt [their unwillingness to participate] was rather demeaning and subversive to many faithful brethren doing their best to magnify their calls."

I continue to be surprised by the ambivalence some women feel to claiming their rightful place of voice and influence in Church settings. Elder Ballard pleads, "Sisters, be prepared both mentally and spiritually to discuss the needs of those who fall within your stewardship. Be bold. Be assertive. Feel confident about raising weighty issues and concerns. You have as much right to input and inspiration as other . . . members." No one wants to go to more meetings than they have to. Neither men nor women. Elder Ballard does not mince words, though, when describing the importance of our decision-making councils and "problem-solving teams": "Satan does not want us to figure out how to effectively use the council system. . . . To be perfectly candid, I sometimes have a difficult time understanding why so many of our [male and female] leaders fail to see the vision of how working together through councils can enhance their ability to accomplish all that the Lord expects of them in their respective stewardships."

We've explored elsewhere how female leaders are essential parts of the council system because they broaden the base of experience and perspective in the search for solutions. Even though their leadership extends over all members of the congregation, female leaders have special insights into half of the congregation that could strengthen the entire community. We women may think we could use that time more effectively at home or at work or school; we may think the meeting is useless or poorly run. Women may be uncomfortable or unsure of how to work with men or how to feel heard in a mostly male meeting. We may think we can get more done working just with women and that we can get around men approving decisions. But a woman's presence at a meeting isn't just about her; it's about being the voice of the women she's divinely called to represent. If for no other reason, women should be active participants in meetings because the symbolic nature of having women in those meetings is important to those who may feel invisible, unheard, or unappreciated. Sisters, let's show up. Let's show up so that we are top of mind with our male leaders. Let's show up so they know whom they can depend on. Let's show up so that we will be trusted when the decisions fall to us. Let's show up, if not for ourselves or even for the women under our stewardship, but for those who come after us, so that no one in the future will question whether or not women have a voice in our faith.

I have noted that women's ambivalence to embrace their voices at church is endemic right down to the simplest structural practice: One Sunday while I was visiting a ward, the sacrament meeting program featured an all-female speaker line-up that was not the Relief Society presidency or any special auxiliary program. It was simply a program of female speakers. After inwardly cheering at this unusual occurrence, I was saddened when the first speaker got up and, only half in jest, quoted Paul from First Corinthians 14: "Let your women keep silence in the churches: for it is not permitted unto them to speak." An all-female program felt uncomfortable even to the female speaker, and it seemed this was her attempt to diffuse any authority she might be perceived to claim as a woman speaking in church.

A man described a similar experience in his own ward:

> On one Sunday in my ward, the final assigned speaker was a woman. She seemed flustered to be in the last slot, was apologetic to the audience and lamented that we weren't going to get the final word in the meeting from a priesthood holder. And then she gave her talk.
>
> The stake president happened to be visiting, and after she finished he stood to make a few comments. He thanked her for the talk, and acknowledged she was just being self-deprecating. But he said it was his responsibility as presiding officer in the stake to correct misinformation. He then affirmed that there is nothing wrong with scheduling a sister to speak in the last slot in sacrament meeting, that that is perfectly appropriate. When we don't do that, it is just a tradition. He especially wanted the Primary girls and the Young Women to understand that they have the same responsibility to teach the gospel as the boys do.

I want to shout "Hooray!" and "Bless you!" to that wise stake president, and add my own plea to women to claim their voice. We have a responsibility, a right, a privilege, a power that is ours to magnify. Another stake president requested that high councilors' wives speak with them when visiting wards, but this particular stake president had to discontinue the practice because the wives hated speaking so much and complained to him so bitterly. While this arrangement could have been a burden on wives with children or other callings (and could have, I believe, been successful by having other women leaders instead of wives speak with the high councilors), I can't help but feel saddened by the end of that practice. What a shame the women of that stake would no longer be able to see and hear other women being involved and invested in stake leadership, or to see the stake's endorsement of women's own ecclesiastical abilities.

A Primary president told me it was a custom in her Primary to have a child explain the context, speaker, reference, and personal meaning of a selected scripture from their Book of Mormon reading program each week. The president was surprised when the counselor she had asked to guide the children in this process backed out, citing a lack of confidence with the scriptures. "Women are sabotaging themselves!" this president exclaimed to me passionately. "Why are we not confident scriptorians?"

Even at the general leadership level, women's tendency to shy away from doctrinal or authoritative subjects has provided fodder for the "Equality Is Not A Feeling" series: Using the number of verses cited per page as a proxy for the doctrinal richness of a talk, the bloggers have analyzed that female speakers in general conference cite less than *half* the number of scriptures that male speakers do. Why do we do this? Is it culture? Practice? Doctrine? Some mash up of all sorts of expectations and influences? Perhaps Young Women and Primary speakers have traditionally spoken to their constituents and thus simplified concepts for their younger audiences. But emphasis on the general level of broad stewardship, such as we've seen in the past several general conference talks by female leaders, suggests that might be changing.

One newly called Primary president explained her personal hurdles this way: "For myself, and I think for many women, we often undervalue our own input and fail to speak up. I am often stuck in second-class status mentality, thinking that someone with more experience by virtue of a mission or leadership experiences within the Church will know more than me. I'm working on trusting my intuition and the guidance of the Spirit as I tackle my first calling as an auxiliary president."

This Primary president mentions not serving a mission as a trigger for "second-class status mentality." Over the past year, I have been part of numerous conversations speculating that women's confidence in themselves as scriptorians and leaders will skyrocket as a result of so many more sister missionaries having studied the scriptures deeply. While I do think we will see a shift in the coming generation, I'm skeptical this shift will result in anything meaningful unless we as a community celebrate their confidence, nurture it, and find a place for it to take root in the Church experience they return to. Their confidence won't do any of us any good if the culture they return to doesn't value what they have to offer. Older women today can help clear the paths of influence and voice—set the expectations now that this is how women engage with the Church structure—so that the younger returned missionaries have a place to plant their confidence, scriptural knowledge, and leadership skills.

Andrea Radke-Moss, a professor at BYU–Idaho, is one of many who have been speculating about what might change in our cultural practices as a result of the missionary age change. "I believe the church will have to adjust what we expect of our 12- to 18-year-old girls," she has said. "Right now, the differences between Aaronic Priesthood duties and what we expect of Young Women is so radically far apart that one might expect the Church to adjust some of the Sunday-to-Sunday responsibilities for Young Women, to give them better preparation, service and leadership skills. . . . Will the changes in missionary leadership translate to changes in the larger church? Will missions allow for the exploration of mixed-gender shared governance? Or will missions simply reinforce traditional gendered structures?" Radke-Moss believes "the changes in missionary age and demographic potentially has strong implications for the future of shared governance in the Church."

In fact, that shared governance Radke-Moss envisions may already be evolving in the mission field. The *Deseret News* reported in April 2014 that Sister Molly Fields had been "fasting and praying 'a lot' as she has prepared to do something that a year ago few, if any, Mormon women had the opportunity to do." What Sister Fields was preparing to do was lead a training session at a thirty-seven person mission leadership council. The *Deseret News* summarized the governmental changes already being seen in the missions: "Today, women like Fields serve in new positions as sister training leaders, participate on the new mission leadership councils, train elders and sisters in district, zone and mission meetings, are responsible for the welfare of all other sister missionaries and report directly to the mission president or his wife on sisters' issues." Such changes signal "deep, long-term ramifications."

In a *New York Times* article about sister missionaries, Church public affairs director Michael Otterson also underscored the cultural adaptations that we will see as a result of ministerially trained women. "Culturally there's an understanding that women's roles are going to be more and more important." The new wave of returning female missionaries, he added, would amount to an "injection of really theologically well-trained women" and enrich the Church, "if they can make the transition back."

"If they can make the transition back" is the phrase that we in the missionaries' home wards and stakes need to pay particular attention to. Recently returned sister missionaries I spoke with expressed gratitude for being called immediately to teaching positions in their local wards. Others have been given visiting teaching assignments to new members or less-active members so that they could keep their mission skills sharp. Pragmatically, one returned missionary said of the sister training leader position, "The boys have always used their missions as opportunities to show their management experience on their résumés. Saying you've led a group of other men is good for getting a job. Now women who have served as sister training leaders can have the same advantage when applying for jobs."

When women claim their voices by attending meetings, speaking up in meetings, embracing opportunities to speak about doctrine, and being visible symbols of female participation, they pave the way for their daughters and granddaughters to feel more integrated into the Church's administrative and ecclesiastical dialogues and thus less likely to feel silenced or undervalued. They will be less likely to feel that women in visible positions of Church leadership are there because of the men to whom they are married. Church can be the place where the best of our training and education and experience is shared most liberally, not the place it is shuffled off to a corner because we are women. By claiming our voices, we women can set the stage for that integrated, kingdom-building future that is within reach of all of our daughters. Isn't that a future we want for our girls? Let's be active participants for them, even if it stretches us outside our comfort zones and weighs down on our insecurities and time constraints. The investment is worth it.

Women Working with Women: Celebrating Other Women

"The first half of every meeting I have with my ward Relief Society presidents," one stake Relief Society president told me, "is discussing all the bickering that's happening in their ward Relief Societies . . . who's hurt whose feelings, who's overstepped their bounds, who's feeling left out." Yikes! The other major theme that surfaced in my research on women working with women is that they can have a hard time supporting each other, especially when a woman is perceived to be overstepping her bounds by entering into traditionally male spheres. I hope all Mormon women have had the experience of being in a nurturing, loving, and stimulating Relief Society; I know I have. The ideal Relief Society experience can be a little piece of heaven. Women can be so very good to each other. But as Joseph Smith stated in discussing how women should relate to each other, "The female part of the community are apt to be contracted in their views. You must not be contracted, but you must be liberal in all your feelings." Let's prove the Prophet unprophetic in this one point.

Sister Virginia Perry features as the heroine in one of my favorite stories about a woman demonstrating the farthest thing from a "contracted" evaluation of another: "On one Sunday Sister Virginia Perry, whose husband, L. Tom Perry, was president of the Boston Stake, noticed a woman who had quietly found a space on the back row in the Weston chapel, having arrived a few minutes late for sacrament meeting. She was wearing jeans and a T-shirt and had come on her motorcycle. Sister Perry quickly sensed that the woman felt that she didn't fit in. Everyone else was wearing their Sunday best and was sitting with their families. So Sister Perry left her family alone, went to the back pew, and asked the visitor if she would mind if she sat beside her. When the woman smiled in the affirmative, Sister Perry put her arm around her. The next Sunday Sister Perry came to church wearing Levi's and a T-shirt." How I love Sister Perry's willingness to put aside the trappings of her elevated stake status, any worries about what her peers might think of her, and any expected practices to fully embrace another woman. I'm particularly touched by this story when I consider how the founders of the Wear Pants to Church day bore the burden of "contracted views" in their symbolic attempt to make women like this biker feel less out of place at church.

One woman I interviewed explained that she feels the warning to priesthood holders found in Doctrine and Covenants 121:37—"When we undertake to cover our sins, or to gratify our pride, our vain ambition, or to exercise control or dominion or compulsion upon the souls of the children of men, in any degree of unrighteousness, behold, the heavens withdraw themselves"—is often considered to be only applicable to male priesthood holders, but she believes that women too can benefit from heeding its strong words. She explained to me that because female leadership opportunities are scarce in number (and thus power is concentrated in the hands of just a few), women in those positions can fall into the traps described in the scripture, thinking their authority is actually much greater than it is. In the male priesthood structure, there are many men in local leadership callings and many more in general leadership callings, but for women there are just a few leadership callings, sometimes creating the tendency to inflate the importance of those few.

Almost every ward or stake female leader I interviewed shared a frustrating story of when she was trying to claim meaningful influence or voice and she was roadblocked by another woman. I noticed a pattern in these stories: when a woman is chastised by another woman, it is often when she is trying to step over into territory that falls outside the traditional Relief Society space. For example, one woman, while serving as Enrichment leader for her Relief Society, also planned the ward Christmas party and wanted to count the party as the Enrichment night for December. But despite all the work, the Relief Society president told her it couldn't count as an Enrichment night because the message intended for that month hadn't been shared with the group. This seems so silly to me, but it underscores a damaging attitude that women who look beyond the demands of Relief Society should in some way be penalized.

Despite all this talk of adapting and innovating and claiming our voice, to strive to engage beyond what is expected of women can be seen as overstepping. As I've talked to hundreds of Mormon women and studied women in other denominations as well, it seems to me that women generally feel out the acceptable extent of their power, as is humanly natural. Where is my presence welcomed? What do I have the ability to influence? What tools are at my disposal for making my mark? These are genderless, human questions. But what is at stake in conversations among and about women is the acceptable dimensions of the arena in which they can reach for that influence. The available landscapes for exerting that influence may change from one group of women to another. For instance, one woman may feel that the arena for exerting influence reaches only to the boundaries of the Relief Society's jurisdiction; that is, she may only feel comfortable engaging with a female community and may feel uncomfortable exerting herself outside of those bounds. However, another might feel that her arena extends beyond the Relief Society out to the landscape of the whole ward. These acceptable landscapes, where influence is negotiated and claimed, change from one subculture to another, from one woman to another, and are often tacit and so deeply engrained in cultural practices that they are hardly consciously recognized. But the common theme is that we cling to those arenas, and excelling within them is important to us.

I hear in our leaders' words a plea for women to increase the scope of their comfortable arenas. For example, in a 2005 interview before her death, former Relief Society general presidency counselor Chieko N. Okazaki shared hard words about women's lack of support for other women: "I have to say that, in my sixty-four years in the Church, I sometimes see a little bit of a change that the women themselves prompt, but most of the time, I haven't seen women who would make that change possible. Wherever I go, I think that [women] already know their place. . . . When women get the message that their job is to be supportive and just agree with the decisions of the bishop, they become clams."

In his book *Spiritual Roots of Human Relations*, Stephen Covey warns of how "borrowing strength builds weakness." What he means is that when our identity lies in the position or authority we hold, such as the degrees after our names or the Church calling we hold or being queens of the arenas we command, we ultimately find ourselves even weaker when those trappings are changed or no longer valued because there we have little core confidence. As we see in the example of the Relief Society president and the Christmas party described above, a woman not only builds weakness in herself by reveling in her status, but she builds weakness in the other person because that other person reacts out of fear or deference to the status alone, and not out of freedom and genuine respect.

Covey explains how important it is for a person to fully own her sense of self before being able to help build another. "A sense of possession," he says, "should precede a genuine giving, just as algebra precedes calculus." Perhaps this is what Jesus was getting at when he suggested to Martha that Mary had chosen the "good part": it is not a clean house or a perfect event or a completed checklist that prepares a heart to hear the Savior. Perhaps Mary represents one who is in full possession of herself and a knowledge of her standing before the Lord, and who is thus able to put aside the trappings of tasks efficiently executed without feeling it diminishes her status in any way. There is no indication that Mary felt the need to disapprove of her sister, although they were clearly very different, both with strong qualities to offer the Savior. Mary's quiet confidence allowed her to look beyond what was expected of her as a woman at that time and thereby more fully reap the rewards of being in the Savior's presence.

Honoring Women's Leadership

In his biography of the English writer Samuel Johnson, author James Boswell recalled a conversation he had with the writer. Boswell told Johnson that he had heard a Quaker woman preaching that morning in church. Johnson replied, "Sir, a woman's preaching is like a dog's walking on his hind legs. It is not done well; but you are surprised to find it done at all."

Ouch. Such is the degree of respect that has historically been paid to women at church.

Our last consideration for this chapter offers a gentle reminder that women's stewardship over their divinely appointed role is to be honored and respected at all times. You may remember the example I shared in Chapter 4 about the Young Women's presidency preparing the girls' camp flyer with the notice of "flushing toilets" that was deemed offensive by a male leader. A former ward Relief Society president described approaching her bishop about forming a book club for the women in her Relief Society and other women they might invite. He approved the idea only if *he* could pick the books the women would read. She declined.

More than one person I interviewed mentioned experiences in which female ward music directors had been stripped of rightful decision-making abilities by overbearing male leaders who thought they had the right to choose the hymns and request the special musical numbers because they were the priesthood leaders. Ward music director is a traditionally female calling, and it seems particularly susceptible to overzealous male oversight. As one former micromanaged music director told me, "I was called and set apart to do that one job, and I was doing my best. I didn't have the tools or the confidence to stand up to [the male leader]. So I just sulked about it instead."

Such stories suggest there are instances where we could do better at giving women space to do their jobs. But to be clear, honoring women's voices and opinions is not a growth opportunity for just ward councils or auxiliary presidencies within the Church. University of Cambridge professor Mary Beard draws attention to this "well-known deafness" throughout our culture that is parodied in an old *Punch* cartoon: "That's an excellent suggestion, Miss Triggs. Perhaps one of the men here would like to make it." Beard asks:

> What's the practical remedy? Like most women, I wish I knew. There can't be a group of female friends or colleagues anywhere in this country (maybe the world) which hasn't regularly discussed the day-to-day aspects of the 'Miss Triggs question', whether in the office, or a committee room, council chamber, seminar or the House of Commons. How do I get my point heard? How do I

get it noticed? How do I get to belong in the discussion? I'm sure it's something some men feel too but if there's one thing that we know bonds women of all backgrounds, of all political colours, in all kinds of business and profession, it's the classic experience of the failed intervention; you're at a meeting, you make a point, then a short silence follows, and after a few awkward seconds some man picks up where he had just left off: 'What I was saying was . . . ' You might as well never have opened your mouth, and you end up blaming both yourself and the men whose exclusive club the discussion appears to be.

Hearing authority in a woman's suggestions or opinions goes beyond having her physically present in a council meeting or even seeing her on a stand. As in her marriage, her feeling of worth at church will depend in part on whether or not she is heard as an autonomous and trusted voice. To return to an earlier analogy, her contributions are her gift, offered for the edification of the Church membership and as a submission to her Heavenly Father. If we neglect the influence of her presence, she is left with the "classic experience of the failed intervention," with potentially dire repercussions for her relationship to the Church.

As we leave our discussion about relationships, allies, communication approaches, and interpersonal respect, the following case study demonstrates the power that comes from honoring women's leadership.

People in the Real World: A Women's Gender Forum

Earlier this year, a stake organized a women's conference, as they do every year. While preparing for that women's conference, the stake Relief Society president received a request from a female member: could there be a forum on gender issues as part of the conference?

I had heard of these kinds of unofficial forums happening more and more regularly throughout the country, but since I knew personally some of the women in this stake I was curious about how this one in particular came about and what the outcome was. Through a little networking, I was able to interview the stake Relief Society president, the woman who requested the forum, several of the participants, and the representative of the stake presidency who led the meeting. I share their perspectives here in hopes that others might find value in a similar model. Names have been changed.

- From the stake Relief Society president:

  Two weeks before our conference, a sister in the stake, Anna, emailed me requesting to have a forum on gender issues at our stake women's conference. She requested that President Brown, a counselor in our stake presidency who is particularly attuned to women's leadership issues and has initiated new gender practices in our stake in the past, lead the forum. As I read her email, I was awash with the Spirit telling me how important it was that we do this. I called Pres. Brown, and he was immediately on board.

Within hours of this experience, I attended an eleven-stake training of Relief Society presidencies with Sister Linda S. Reeves, second counselor in the Relief Society general presidency. We were informed that she was here to train us and then we would in turn train our ward Relief Society presidencies. I was so eager to receive this training as I have only been in this calling several months and am feeling a bit lost.

As we met, Sister Reeves stood and looked at us and then said, "The Spirit is telling me to talk on something I had not planned to discuss." She wanted to discuss women and the priesthood and the issues many women are struggling with at this time. She did teaching from the scriptures, shared her experiences with the brethren, and there was a great deal of discussion as well. After almost an hour she again stood there and looked at us and said, "I thought we would move on but the Spirit tells me there is more we need to discuss here. Some of you have not had your chance to talk about this yet." Sure enough, more women stood and spoke their concerns. I cannot begin to tell you how powerful the spirit was in that room. We spent the entire two hours of our "training" discussing the ideas of women and their role in our church. One of the statements I wrote down from Sister Reeves says, "We want to embrace every woman. It's not us vs. them, we are all members of His church, we are sisters, we want to listen and understand." Sister Reeves truly was listening and did want to understand. The spirit was so powerful it was draining me.

It is very clear to me that the Lord cares deeply for each daughter of His and when they are struggling it is of great concern to Him. I don't think it was a coincidence that Anna emailed me that morning and that the spirit spoke strongly to Sister Reeves to spend her training time talking with us about women's concerns. The Lord truly cares.

I am grateful the women of our stake felt they had a safe space to discuss their concerns with gender roles with Pres. Brown at our women's conference. The room was quite crowded and I stood in the hallway to make room for sisters who wanted to be in there.

• From the initiator, Anna:

I recently read the March 1, 2014, *New York Times* article about sister missionaries and their influence on gender roles in the Church. I felt like bells just went off all over in my heart. Although I have been thinking about our gender doctrine and praying about what it means to be a woman, I felt so strongly that we need to make changes now to help women feel more included and empowered. I pump breastmilk during my lunch break at the hospital where I am a doctor, and usually I write clinic notes or follow up on other patient care issues while I pump, but on that day I just couldn't focus on work. There was a space to leave your email address in the online version of the article for further contact with the journalists, and I submitted mine. The journalists received hundreds of responses from Mormon women to their article, prompting them to publish a follow up piece the next day.

But I felt like all this was silly, like Mormon women were giving our voices to the wrong place. I felt frustrated that here were two non-Mormon journalists who were receiving emails and emails from Mormon women wanting change. . . . [B]ut why these journalists? I thought, shouldn't we be working through these requests and concerns at the local levels? The idea of having a session at the upcoming Stake Women's Conference came to me, the idea being to have a very practical session where we could talk about what could be adapted right here, right now in my stake that would help women feel more empowered. I knew President Brown would already be at the Conference, so I thought that perhaps he would be willing to moderate the session, and an additional benefit would be having sisters witness their male leader listening to their suggestions and concerns that, in and of itself, would be empowering. I had the idea for a few days but felt nervous about suggesting it because the conference already sounded so lovely and I didn't want my idea to be a distraction. But eventually I dashed off an email to her with my idea. And then she took over from there and it was such a fast and positive response! So exciting.

It's funny to me that after praying about eternal doctrine, this little meeting about earthly logistics and leadership came to be, but as I've reflected on the experience I feel strongly that it is all part of the same story.

The room for which the meeting was scheduled in was one of the regular sized classrooms. But we quickly outgrew the room and people were spilling out the door by the end. At the end of every woman's statement, others' hands were immediately raised.

Many issues were brought up including women's difficulty discussing intimate relations in front of male clergy, the need to strengthen young women's understanding of the Relief Society, the need to teach men about the importance of and the structure of the Relief Society, the frustrations many women felt that even if leaders listened, nothing would change. Women also discussed how much animosity they felt from other women and how they felt tentative—like they were "walking on egg shells" around many women in their ward because they were afraid of how they would respond if they brought up their concerns about gender issues. Many expressed frustration that people assumed they were unfaithful or "didn't get the gospel" because of their concerns.

Throughout the meeting President Brown stated several times his willingness to be contacted directly or to visit wards or Relief Societies or other forums for ongoing discussion. I think one of the most powerful parts of the session was the way he responded. He was not at all defensive. He did not make excuses or try to explain things away. He listened, was sympathetic, but he didn't linger on any one comment very long and kept the discussion going, allowing as many women as possible to comment.

After the meeting, we gathered in the cultural hall where we sat around our classic round Mormon tables. The air at the table was excited and the conversation lingered on these topics for another hour. Women shared their personal experiences, thoughts, hopes, and frustrations about gender issues both inside and outside the church. Being somewhat reserved and shy in social groups I myself said very little, but I was excited to hear how passionately these women cared about these issues and how excited they were to identify each other—to meet new friends with whom they felt comfortable sharing these parts of their hearts. Their relief at being able to publicly discuss their concerns was palpable, and several times they mentioned how grateful they were that the session had happened and how open President Brown had been.

At many points during this experience I felt nervous about even this simple act and idea. I feel that as Mormon women we often worry too much about what we think of each other and as a consequence lose out on opportunities to be genuine with each other. I want to see and be seen as a disciple of Christ, and I imagine other women in the Church also yearn for acceptance as disciples first without regard to their personal career or family choices. I've been rereading Third Nephi, and the doctrine of salvation outlined in the chapters about Christ's ministry doesn't say anything about gender identity or roles. It talks about faith, repentance, etc.—steps we all take and learn in unique ways—but yet we feel a need for validation along our path in order to feel hopeful that we may obtain the promises we desperately long for. What I've been reminded of during this experience, as I am so often in this church, is what great power there is in talking face to face to others about the closest issues to our hearts. I am reminded that sharing burdens with each other allows us to lift, succor, and validate each other and find our way forward toward Christ, which is the essence of the baptismal covenant. I am reminded that when we are seen through a glass clearly—not darkly—and when we see others the same way in open expression, our hearts are filled with greater love and understanding. I hope that women in our stake at the session and other women worldwide who attend sessions like this can, through open discussion, strengthen each other, succor each other, and help create space for each other in their communities so that each sister will continue to choose this gospel and its rich community of sisterhood and brotherhood.

- From President Brown of the stake presidency:

I was honored that I was the guy the women wanted to hear them out. I try to live my life in a way that can bring out women's full potential. I've never pounded the pulpit on this issue, but I've done it behind the closed bishop's door all the time. I can't make a difference whipping people up into a frenzy, but I can change things from the inside.

The gender forum at our stake women's conference didn't have an agenda. It was just a conversation. It was an opportunity for the women to share how they're feeling about their place in the Church, not just among themselves but directly with a male leader. We didn't have a list of next steps that came out of it. I didn't do anything proactive; I was just responsive to what they told me. It was far more important for the women to talk than for me to talk to them.

The tone was grateful and appreciative, not angry or accusatory. They said they'd never had a place to express their feelings like this before to a male leader without any fear of being reprimanded or patronized. I was so glad to do it. I was so glad they knew that I was the guy to call.

- From a participant:

I was really happy the meeting was happening, but I felt everyone was walking on eggshells until I said some hard things. President Brown said he was going to have the stake presidency wives speak more often. I responded by saying I didn't just want to hear from the wives of the male leaders. It doesn't help if a woman only gets to speak because of who she's married to, not because of what she's done. That doesn't make people feel better. After that, the comments really opened up.

This stake presidency has done some creative things in the past: for instance, our stake relief society presidency sat up on the stand during a stake conference a couple of years ago. But then that hasn't happened again since. I hope that after this meeting, we will see changes like that made consistently so they just become new traditions.

Chapter Eleven

Process

"Ideals are stars to steer by; they are not sticks to beat ourselves with."
Barbara B. Smith, Relief Society General President,
Ensign, March 1976

Once we've prayed and meditated about needs and possible solutions for our target audience, and once we've identified allies and lines of communication that might aid us in implementing an adaptation to gender practices, it's time to execute.

The three-hour block of meetings on Sundays represents the critical time for us as leaders and members to employ adaptive gender practices. There are, in addition, meetings of smaller groups that immediately precede and follow the three-hour block, and of course there are midweek activities and meetings too. But the Sunday gathering time provides the bulk of communal worship and thus communal practices, and so much of the discussion in this section will be focused on what we can do during our Sunday meetings.

In my research, I've been heartened by the range of specific practices that are currently being employed across the country to successfully magnify the impact of women at the local level. These ideas are what are working for stake presidents, stake Relief Society presidents, bishops, ward Relief Society presidents, Young Women and Primary leaders, and members with no official stewardships at all. Like all of the ideas and stories I've included so far, I share these with the intention of expanding our repertoire of tools for meeting the needs of our sisters and brothers and alerting us to pitfalls. Some practices mentioned here may spark a thought or an idea for you; others may seem irrelevant or impractical for your specific situation. All are intended to expand our spiritual imaginations and open our hearts to what is possible.

Let's start with what is happening in our Sunday meetings.

Making Women More Visible in Our Sunday Meetings

Sacrament meeting is the focal point of our Sunday worship; it is the reason for gathering. Taking the sacrament is the most important event of the week for each of us, and nothing should detract from our ability to take the sacrament bread and water in reverence and meditation. However, surrounding this sacred ordinance, we have traditional as well as doctrinally decreed ways of gathering and worshipping in community. What we see, who participates, and how we feel during these surrounding worship practices can have an impact on our relationship to our faith and on our ability to take the sacrament with the right attitude.

It is easy to spot the men when entering the chapel and preparing to take the sacrament: the bishopric is usually gathering up on the stand, the Aaronic Priesthood holders are preparing the trays of bread and water on the sacrament table, perhaps a few older boys or men are gathering other priesthood holders to pass the sacrament. In my ward, the greeter is a man who passes out programs and welcomes us as we enter. As the meeting progresses, those bishopric members stand to give announcements, announce new callings, and set out the program of worship. Those boys walk around the congregation, tasked with the sacred job of distributing the tokens of the Atonement. On fast and testimony Sundays in my ward, two young men stand holding portable microphones at the front of the chapel, ready to bring them to the older people in my ward who wish to bear their testimonies from their seats. My ward's chorister is usually a man. The ward membership clerk—a man—walks down the aisles during the meeting, counting those in attendance.

Where are the women? Little in this tableau indicates the tireless backstage work of the ward's women and girls in pursuit of our spiritual health. Nothing acquaints me as a ward member with those women under whose stewardship my well-being falls. Little indicates the marvelous cooperative counseling that may have taken place just shortly before between the women and the men of the ward. In my ward, the organist is a woman. There may be a woman on the stand who participates as a speaker in the program. Or there might not be. But a visitor or new member with far less understanding than I would be justified in suspecting women do not participate in the administration of the Church from the brief scene I described.

Bishops around the country are making an effort to have the women, and particularly the Young Women, become an essential fiber in the visual tapestry that is sacrament meeting. Several bishops I spoke to have asked the Young Women to act as permanent greeters, saying that the ward family feels like they can now more readily identify and feel a connection with the Young Women of the ward as they do to the Young Men who pass them the sacrament every week. There is the example of the bishop who asked the Young Women to contribute the bread for the sacrament table, as I described earlier. I was told of a Young Women activity that was a behind-the-scenes tour of the Sacrament: the girls baked the bread, then the Young Men showed the Young Women how they prepare it, where they prepare it, and how they clean up. Another ward has asked the Relief Society to perform a simple women's choir number one Sunday every month—no rehearsal required, but the women routinely have an opportunity to stand before the congregation.

Mixing up the speaker selection and ordering is a practice that many bishops I spoke with are either informally or formally implementing. One bishop said that when asking a couple to speak, he deliberately tells the couple that they can decide which of them speaks first. Although he's only had a few couples opt to have the woman speak second, he feels it breaks down the expectation that the woman will be the "two-and-a-half-minute youth speaker" and the man will give the doctrinal sermon. Another bishop said, "We've made a conscious effort when planning our programs to focus on who's the most experienced and flexible speaker. We put that speaker last so that the last speaker can be a person who can adjust their talk on the fly as the time demands. Usually that's a woman."

A member of a New York City ward described another practice of speaker selection:

> My bishopric never assigns married couples to give sacrament meeting talks. Ever. Talks are given by a selection of three people, men and women. Sometimes two of the three are a couple if they're new to the ward, but usually it's just three people unrelated by marriage or calling. I love this because in the Church, men speak all the time as conductors of the meeting or the High Council visitor, etc. Women only speak when they're up there with their husbands, or if they're the single woman who's stuck in the youth speaker slot. What I always take away from that arrangement is that women only have a message to share if they're married or have an "important" calling, and it certainly means that women speak less often than men. With this arrangement of unrelated people speaking, the messages of the gospel are shared without any subtext.

I also find this practice appealing because one couple isn't overburdened on a particular week with both adults assigned to give talks. It relieves the problems of having both spouses find time to prepare midweek or having to shuffle kids around during the meeting itself.

As I've mentioned previously, all-female programs seem to be becoming more and more common, and not just because it's the Relief Society's yearly turn. Assigning women to be the only or final speakers sends a powerful message to women themselves that they are trusted as theological thinkers, ecclesiastical leaders, and doctrinal authorities, even if they are not assigned to official female leadership positions. It is also important, however, to give those who are official female leaders a voice and platform in a sacrament meeting setting so that the men and women in the congregation can learn to recognize them and trust them as respected stewards. A Primary president shared with me her own efforts to acquaint her ward with the female leadership:

> In December, while the bishopric was preparing a ward theme and agenda for the new year, I felt impressed to suggest to our bishopric that it would be helpful to have the male and female organizational presidencies (Relief Society, Young Women, Primary, Elders Quorum, High Priest, Young Men, etc.) be introduced to the ward and speak on how their organization strengthens families, which was our theme for the new year. This would help ward members see and get to know the names and faces of those who serve in each capacity. I emailed the suggestion to the bishop and the counselor I work with in the Primary. They thanked me for the suggestion, and I let it go without any thought of taking it further.
>
> A couple of weeks later in ward council, one of the bishopric counselors proposed assigned Sundays in January for each quorum and auxiliary president to speak on how their respective church program strengthens families! On those January Sundays, I enjoyed hearing from each of the presidents. Very thoughtful talks. It was so nice not to hear a month of New Year's resolution talks like every other year! As the first speaker myself that January, I had each of my presidency members stand in their pews as I introduced them at the beginning of my remarks.

The desire of female leaders to have regular opportunities to address the wards was a theme I heard from almost every Relief Society, Young Women, and Primary leader I spoke with. One stake Relief Society president explained to me,

> I've only been asked to speak in Sacrament meetings three times in the four years that I've been in this calling, and those have only happened because an assigned speaker got sick and I pushed my way in as a fill-in. I want the women of my stake to know I'm there for them. I want them to know they

can look to me to have their best interest at heart. I want them to know of the power and potential of Relief Society, of the amazing organization they're a part of. I talk to the ward Relief Societies during ward conferences, but I don't have a consistent time or place when I can communicate to the women of my stake. I'd say maybe a third of the active women in my stake could identify me as the stake Relief Society president, and that's even with me being a really outgoing leader!

Some wards are using the monthly high councilor visit as an opportunity to introduce female leadership to the wards. The stake Relief Society president quoted above told me how much she would love to share the responsibility with the other female leaders of speaking to the different wards, but her stake president isn't ready to adopt the practice yet. If one president or counselor from each female-led organization rotated speaking with a high councilor each week, the burden wouldn't be too great on any one person, and the wards would see a regular carousel of female stake leaders accompanying the male stake representatives. A number of stake presidency members reported this arrangement working very well in their stakes, while others said they preferred to stick with the more traditional practice of having returned missionaries accompany the visiting high councilor. While these return missionary speaking companions are now typically male, more and more will be female, provided that the high councilor is comfortable asking a twenty-one-year-old woman to accompany him. This may be unlikely for some high councilors and thus continue to result in all-male programs unless there is some stake mandate in place to equally distribute the sister and elder missionary speaking companions.

In my own ward conference this year, I noticed that the female leaders of the Relief Society, Young Women, and Primary stake organizations who came to participate in our ward conference were not even introduced by name during the sustainings at the beginning of our sacrament meeting. The deacon's quorum president had stood up and been sustained before the first woman was even mentioned. And then the stake auxiliary presidencies were part of the "as presently constituted" collection of sustainings at the end of the long list. I would have very much liked to know those women's names and have been able to identify them in the congregation. Reports are reaching my ears frequently of stake Relief Society presidents being routinely introduced in stake conferences or sitting on the stand during stake conferences for the congregations to see and recognize. Having female leaders sit on the stand during stake conferences seems like a natural extension of the practice at the general Church level, where the female leaders sit with the general authorities at the front of the Conference Center during all four general sessions of Conference. In fact, should we at all question our general leadership's dedication to women's visibility at General Conference, the entire Relief Society, Young Women, and Primary general presidencies were moved to the middle section of seats in April 2014—directly behind the Quorum of the Twelve Apostles—and, for the first time, the apostles' wives also sat on the stand.

In that spirit, a friend described to me the unusual practice employed at the release of her father as bishop: "When my father was released, the stake president asked the bishopric *and their wives* to all stand for a vote of thanks, and then he asked the new bishopric and their entire families to stand and be sustained. I cried to see my mom and dad standing there together. My parents were both so invested in the calling—it felt right for them to stand and be released together."

As I've spoken to members about these expanded gender practices over the years, some have expressed the feeling to me that having female greeters, having Young Women hold the microphone for testimonies, having Relief Society presidents sit on the stand for conference meetings, etc. are hollow symbols of no substance or else paltry bones thrown to women by the men who continue to have the real power. On the flip side, others have wondered why they should even extend the effort to adapt practices since women should be satisfied by our revolutionary gender doctrine and not need "worldly glory" and attention. In the face of these objections, I reiterate my belief that visual representation matters deeply. Weaving girls and women into the Sunday experience is an important way to recognize and respect the work that so many women and girls are already doing behind the scenes. If women are out of sight, they are out of mind. Conversely, if we see women actively participating in the preparation and execution of our most important weekly worship, we are more inclined to understand and appreciate the depth of women's contributions.

Youth: Providing Equivalent Opportunities

I recently found myself at sacrament meeting a little early, sitting next to one of the young women in my ward whom I barely know. We chatted a bit before the meeting, shuffling around to make room for my kids and discussing her early mornings on a sports team at school. When the meeting started, the bishop mentioned a Young Women activity in the announcements. My new friend leaned over to me: "I'm so over Young

Women activities. All we do is bake cookies and visit retirement homes. The boys have gone night skiing and hiking up Mt. Timpanogos and off-road biking. I'm sick of them getting to do all the fun stuff!" I was startled by her unsolicited revelation and humbled by the realization that our discussion here is needed in my own backyard.

Perhaps no effort is as crucial as those geared toward helping our young women know not just their personal worth, but their potential to be valued and vital contributors to their religious community throughout their futures. And yet between the milestones offered by priesthood progression—from deacon to teacher to priest and the accompanying community responsibilities associated with each—as well as the well-oiled machine of the Boy Scouts program, our young women are especially vulnerable to not receiving the same kind and degree of support as our young men. Although the Young Women program has age-adapted classes, the doctrine around women in our theology is unique, and Personal Progress approximates the skill building of Scouting, too many girls and women feel that Beehive, Mia Maid, and Laurel are consolation prizes for not being deacons, teachers, and priests.

It doesn't have to be this way. By looking at the structures and practices of both the Young Men and Young Women programs and relying on a little inspired imagination, leaders and members can identify areas that might lack parity and do much to rectify them.

The budget available to each auxiliary is an obvious place to start. Former counselor in the Relief Society general presidency Kathleen Hughes describes her process of identifying the Young Women budget as an area of tension in her own ward and considering an approach:

> My interactions with Priesthood leaders have been uniformly positive. That is not to say that I never disagreed with them. (Anyone who knows me, knows that I have opinions about things.) But I have found that Priesthood leaders would listen when I expressed my opinion or when I raised a concern.
>
> I particularly recall an occasion when the Bishop announced in Sacrament meeting that the young men in the ward would be given the opportunity to raise money for their activities by placing flags in the front yards of homes within the ward boundaries. All members and neighbors were invited to give a particular amount of money to the young men and in return, on special national holidays, the flags would be placed in their yards. I had recently been released from serving in Young Women, and I well knew how little money there was available for their activities. I was upset. And during the week, as I thought about the announcement, I became more upset. Finally, my husband

said, "Kathy, go talk to the Bishop. He'll listen to you." So, I called his office
at work and made an appointment to visit with him. I laid out my concerns
and my rationale for why the planned money-raising activity for the Young
Men seemed unfair. He listened, asked some questions, but made no commitments. I could do nothing more. I wondered if my meeting had done any
good, and when I heard nothing from him, I began to think that the original
decision would stand. But, a week later the Bishop sat down next to me before
Sacrament meeting and said, "Kathy, I just want you to know that we are
going to involve the young women in the project. And you were not the only
woman who came to see me. I heard from several!" Courageously, but courte-
ously advocating for those we are called to serve had made a difference. I have
consistently found that to be true.

Equal budgets for boys and girls sends an important signal that one group's
spiritual development isn't more important than the other's.

Because the Boy Scouts program is so entrenched in our young men's
Church experiences here in the United States, they benefit from the extensive organization and legacy of that program. Thus there are events
and practices associated with that association that have no parallel for
the girls. (And children are quick to notice this and remind us of it: for
example, when the Primary president in my ward recently started a sharing time activity by saying, "You boys know from Scouts how to make
a fire, right?" and an eleven-year-old girl piped up, "Hey, I know how
to make a fire too!") The Blue and Gold annual banquet, for example,
requires extensive ward resources of time, talent, and even money, but no
such time, talent, and money are similarly designated for the Activity Day
girls. With less structure and heritage than Boy Scouts, Activity Days are
only as good as the leader's initiative. My own daughters' experiences in
Activity Days have run the gamut: from painting nails and applying facial
masks to touring Temple Square. While I treasure the opportunity my
girls have to develop friendships with other Primary girls their age and
with admirable leaders, I'm not sure what to say when my oldest daughter
asks why some boys show up to church in special blue uniforms and have
their own banquet to honor them. Similarly, when my daughters heard in
Primary about the father-and-sons campout, they asked my husband why
they couldn't attend too. He said there was no reason, so they went with
him. If there are objections to including girls in what some consider to
be meaningful father-and-son traditions, then start a father-and-daughter
campout too. Or a mother-and-daughter campout. Or a mother-and-
daughter night at a soup kitchen. Or hike. Or lake excursion. One ward

created a summer day camp for both the Cub Scouts and the Activity Day girls to attend together.

The point is not that the events have to be the same, but that the girls need to be able to feel equivalent investment and significance in the events. They need to be able to say to themselves, "I don't feel left out of the father-and-sons campout because my father (or mother) and I get special time together during the (fill in the blank) church activity, which is just as exciting or interesting to me as what the boys are doing." Several reports have reached me of successfully integrated Pinewood Derbies, where both boys and girls participate. A proud mom shared with me the photo of her daughter's car, carved and painted to look like a delicious double decker ice cream cone. But one Primary president didn't have such a happy ending: when a girl took first place in the race, a mother of a boy approached this Primary president and asked, "When is it going to be about the boys?" Although this response baffled the Primary president (a woman particularly attuned to these issues we are discussing here), our perspective as parents of boys or girls colors our perception and our sensitivity to the messages our children receive. But again, alternate solutions can be found if there are sensitivities. What about a separate girls' Pinewood Derby on the same night where the boys cheer on the girls and the girls cheer on the boys? Or what about a wooden boat race for the girls or an Olympics activity with three-legged races and obstacle courses? If there is a feeling that the separate gender experiences are valuable and thus the activities should not be integrated, the ideas are endless.

One reason some people advocate for boys and girls to participate in the same activity as opposed to different, gendered activities is because different activities can rarely be objectively deemed comparable if they are defined by gender stereotypes. For instance, we may find ourselves saying, "Well, the boys have the Pinewood Derby but the girls get to make scripture bags." Who says those two things have parity? Who says a girl won't feel the Pinewood Derby to be a closer expression of herself and more appealing than making a scripture bag? Also, Pinewood Derby, like Boy Scouts overall, has a heritage, a brand, a code word that sends ripples of understanding through our whole community and binds us together. Unless making scripture bags has that same longevity, that same nostalgia and parental bonding opportunity, it does not have the same emotional payoff for the girls. As another example, one of my husband's most profound memories of his youth was climbing Mount Rainier at age fourteen with his Scout troop, which was composed of the young men from his ward. Did the girls in his ward have an equivalently challenging and emotionally maturing activity themselves? The answer is likely no.

When planning different but gendered activities, we have an obligation to look beyond gender stereotypes and find options that build similar skills in boys and girls, create similar community bonding, offer similar opportunities for spiritual growth and quite simply are just as much fun. We have an opportunity in our youth activities to challenge gender stereotypes and help our children become better prepared for their futures. Let's have boys babysit as we prepare them for their essential roles as fathers. Let's plan a Young Men cooking class. Few men will not have to or want to cook for themselves or their families in our rising generation. Let's have the girls hike Rainier. I've personally participated in Young Women career nights. What a joy it was to see young women preparing for their futures in expansive and empowering ways as they contemplated their skills, their priorities, and their dreams. Because of activities like this, the Church will be the support system they turn to when making deliberate choices about their lives, not the limiting factor they blame for pigeonholing them as people they feel they are not.

The opportunities to recognize girls' progression through Primary and Young Women are broad and relatively untapped, whereas the progression of a boy through Aaronic Priesthood quorums is a communal cause for celebration and support. How the girls' progression is recognized currently varies wildly from one ward and stake to the next, based on the disposition and priorities of the leaders. One man describes an effort to recognize the girls with equal enthusiasm to the boys when they progress within their own program:

> This past year in my ward, several girls completed their Personal Progress requirements and were to be given their recognition award. In the past, I've seen bishops call the girl up from the audience, congratulate her, hand her whatever, and that's pretty much it. But this time, my bishop went out of his way to make an appropriately big deal of their awards. He had the girls, their parents and their Young Women's president sitting on the stand at the beginning of sacrament meeting. He gave a sort of mini-talk, explaining the program and its requirements. Then he called each girl up and had her speak about what she had learned or her favorite part of the program. There were hugs with parents and leaders. I would estimate he devoted a full ten minutes of our meeting to honoring these young women, and frankly I have never seen anything like it. But it occurred to me that of course that's the way we should be doing it.

What a beautiful way to extend the confidence-building attention boys enjoy in their Boy Scout courts of honor to girls. Another bishop told me he asks the congregation for a sustaining vote when a young woman advances, and publicly gives her a certificate the Church makes available for this purpose. And this mutual approbation doesn't need to be a one time thing: one Young Men group reported that their next activity was to attend the Young Women New Beginnings evening to see the girls get their awards. This feels to me like a healthy way to show cooperation and collaboration, while still maintaining spaces for boys and girls to develop among their own. Although community recognition is important to building a feeling of support and acceptance within a young girl, families can privately take on the task of recognizing these milestones by having equivalent celebrations when a daughter enters Young Women as when a son receives the Aaronic Priesthood. One couple has a special family ritual of taking their twelve-year-old son *or* daughter on an outing all their own to discuss the years and responsibilities that lay ahead.

As I have pointed out before, except for local Primaries, there is no place in the official governmental structure of the Church where a boy or man is obligated to respect the administrative or ecclesiastical authority of a woman. The teen years are a prime time to ensure that boys never feel dismissive of a female leader, even if they are never under her particular stewardship. It should never be okay for a boy or man to take a bathroom or snack break when a woman appears on the television to speak at general conference. The training to prevent that has to start young by giving boys experiences where they learn to trust the spiritual guidance of women who are not their mothers. Efforts in this regard that have been reported to me include having the Young Women presidency teach Young Men classes periodically, or the young women themselves teach or lead youth activities.

One woman, a mother of sons, told me of a sacred experience she had as the Eagle advisor in her ward, a position she volunteered for when she saw that the boys in her ward weren't getting the support they needed to finish their Eagle projects. In one year, she shepherded ten boys to receiving their Eagle Scout award, and in the process, these teenage boys had the rare experience of working with and trusting a woman (who was not their mother) as a spiritual guide. The partnership was a treasure for both this woman and the boys:

> It was probably the most spiritual calling I have ever had. The reason was that I would sit with the boys, and we would pray together about their proj-

ect once a week. We would see so many roadblocks come up standing in the way of their completing their projects. . . . But I would remind each boy that he had felt the Spirit when he chose that project, he knew Heavenly Father wanted him to do this, so we could find a way to overcome this hurdle. We would pray before making calls and reaching out to people. It was just miraculous. I hadn't seen miracles like this since I had been on my mission. This was one of those times that I understood that the Lord really is training these boys and that I could help them tap into the powers of heaven. Each one of them was so overwhelmed by what we were accomplishing through prayer and faith. As they saw they could really call down the powers of heaven, they gained faith that they could call on Heavenly Father throughout their lives.

She continues to describe the relationship with the boys' male leaders:

When I started working with the boys in this one-on-one way, I got pushback from the Scout leader and the quorum advisors. I thought, What? What's the problem? What they said was, "We don't want this to become a competition about who's going to get their Eagle first." And I remember so clearly saying, "How come that's wrong?" I could see on their faces and in their voices that I was entering into a male dominated organization. I felt their anger. There are men all over Scouting. And here they've got a woman coming in and ruffling feathers, and they weren't happy. So I thought, "Okay, I've got to back off and figure out how to get this done." And I did. I changed my tactics. I was most productive working one-on-one with the boys, but I did have to spend time too building the trust of their other male leaders. They simply weren't used to supporting a woman's stewardship of their boys.

Youth: Interviewing Young Women

One of the more sensitive subjects today is that of teen girls being routinely interviewed privately by male leaders to receive limited-use temple recommends or to discuss youth standards. We understand that these interviews are part of the bishop's ecclesiastical responsibility and that, overwhelmingly, these are wonderful men who would never dream of doing anything untoward to a teenage girl. However, even with another man chaperoning in the hall outside, some parents and youth feel uncomfortable with the idea of any man having the responsibility of asking a teen girl questions about her relationship to her body. The concern isn't as much about the possibility of physical inappropriateness as it is about the rhetoric. How can a middle-aged man discuss moral standards with a young girl—either hypothetically or in response to her lived experience—without it feeling supremely awkward at best and manipulative, shaming, and invasive at worst? It is a very difficult task. In addition, teens in America today live in a culture that, for better or worse, empowers them to own their own sexuality. Their sexual lives are not, they believe, subject to community discussion or oversight.

These interviews also present one of the only times where Church guidelines sanction adults and children of the opposite sex to be alone together. In the Primary in which I serve, for instance, our male teachers are all assigned to teach in pairs or trios, and we have to leave the classroom door open to the hall if there is only one man in the room with the children. One stake Relief Society president told me how the Church's facilities department came and added glass windows to every classroom door in her building so they could be seen into at all times. We don't even allow male missionaries into the homes of single women, and missionary companionships themselves are precautionary structures in addition to being ecclesiastically mandated. Those kinds of precautions to avoid even the appearance of anything untoward, thankfully, come naturally to us.

So in this respect, it is understandable that male leaders asking teen girls about their personal lives would feel uncomfortable to some. Of course, we believe these men are acting as representatives of God in ecclesiastical callings for which they have been set apart and designated with priesthood keys, not just some random middle-aged man asking a girl private questions. But we live in a world where parents have to be hyper-protective of their children, and some girls and parents are suggesting options. Could another female leader—perhaps someone of the girl's choosing—be present in these interviews? Could the bishop's wife herself be present? If the girl prefers her mother attend, is that a possibility?

When journalists Jodi Kantor and Laurie Goodstein invited Mormon women to give input about practices they would like to see changed for an article they were writing for the *New York Times*, requesting a female presence when discussing personal matters with male leaders was the most common theme. One stake president in California, after speaking with many of the college students in his stake and recognizing how important this was to them, now allows girls and women to request a female companion of their choice to attend worthiness interviews. In wards and stakes where this is not currently allowed, I have heard heart-breaking stories where this issue has created unresolvable wedges between families and their Church community. In one such story, a father told me that he, his wife, and his daughter agreed that the daughter would always have a female leader present when being interviewed. The bishop refused to accommodate their request when it came time to interview her for a temple baptism trip, which made the other young women feel like they had to take sides. Apparently, they sided with their friend. The father continues:

> My daughter is their natural leader. They attended a large public school with a handful of LDS students and a third of the students bused in from impoverished, violent neighborhoods. My feisty and fearless street-smart daughter watches out for her friends and fights their battles and has spared them from beatings and molestations more than once. The other Young Women said they would not attend the temple without my daughter.
>
> The bishop decided to interview my daughter with my wife present. I was honored to stand with my daughter in the temple baptismal font later that week, and it brought back sacred memories of her own baptism four years earlier.
>
> Perhaps this would be a good place to end the story, except it didn't end there. After the temple trip, the bishop requested our permission to do a retroactive, "proper" interview alone with my daughter and said that he was not going to compromise the policies again. We did not agree.

Long story short: the mother now attends a different church. What a mess. My heart goes out to the family and the bishop, as I'm sure many of ours do. Answers for this one are beyond my suggestions except to encourage extreme compassion and sensitivity to families' concerns and bishops' responsibilities alike.

Youth: Preparing Young Women for Church Service

As a member of my ward's Relief Society presidency while in college, I was responsible for introducing the freshman girls to Relief Society. I quickly discovered for myself what Young Women general president Bonnie L. Oscarson has said: "Our young sisters frequently feel as if they don't have a place or anything in common with those in Relief Society." Not only were our freshman girls leaving home for the first time, many coming thousands of miles away from home to a campus where Mormons were a tiny fraction of the population, but they were expected to transform overnight from working on Personal Progress to talking about babies and financial woes with the graduate students, professors, and other married women in our university ward. I struggled to keep our youngest sisters engaged in our Relief Society and feeling like they had the same sense of purpose and belonging that they had experienced in Young Women.

President Oscarson has encouraged us in the Relief Society community to work particularly hard at transitioning the young women:

> Before they turn 18, [our young sisters] need Young Women leaders and mothers who will joyfully testify of the great blessings of Relief Society. They need to feel enthusiastic about becoming part of such a glorious organization. When young women begin attending Relief Society, what they need most is a friend to sit next to, an arm around their shoulders, and an opportunity to teach and serve. Let us all reach out to help one another through the transitions and milestones of our lives.

Local leaders have discovered the importance of transitioning young women and are taking President Oscarson's words to heart. Many local leaders have already recognized the discrepancy between our Young Men and Young Women programs in preparing our youth for the expectations and opportunities of their adult Church service: young men are included in priesthood quorum opening exercises from the age of twelve, and they are formally assigned as home teaching companions. Young men have an integrated experience from the age of twelve on as they progress through their priesthood quorums, understanding that their service and responsibilities as a youth evolve into similar adult responsibilities. In contrast, young women can go through the entire Young Women program without ever collaborating or coordinating with the Relief Society. (In the process of writing this book, I realized that the official Church style guide includes an entire chapter on Scouting terminology—how to use the terms, write them correctly, etc.—but Activity Days is not mentioned once, suggesting how rarely we talk about the girls' program in official publications.) In my interviews, I was delighted by how frequently local leaders have recognized that visiting teaching provides an easy avenue for giving young women experiences that are similar to those of the young men and also helps prepare them for the expectations and joys of Relief Society. One bishop explained how he and the other leaders in his ward saw visiting teaching not only as an answer to Relief Society transition but to the needed preparation of young women for their missions:

> Most of the young women in our ward have expressed a desire to serve a mission now that the age has been lowered for service. While reflecting on how to help the young women prepare to serve missions, our bishopric and Young Women President independently felt inspired to assign them to serve as visiting teachers. I asked one of my counselors to ask the Young Women President about trying out assigning Laurels to visit teach, and she said that she had been preparing to ask us about that and wanted the Mia Maids to

do it as well. The Young Women President and Relief Society President have been working together to make assignments and they are starting to visit. The handbook does not specify that young women should or should not be visiting teachers.

A stake president came to similar conclusions, also when focusing on how to prepare young women better for missionary service.

> Every stake presidency has their "inspired priorities" because we can't do everything. One of our areas of focus was that we wanted to prepare our young people and our old people for missionary service. We realized that with the accelerated timetable for missionary service the home is now the MTC, and the seminary is now the MTC. When the age change happened, I realized that unless we're preparing our young women as much as we're preparing our young men, we're falling short. There is the opportunity and the responsibility now for everybody to be a preacher and a theologian.
>
> One of the great advantages our young men have is that every month they have a chance to go and minister through home teaching. Of course the program isn't always executed perfectly or sometimes they just sit there or mumble a closing prayer. . . . [B]ut when it works well, it really, really works well. It was during a stake council meeting that I had this feeling: we should have our young women do this as well. We already have a program in place: visiting teaching.
>
> I went through the handbook. I couldn't find anything that proscribed young women visiting teaching with Relief Society sisters. I think going through the handbook is always a good practice because a lot of times things are rooted in tradition or folklore or it's just the unwritten order of things, which is important, but many times the handbook is silent and we are free to make our best decisions.

Despite broad enthusiasm for the change within his stake, this stake president clarified that the transition has been slower than he would have liked. Adapting programs undoubtedly creates growing pains, but following inspiration and administrative imagination will undoubtedly result in better preparation for missions and Relief Society membership for the girls in these wards and stakes.

Rhetoric: Empowering or Dismissing Women through Our Words

Looking objectively at the way we speak and address each other may be the hardest job we have tackled yet in adapting our practices to be more inclusive of women. We speak every day, extemporaneously, without always having the benefit of being able to think and plan ahead of time what we should say and how it might affect others. Words build up, of course: they empower and praise and build confidence. But words can tear down, too, even if they're not intended to; they can have unanticipated consequences, they can reflect biases and subtexts in ways we might not even be aware of, and they can reveal our true natures even when actions do not.

Unfortunately, the rhetorical practice of silencing women reaches back to the beginning of Western civilization as we know it. Think back to your high school English classes. Did you ever read Homer's *Odyssey*? It's one of the earliest known examples of Western literature. At the beginning of Homer's *Odyssey*, and thus at the beginning of Western culture, we have the first recorded example of a man telling a woman that her voice should not be heard in public: Telemachus, Odysseus's son, is singing to guests about the trouble his father and the other Greek heroes are having returning home from wars. Penelope, Telemachus's mother and Odysseus's wife, comes down from her room, doesn't like the sad songs she's hearing, and in front of the guests she asks her son to choose a more cheerful number. Telemachus responds to his mother, "Mother, go back up into your quarters, and take up your own work, the loom and the distaff. . . . [S]peech will be the business of men, all men, and of me most of all; for mine is the power in this household." And so she is shuttled back upstairs.

Happily, few American men today would attempt something so brash as Telemachus's silencing of his mother. This drastic remonstration of a woman's public voice would not be an acceptable practice in our Church or societal culture today. But at the dawn of Western culture, women's voices were actively silenced and the process of growing into manhood, as understood by Homer and most of the ancient world, included claiming a public voice and superiority over even one's own mother.

The remnants of those practices, so recently discarded in the full scope of history, linger insidiously and unconsciously in our communication with each other. For instance, Deborah Tannen explains that the modern stereotype of the "nagging" woman may "result from the interplay of men's and women's styles, whereby many women are inclined to do what is asked of them and many men are inclined to resist even the slightest hint that anyone, especially a woman, is telling them what to do." Nagging is the result of a woman repeating a request over and over, because she is not getting a response and is convinced that her husband would do what she asked if she only made it clear how important it is to her. But the man may subconsciously resist following orders and thus instinctively wait before fulfilling the request, in order to imagine he is doing it from his own free will and not out of coercion. Each time she repeats the request, he puts off fulfilling it, prompting her to request again. The result is that women have borne the brunt of the stereotype, even though long-standing communication styles in both genders are to blame. Women bear the brunt of these rhetorical stereotypes because it is women who approach an overwhelmingly male cultural discourse and try to have a voice within it. Men rarely find themselves among a dominantly female culture, needing to fit their voice into that female conversation.

Within Church culture, we have a rich tradition of telling women that we love and appreciate them, from the pulpit and one-on-one. Both men and women do it, we do it often, and we do it well. What more is needed? For some women, nothing. They feel wrapped in the loving embrace of a community and they feel that their contributions—even the daily, thankless tasks of motherhood or selfless service—are recognized and appreciated. Recognizing and appreciating the at-home mother or the woman in the background is something that we as a people excel at, sometimes uniquely, in the world today.

However, there are a couple of unexpected pitfalls in this approach that tend to haunt some women. The first is that we may subconsciously believe that verbally appreciating a woman's background contributions is reward enough for her efforts, and that greater visibility, responsibility, or reward are unnecessary and even inappropriate. Most of us would not do this consciously. But we have ingrained in our cultural imaginations the proverbial image of the "angel mother" who never seeks attention or asserts herself equal to or above her children or husband. Essential to the image of the angel mother is a soft voice, a backseat influence, and contentment with not receiving recognition outside of a close circle of family and friends. For some, any woman who seeks to separate herself from this ideal is somehow suspect. We're not sure how to reconcile the capable, educated, and ambitious women we have in our congregations with the subconscious programming that tells us women shouldn't *need* to be considered as independent and valuable contributors, because that's not something their personality demands. The days of that undercurrent are over. And we can reflect our dedication to women being independent and valuable contributors in the language we use to give them the public recognition.

Group appreciation also has the tendency to oversimplify and generalize the contributions for which women are being valued. If women are formally appreciated for being nurturing, patient, and virtuous, there is the danger of assuming that every member of that group shares those characteristics in common with every other member. Thus women who do not consider themselves inherently patient or virtuous or creative or spiritually in tune or whatever the laudation might be are actually devalued and destabilized in their own perceptions of themselves, rather than built up as intended. At worse, they can feel like only one kind of woman is appreciated or acceptable, and they are not that woman. Sister Patricia Holland herself humorously declares that she was "threatened to the core" by her inability to like a characteristically feminine activity: sewing. "Can you imagine my burden over the last twenty-five or thirty years, 'faking it' in Relief Society sessions?" Other women might be "threatened" by their inability to enjoy small children or be a warm hostess or to keep a clean house or like pink or enjoy cooking or any number of group-positive characteristic women are assumed to have in common. On the flip side, women who enjoy public speaking or negotiating or leading teams or playing sports may feel they are being unnecessarily barred from being these things in a Church setting because those are things men are more likely to be appreciated for.

This is not to say that the good qualities of our members shouldn't be celebrated and acknowledged. They absolutely should. But the danger is that when we appreciate women for general qualities, we may feel it lets us off the hook for appreciating other, more individual qualities. We may believe that because we've appreciated women for being the things all women are, we don't need to dig any further into her unique identity to find not only what distinguishes her from men but what distinguishes her from other women.

Freeing women from tasks that are not considered to be in their general stable of strengths may have once been considered chivalrous, but the result today is that we silence women's voices. We may do so with a well-meaning spirit of beneficent protecting, but over the long run, a woman may feel she's been "protected" from having the kind of public engagement that would actually magnify her potential, and she may feel cheated. If a woman absorbs the message that, as Telemachus says, "speech is the business of men," it doesn't matter if she receives that message by being reprimanded by a son or by being protected by a husband. She is metaphorically shuttled up the stairs all the same. We can, again, reflect our dedication to women being independent and valuable contributors by assiduously avoiding language that suggests they are being protected from the realm of men.

Lastly, there is the ironic twist that when people are praised for things that they don't believe about themselves, the praiser is ultimately dismissed as an unreliable source. For example, I learned long ago not to trust my husband when he tells me my hair looks great. Early in our marriage I would ask him, "How does my hair look?" as I would ask a girlfriend. He answered me honestly, so sometimes he'd say, "It looks a little funny today." After a year or two of tears, he learned that if he just told me my hair looks great every time I asked, I would be happy. Of course now, many years later, I don't trust his evaluation of my hair at all! There are some days that I *know* that my hair isn't cooperating, so when he tells me it looks great, I don't believe him. In a more serious vein, if a woman doesn't believe herself to be a good nurturer, then those who tell her she is will eventually become untrusted sources. This is one of the reasons it is so important to have our actions and beliefs align with our words: words can actually have the opposite desired effect if not supported by the long-term actions that build core confidence.

It's impossible to pin down every guideline for how men could more effectively talk to and about women. The first step is purely awareness and cooperation between men and women to bring examples to each others' attention. Both men and women can educate themselves to look for the pitfalls we all fall into by reading works by Tannen and others in the linguistics or psychology fields. And we can dedicate ourselves to helping each other identify and solving the rhetorical patterns that may constrict women's value. For example, a member of a stake presidency described to me one practice his stake has adopted for including women rhetorically in priesthood blessings. "We tell all of the priesthood holders in our stake," he told me, "that when giving a father's blessing they should always reference their wife: 'I'm giving you this blessing in the presence of your mother who joins her faith with mine to work in unity and as an equal partner. Our faith is united in this moment. . . .' And then proceed with the blessing. When men are blessing babies, we ask them to do the same thing: 'The name that your mother and I choose is . . .' There are lots of opportunities to acknowledge the woman's faith and the importance of her presence in priesthood blessings."

Hearing, seeing, and including women isn't just about putting out more videos about them or giving them a seat on the stand, as important as those things are. It's about asking ourselves whether or not we hear women's contributions as authoritative. It's about asking ourselves why we take a bathroom break during the female speaker in general conference. It's about rooting out those hard-wired perceptions that make us believe women "nag" while men "assert." It's about ridding ourselves, once and for all, of the pernicious belief widely held by the Greco-Roman founders of our oratory and linguistic culture that women who speak publicly are "pernicious freaks," as one ancient Greek scholar called women who advocated to speak in their senate. We've only been at this cultural shift for a fraction of our known history; we cannot have rooted it out entirely already, but we are getting closer. Our language is the oldest, deepest, most entrenched way we reveal our beliefs about another person: Is she worth listening to? Is she respected? Is she capable? Our words will speak volumes.

Rhetoric: Seeking Doctrine in Female Sources

Several years ago, when I was still new in my study of Mormon women's history, I was invited to a special event in Brigham Young's Lion House to celebrate the release of the Nauvoo Relief Society Minutes into public accessibility. As part of the evening, an actress dressed as Eliza R. Snow came to the little dining room where we were gathered on the upper floor of the building. I was completely captivated: posing as Eliza, the actress recited Eliza's own address given in the Ogden Tabernacle at a Relief Society meeting on August 14, 1873. Eliza had just traveled through Europe and the Middle East for several months visiting dignitaries and missionaries, and culminating in a trip to the Holy Land. She had written letters home from time to time, which had been published in the *Woman's Exponent* magazine. This is what Eliza said to the women of Ogden and to me that night:

> We [women] are to be progressing, and growing better. If we have done well today, we must do still better tomorrow. We believe in eternal progression. It will not do to say that we have so much to do that we cannot do anymore, because the works and duties for women in Zion are constantly increasing. Nowhere on the earth has woman so broad a sphere of labor and duty of responsibility and action as in Utah.
>
> I tried in many instances to make people believe that women in Utah had more freedom than women had anywhere else on the earth. But they

thought that they knew better than I did. I told them how long I had lived with the people, and that I ought to know better than strangers.

To be sure we have trials, but what are they? I want to ask my sisters now a serious question. When you are filled with the Spirit of God, and the Holy Ghost rests upon you—that comforter which Jesus promised, and which takes of the things of God and gives them to us, and shows us things to come, and brings all things to our remembrance—when you are filled with this spirit, do you have any trials? I do not think you do. For that satisfies and fills up every longing of the human heart, and fills up every vacuum. When I am filled with that spirit my soul is satisfied; and I can say in good earnest that the trifling things of the day do not seem to stand in my way at all. But just let me lose my hold of that spirit and power of the Gospel, and partake of the spirit of the world, in the slightest degree, and trouble comes; there is something wrong. I am tried and what will comfort me? You cannot impart comfort to me that will satisfy the Immortal mind, but that which comes from the fountain above. And is it not our privilege to so live that we can have this constantly flowing into our souls? To be sure we have many of the crosses of life, but what do we meet them for? Are they for our own good and benefit or do we meet them all as for Zion's sake? Do we let Zion take full possession of our desires, our ambition?

I had tears in my eyes as she finished. I had not known that Eliza, or any of my spiritual foremothers, had spoken so forcefully about points of doctrine, had appealed so forthrightly to "labor," "responsibility," and "action." It was not a rhetorical style that I was accustomed to hearing from contemporary female leaders. I was moved not just by the words, but by the fact that a woman had said them, right there in front of me. She didn't look like me, dressed in her petticoats, but she *was* me still. I loved her and listened to her, and later studied her, as I have with very few men. This is the power of teaching doctrine by women to women.

Prior to 1997, the Relief Society had its own class manual that was written by members of the Relief Society board. These were manuals that were produced by women for women, and were compiled with women's needs and responses in mind. They included literature lessons, mothering lessons, practical guidance, as well as spiritual food for thought. The Relief Society also published its own magazine prior to 1970. One elderly woman says, "I used to love to lie on the bed at my grandmother's summer sleeping porch and read her old *Relief Society Magazines*. I was sorry to see them go. They gave women a voice." When going through my husband's grandmother's house, I found her own stash of the *Relief Society Magazine* and spent hours pouring over the Eliza R. Snow Poem Contest winners, the reports of women's accomplishments in the "From Near and Far" section, and the Theology lessons. Between these manuals and magazines, women had a body of literature and an outlet for their written word that allowed them to talk to themselves about themselves.

In 1997, President Gordon B. Hinckley wanted to address the needs of a global, growing Church, and specifically the fact that many homes outside the United States didn't have a doctrinal book in them. He wanted every member to have a book in which the prophets speak about doctrine, and thus the *Teachings of the Presidents of the Church* series came into being. With the advent of this series, the Relief Society and priesthood manuals became one and the same, streamlining the educational experience for men and women, and allowing men and women to share what they learn in their classes with each other. The series also had the desired effect of giving members worldwide direct access to the words of the prophets.

There was a cost to the new series though: for fourteen years, our manuals have represented exclusively male voices. There is nothing in our Relief Society or priesthood classes that represents, honors, or nurtures the voice of women on theological or social issues. In addition, the tradition of assigning speakers to talk on recent general conference talks also puts women at a disadvantage: with only 9% of general conference talks being given by women, it is statistically unlikely that a speaker will expound on the words of a female leader to the congregation. In fact, I have personally never heard a sacrament meeting speaker or Relief Society teacher speak about a general conference talk given by a woman. This means that the responsibility is ours then, as individual members and leaders, to bring in the voices of women to our lessons and talks. And some leaders are taking this responsibility seriously: one bishop made a point of telling me that he routinely assigns female leaders' general conference talks to the men *and* young men in his ward as the subjects of their talks. Several others told me the same.

Of course a teacher or speaker must start with a conviction that quoting from women and representing women as theological authorities (even if not administrative authorities) is important. And if it is so important for women, it is also important for men who will benefit from the exercise of being exposed to ideas that reflect a perspective and voice different than their own, as women routinely are when listening to the perspectives of men. I hope that there is little question at this point about why this is important. But where do men and women go to find those female words of wisdom and truth that they can use in their teachings?

At the temple recently, I received a list of initiatory names that had no dates or places associated with them, and I confirmed with the temple worker that they indeed had no more information on these women than what I saw. I mentioned this to my husband later that day. My husband, who works in the family history industry, told me he wasn't surprised. Women have been so poorly recorded throughout history that we have a dire shortage of specific names, dates, and places for them in the historical records we use for our family history work. My heart ached for these unidentified women who were just names on a page. I was reminded of the Lord's words in Isaiah 49: "Can a woman forget her sucking child, that she should not have compassion on the son of her womb? yea, they may forget, yet will I not forget thee. Behold, I have graven thee upon the palms of my hands; thy walls are continually before me." The lives of women in the past—not to mention their wisdom, their thoughts, and their accomplishments—are almost invisible to those who don't actively seek after them. Or to those, like Harvard historian and Mormon woman Laurel Thatcher Ulrich, who use brief diary entries and birth and death records to piece together whole lives, as she did in her Pulitzer Prize-winning book, *A Midwife's Tale*.

This is the landscape we face when we seek out women's words from past generations. Happily, our culture deeply values the journals of our pioneer foremothers, and we have a more than 150-year history of female leaders speaking publicly. But the average member assigned to give a talk or lesson is unlikely to know how to access the words of these women. For instance, a search for Eliza R. Snow, probably the most prominent and well-known female leader from our history, yields zero results on LDS.org under "general conference," zero under "scriptures," two under "magazines," and only a handful under "manuals." Many of those manual references are from seminary Church history manuals, but some are from the 2011 book *Daughters in My Kingdom: The History and Work of Relief Society*. This book—it is never called a manual in the description—was a celebrated step in giving women of today a resource and voice. Not only did it provide one of the robust official Church resources we have for statements by and about women in the Church, but it also publicly acknowledged a specific author, Susan W. Tanner, crediting a woman's name to an official Church document. Men and women alike are turning to this book to augment their lessons and talks with statements and thoughts by women.

I have found the idea of using *Daughters in My Kingdom* as a source text for talks and even classes is quite well established, just three years after its publication. A stake Relief Society president described to me the class she initiated around the book: she held a special class every Thursday morning for eight weeks. They had over one hundred women attend regularly. (My own stake did something similar.) The stake Relief Society president created a blog to go along with the class on which she posted scholarly articles and posts from LDS blogs that went along with what they were studying.

But, as I have mentioned, we don't need to limit *Daughters in My Kingdom* to something just for the ladies. If we are to work cooperatively as men and women, and not just consider women as a special interest group within the larger Church membership, men too need to value and use the words of women. A woman shared with me the action her husband took upon reading the book:

> When *Daughters in My Kingdom* came out, my husband looked through it and said, "You know, I'd really like to teach this in the Elders Quorum." He's not currently called as an Elders Quorum teacher so he asked the Elders Quorum president for special permission to teach it as the first Sunday lesson each month for a year. The Elders Quorum president liked the idea, went to the bishop, who also liked the idea, and so for the past several months, my husband has been teaching the Elders Quorum the history of the Relief Society using *Daughters in My Kingdom* as the source text. Maybe next year, our Relief Society will take the cue and do it as well.

I recently poured over a new and unheralded section on history.lds.org: Women of Conviction. Although launched with only eleven articles, the section signals several important trends. Many of the articles are written by and publicly credited to women. The importance of "lady missionaries" is discussed in detail, going into detail about specific early women such as Inez Knight and Lucy Jane Brimhall, who were the first women sent abroad to proselytize in 1898. It credits Lucy Mack Smith, whose image in our cultural consciousness is more of a supporter keeping the home fires burning, as the first domestic proselytizing missionary, traveling to Michigan with Hyrum Smith in 1831. It tells of Mildred Randall, who, in 1873, became the first married woman to be called on a mission without her husband. It includes video interviews with female leaders who are not in official positions anymore: Julie B. Beck and Bonnie D. Parkin are not our current leaders, but interviews with them are still featured on the site. This is important because we don't have an emeritus status for female leaders and they are rarely publicly visible after they leave their callings.

Another resource accessible to the general membership is the Deseret Book series, *Women of Faith in the Latter Days*, a seven-part series edited by Richard E. Turley Jr. and Brittany A. Chapman of the Church History Library. Working chronologically, Turley and Chapman have compiled biographical sketches of hundreds of women from our earliest Church history that are a treasure trove of experience and insight. Although teachers and speakers will have to cull the narratives to find stories that fit with particular themes, the effort is worthwhile. For instance, I was particularly moved by the words of Sarah Sturtevant Leavitt (1789–1878), a member missionary who lived in Mayfield, Ohio, ten miles outside of Kirtland. I very much look forward to using this excerpt from her autobiography in a lesson or talk about missionary work one day:

> I wanted very Much [to] get the good will of My Neighbours for I knew that I could have no sucksess in Preaching Mormonism unless I did and I was So full of that Spirit it was hard to hold My Peace. Consequently I Mingled in the Society of all, was Cheerful and Socialle as tho [I] was a great friend but keeped on the Side of truth and right. I would go in to the Tavern when they had Balls and help Set the table and wait on Ladies and was very Socialle and talkative and by being free with all, I soon got the good will of some of them. If we had commenced telling them of there faults and that they were all wrong which was the case and they Must repent or the would be Damed, we could not have got along in the place. . . . We were Wached Mighty close to see if they could discover any Dishonesty in our Dealings, but as they could find nothing to complain of they thought they would Let live.

The image of this frontier woman setting up the balls for the billiard games in the local tavern has stayed with me since the day I read this. Perhaps Leavitt's experience touched me so deeply because I was raised in New York City and went to dozens of parties in high school and college where my friends were drinking while I "keeped on the Side of truth and right." I don't think the image of her in the tavern would have had the same impact on me if she were a he.

About four years ago, in the springtime as Mother's Day was approaching, I became aware of a slim booklet called *Words of Wisdom: A Collection of Quotes for LDS Women* that had been compiled and put online for public download by an LDS women's group. The seventy-eight-page booklet was organized thematically, covering agency, diversity, faith, motherhood, leadership, scriptures, service, trials, etc. There were a few

statements about women by male speakers, but overwhelmingly the selected quotations were by current and past female leaders. I sent an email
to my bishop, although my calling at the time was Sunday School teacher.
Mother's Day is a tricky thing to celebrate with universal approbation, and
I suggested that he consider downloading the PDF of the booklet, which
included a lovely cover and table of contents, as a gift for the women of
our ward for Mother's Day. I was a little nervous that he might not get past
the name of the group that had compiled the booklet—WAVE, Women
Advocating for Voice and Equality—but I assured him that I had reviewed
every statement and found it to be one of the most helpful repositories
of our female leaders' voices that I knew of. Imagine my delight when
Mother's Day morning, the young women of our ward distributed printed
copies of the booklet to every woman in our ward. Many of the statements
at the beginnings of this book's chapters were first introduced to me by
this booklet. And that bishop had my devotion from that day forward.

There are dozens of books that compile the excellent talks from BYU's
annual Women's Conference, and there are treasures from women like
Chieko N. Okazaki and Sheri L. Dew on the shelves of Deseret Book.
But there are still several challenges in the way of those who wish to quote
from women: First, there are still almost no statements by women in our
official Sunday School, priesthood, and Relief Society manuals, so the
burden lies with us to search through the resources we do have to add
women's voices. Second, the volume of books and statements by women
that we do have are often addressed specifically to women, and so we have
to work extra hard to find statements that are either gender neutral or that
could be relevant to both men and women. Third, there are currently no
online repositories—even LDS.org—where we can go to find our female
leaders' talks categorically and systematically organized and publicly available through an online search, and the volume of those talks and books is
still a fraction of what is available by men. Fourth, we have to overcome
the deep-seated cultural bias that statements and talks and books by men
are universally applicable, but statements and talks and books by women
are for a subset of the population: women. One of the most important
truths when talking about quoting women is that women's words and
thoughts can impact and have value for men, just as men's words have
impact and import for women.

I recently saw a Facebook posting from a male Church employee proposing Eliza R. Snow as the subject for next year's priesthood and Relief

Society manual. The comments, several from other Church employees, took off in an excited burst of suggestions: how about Emmeline Wells? Vilate Kimball? Wives of the prophets? People posted links to the *Woman's Exponent* archives at BYU and *Eliza: The Life and Faith of Eliza R. Snow* by Karen Lynn Davidson and Jill Mulvay Derr. The excitement about the possibilities convinced me there is a hunger to know these women, to have their words become integral to our worship and spiritual education.

Rhetoric: Honoring Names and Titles

I carry two family names: Neylan was my paternal grandmother's maiden name, and as she was an only child, the name as a surname died with her. Her father had changed the spelling from Neilan to Neylan when he redefined himself from an Irish immigrant to the lawyer and best friend of William Randolph Hearst. My paternal Scottish side is represented by my last name, McBaine, and I take pride in that immigrant story as well: the University of California at Berkeley's Boalt Law School hosts the McBaine Moot Court Competition, named after my other great grandfather. As the only member of the Church on my father's side of the family, those two names are a constant reminder for me of the responsibility I have to my ancestors.

The idea of keeping my last name evolved naturally because my mother herself used her maiden name for most of my childhood. As a professional opera singer, her stage name was her maiden name. But I didn't consider keeping my name seriously until I met my future husband, whose last name was Smith. Neylan Smith? I cringed when I thought of losing the Scotch-Irish lilt of my full name, especially when the alternative was Smith! But it was my husband who mentioned it first: he had just returned from his mission to Spain, where the custom is for husbands and wives to keep their own names and the family to be referred to by both names. In a romantic effort to bring a little of his beloved Spain into his marriage, he requested I keep my own name. Done.

A belligerent statement against the shackles of married life? An effort to distance myself from the unity of marriage? Not at all. More like a tribute to the people and the cultures that have made us who we are and to whom we owe a debt of gratitude. But I found that conviction challenged from the moment we announced our engagement: a friend told me we wouldn't know who we belonged to in the eternities if we didn't share a name. And the ward clerk in our first ward as a married couple told me it was "illegal" for me not to take my husband's name. We had to waste the bishop's precious time to get special permission for me not to be listed in the ward directory as Neylan Smith, and even then, and in most wards since, I have been listed as Neylan McBaine Smith even though Smith is not on Church or legal records.

My mother and stepfather are currently on a mission. When they married, my mother again kept her maiden name, and they received no pushback when requesting missionary nametags for Sister Bybee and Elder Ford. But they have had a number of experiences of their own that demonstrate our cultural confusion around the changing traditions. For instance, an older man was giving a talk in a chapel to all the senior missionaries, and my parents were sitting in the first row. So the man at the pulpit was close enough to be able to see their nametags. As he talked, he kept glancing down at my parents, who were holding hands. At one point he stopped in the middle of his talk and said, "Are you two married?" "Yes," they answered. "But your names are different," he continued. "Yes," they answered lightly. "You can't do that," the man said before the awkward pause ended and he returned to his talk. In addition, all letters and emails both from the Church and from the local mission are addressed solely to my stepfather, Elder Ford. My parents are unsure if this is because mission communication always goes through the man or if it is because my mother isn't listed in records under his name, but the result is that she is never communicated to directly.

Although there are understandable logistical complications to listing two names and keeping records straight, the Church manages to honor the different naming conventions in other countries, so it shouldn't be too much of a stretch to do it in the United States if those of us handling local records are willing to do so. Those who have different names also have a responsibility to do the extra work of assimilating others to the practice. For instance, my daughters' middle names are all McBaine, and we use their middle names at their schools and on nametags so teachers and other parents know those kids go with me. Additionally, we have a "pet name" for our family, the McSmiths, that gives our friends a shorthand for referring to us. One year, when we casually signed our Christmas cards "The McSmiths," someone wrote me asking if we had officially changed our family name to this mashup. I am grateful when anyone takes the time to address a letter to the Smith/McBaine family or the McSmiths (as opposed to The Smiths) because it shows me that they respect our decision as a family. A friend who uses her maiden name told me that a guest recently said the prayer before a dinner party at my friend's house. She referred to both surnames of her hosts. "I could have kissed her!" my friend recalled.

Are names and titles important in our Church culture? We know from the temple and the scriptures that names themselves are of vital importance in our doctrine. And we have a deep tradition of using honorific titles that identify priesthood positions for men that stem back to the days of the New Testament. Elder, bishop, and president are just some of the titles liberally used in our administration system that we believe mirrors the organization originally established by the Savior himself. Each title designates a different level of priesthood progression, a different stewardship, and different set of keys authorized to be accessed by that man. The organization runs on understanding of and deference to those keys, and we know from the temple that creation and progress happen in a similarly systematic, organized fashion. One woman who hyphenates her maiden name with her husband's last name told me, "When I was an ordinance worker, people would give me guff about my hyphenated nametag, and some of the other women ordinance workers outright refused to use my full last name. And I would think, 'We go through all this trouble to search out the names of the deceased, say them aloud as best we can, and carry them through the temple one by one to honor them and love them and serve them. But we can't be bothered to love the living by uttering a few extra syllables?'"

So yes, names and titles matter.

At least, they have significance for men. Despite ample use of the terms "prophetess," "priestess," and "presidentess" in the early documents of the Church, including the Nauvoo Relief Society Minutes, there is only one name or title by which women are known throughout the Church today: sister. While this title holds within it the entire truth of the plan of salvation—that we are all children of heavenly parents who love us and want us to return to them—it also means that the various stewardships and types of contributions made by women get lumped together in an indistinguishable mass.

Several years ago, when Julie B. Beck was general president of the Relief Society, I was sitting in a meeting at work with several employees of the Church whom I did not know personally. At one point in our discussion, one of the men referred to "President Beck." In my mind's eye, as the conversation continued, I imagined we were talking about Julie B. Beck, presidential representative for half of the Church. It took me about thirty seconds to realize I had no idea what the man was talking about, because he was referring instead to David L. Beck, general president of the Young Men.

The experience was a wake up call for me. When the colleague referred to President Beck, it didn't occur to me that this wasn't Julie Beck's title. My subconscious assumed that because she is the president of the women's organization, she, like Emma Smith of old, would be called President Beck, especially since in sheer size, the Young Men organization is considerably smaller than the Relief Society. Then I realized that I had never actually seen or heard her referred to that way. Why not?

Technically, I understand that the answer is that we've adopted titles in the contemporary Church to indicate the priesthood line of authority, and women are not a part of that line. They do not share those priesthood keys, which Sheri L. Dew has defined as "the manner through which the Lord authorizes and disperses His power and authority throughout the Church for both men and women." But I cannot help but wonder if it would take away anything from the honor of the priesthood if we gave women similar, but purely symbolic, honor through titles of their own. I don't think it would, and I think it would help magnify women's stewardship and visibility.

Symbolic titles for women could help define and give greater shape to the role that some women play as they support their husbands who have titled callings. For instance, blogger Alison Moore Smith recalls, "When I was in college, Dad was called to serve as a branch president at the Missionary Training Center. My mom was expected to attend and serve, and she did. My dad was given a missionary nametag. So was my mom. Hers said, 'Sister Moore — Wife — Branch Presidency.'" Smith has the nametag to prove it. We use the terms "mission mom" or "ward mother" informally and inconsistently, but the casual use of the terms belies the commitment many of these women make to their callings and those of their husbands. "Temple matron" seems more codified; it appears on name badges as an identifier of the woman's job, although not as an honorific title. Smith lightheartedly ponders the use of those titles for women: "I suppose ['matron'] is a title (although I've never heard anyone in such a position addressed as 'Matron Thompson'), but really it just means 'sober, middle-aged, married woman.' Which is kind of like giving a guy the title of 'geezer.'" Referring to "my mission president's wife," a common appellation, also undermines the tremendous commitment of the woman, underscoring the fact that she is only there because of who she's married to and not because of the contributions she herself is making to the mission. Smith recalls: "The husband of a friend was called to serve as a mission president. As I witnessed the preparations to leave for three years, packing up an entire home, learning a new language, leaving friends and family, it was obvious that the woman was making as serious a commitment as the man. But she wasn't given a calling or title to go with it. In fact, her service was barely recognized other than her support role."

So what are we to do? I have suggested publicly that in our local communities we refer to the Relief Society, Primary, and Young Women presidents as "President So-and-So." (I haven't come up with an elegant suggestion to replace "matron.") I can't find any official request not to do this. But of all of the practices I have mentioned publicly in the past, this suggestion has generated the most negative feedback. One person said, "I have been thinking about the use of titles in the church, which is an American cultural habit. I would rather we eschew titles altogether. I seem to recall the early leaders were Brother Joseph and Brother Brigham." Other people have told me that insisting on titles just ossifies the idea that some people are "in charge" of others, even if those people are women. Yet another told me that titles just distance us from the people we serve and are inappropriate altogether for the servant leaders we strive to be. I even read a parody online that mocked the idea by imagining a ward council where everyone was calling everyone else "President" and no one knew who was talking to whom.

While I think there is truth in all of these points, the inescapable fact is that we are working in a hierarchical organization, and if we want to have a seat at the table we have to play by the rules. And the rules are that those with stewardship who have been set apart to play divinely appointed roles in our religious communities have been called, since biblical times, by special titles. Yes, in the early Church, the prophets were Brother Brigham and Brother Joseph, but at that same time we had Presidentess Smith and Presidentess Snow. Why have titles increased in importance for men and decreased for women?

Another reason to consider this practice is that it seems to be employed at the level of general Church leadership. In his April 2014 talk at general priesthood meeting, Elder Dallin H. Oaks quoted general Relief Society president Linda K. Burton. Of course I was delighted that Elder Oaks quoted a woman in his talk ostensibly addressed to men, but more interesting to me was the fact that Elder Oaks in his live address prefaced the quote by saying, "President Linda K. Burton of the Relief Society said . . ." Elder Oaks himself called her President Linda K. Burton! But in the official transcription of the talk, the phrase was changed to "Relief Society general president Linda K. Burton said . . ." While the change may have been made to align with editorial standards, it seems significant that the Apostle's personal references reflect a use of titles that we on the local level do not employ.

Rhetoric: Men Speaking About and To Women

There are customary times when men are required to speak to an exclusively female audience: the First Presidency address at general Relief Society and Young Women's meetings, now Women's Meetings, is the prime example. There are occasions on the ward and stake level too when bishops or stake presidents address Relief Society groups. There are other times when men elect to talk about women to a mixed audience of men and women, such as in Elder Quentin L. Cook's April 2011 general conference talk, "LDS Women Are Incredible!" or Elder D. Todd Christofferson's October 2013 talk, "The Moral Force of Women." In my personal memory, there is only one time I have heard a woman address men exclusively in a Church setting: Young Women general president Elaine S. Dalton spoke to "our sons and to all fathers" in her October 2011 general conference talk, "Love Her Mother."

Several male leaders I interviewed felt awkward about addressing all-female audiences and admitted they were unsure what to say to these groups. Despite the hesitancy, I found two excellent suggestions rose from my conversations with these bishops and stake presidents. The first tactic I found that men can use to effectively talk to women is to sidestep the "I'm a man talking to women" approach entirely and focus instead on gender-neutral doctrine or scripture. Just because a man is talking *to* women doesn't mean he has to talk *about* women. Focusing on pure doctrine and delving deep into scriptural truth with the women signals a trust in their ability to be theological thinkers and contributors and encourages them to be scriptorians in their own right.

The second tactic a bishop or stake president may take is to use his time with women to tell them what he's telling the men in their own meetings. One stake presidency member told me, "I tell the women how we're encouraging the men to prioritize: Their wives come first, then children, then their employers, and then their church responsibilities. I've told women how we encourage men to care for their children, to be nur-turers, to read to their children, make every effort to be home for dinner. They know they have full claim on their husbands, greater claim than any church activity. I hope they feel empowered to know how their hus-bands are being counseled." This approach signals transparency between the sexes and doesn't make the women feel at all like a man is teaching them how to be women. These male leaders seem to be sympathetic to the concerns of women such as this blogger:

> What concerns me is the abundance of counsel from men directed toward women on what it means to be a woman, with very little reciprocity. Too much emphasis on men teaching women how to be women may foster unhealthy attitudes and subtly encourage women and girls to look to men for approval, guidance, and authority as they form self-conceptions and life goals. We must wholly understand that we are important, not because of how much men value us or what men think of us, but because of who we are as humans on planet earth and daughters of God. I worry about the effect on dating and marriage as two young people enter a relationship, the man having learned from male ecclesiastical leaders how to be a man, and the woman having learned from both women and men.

The blogger continues with her own vision of reciprocal rhetoric:

> I would like to see something more balanced. Imagine the power that could be unleashed if women, drawing on inspiration from heaven and a wealth of experience, occasionally instructed men on how best to fulfill their roles as husband, fathers, and priesthood holders. I am accustomed to congregations of women learning from words of wisdom and encouragement spoken by a man of God. But I have this other vision in my mind—a vision of a group of men sitting and listening to a woman whom they love and respect, a woman of God, in full acknowledgement of her divine calling and gifts of the Spirit. Maybe she would be teaching them about her experiences in drawing on priesthood power, or how as men, they can better assist the women of the Church, or how better to honor their roles as fathers and husbands. I believe that a woman addressing a priesthood meeting would bring great blessings and a needed balance as men and women strive to work together and under-stand one another.

Even if we still have few examples of women teaching men, the re-sponse to women teaching other women about doctrine—even doctrine traditionally assumed to be most applicable to men, such as the priest-hood—seems overwhelmingly favorable. One woman rattled off to me at least half a dozen recent talks by female Church leaders that have discussed the doctrine of priesthood and had particular weight and meaning for her. Significantly, none of these talks by female leaders had come from general conference; rather, the woman mentioned President Linda K. Burton's May 3, 2013, talk from BYU Women's Conference, where she encouraged women to memorize the oath and covenant of the priesthood as found in Doctrine and Covenants 84. Also, she mentioned Relief Society general board member Sandra Rogers's April 14, 2013, talk at the Relief Society training meeting, where she talked about women accessing priesthood power, as well as several other talks that had occurred in women's training meetings or women-only conferences.

The assumption that men can teach both men and women but women can only teach women is so deeply ingrained in our culture at large that most of us have probably never even considered its implications. It was this cultural undercurrent that catalyzed Margaret Thatcher to don her '80s power suits and take voice lessons to lower her speaking voice to sound more like a man. It is the force behind a whole industry of business books with titles such as *Lean In: Women, Work and the Will to Lead*; *Dare: Straight Talk on Confidence, Courage, and Career for Women in Charge*; and *Why the Best Man for the Job is A Woman: The Unique Female Qualities of Leadership*. So when a man comes along who does not teach women about themselves but rather seeks to be taught by them, miracles can occur. This woman described one such miracle.

> It's remarkable how answers come in the most unexpected ways, sometimes long after you've given up looking or hoping for them. I've struggled with eating disorders and seemingly intractable anxiety about my looks since I was 11 years old. Over decades, I've learned to sort of manage those feelings, but they're never very far below the surface, and I'm particularly aware of them now as I try to guide my young teenaged daughter through those years that were so devastating for me. I have often worried about the ways Mormon culture can contribute to these feelings, with makeover night activities, and "modest" fashion shows and lessons about the importance of attracting a husband. I've never felt like I could adequately convey how painful it was to be a Mormon girl who isn't especially pretty to any Mormon man.
>
> But recently, a man whose name I don't even know bore his testimony in a ward we both happened to be visiting for the day, and I found that hard, cruel knot in my heart unraveling a little. I was surprised when a man stood up and said he wanted to bear his testimony of Girls' Camp. He went on to say that he felt a bit strange relating this story as a visitor in a ward where he

didn't know anyone, but that the experience was burning inside him and he needed to talk about it.

He said that he had been asked to give a talk at girls' camp and felt sort of silly about it. He's a Management professor at a business school, and he didn't know what he might possibly have to say that would be worthwhile to these girls. He remembered some recent conference talks about preparing by simply working harder to be able to perceive and welcome the Spirit, so he spent a lot of time trying to prepare without really knowing what he should talk about, reading scriptures and praying and finally just desperately hoping that it would be given to him "in the very hour" to know what he should say.

When he got to camp, he began by reading a page of quotations about light, and asked the girls to write down one sentence or phrase that really stood out to them, and then write a paragraph or two about it. And then he asked them to talk about what they had written. They spoke for several minutes about light and intelligence and love and truth—the sorts of things he was kind of expecting. Finally, one girl said, "You know, I don't think of myself as beautiful, but I feel really beautiful right now." Seven or eight girls, he said, took up the theme of beauty, which would never have occurred to him in the context he had been thinking of, but he realized that this was the deepest need of their souls. He related, with deep emotion, how he had been given to understand that these girls are "pulverized" (his word) by constantly having crushingly impossible ideals of beauty flung at them from every side, and that this was the pain they needed to have healed by the Atonement. And then he testified that he had seen that healing happen, at least briefly, as they saw themselves in the context of the kind of light the scriptures describe. He expressed gratitude for wise counsel about receiving revelation if we will really love those whom we prepare to teach, and concluded that he was grateful for having had his prayer answered, having known without knowing how to open that door for the young women whose souls he had been privileged to glimpse that day.

I spoke with him briefly afterwards, to tell him how much I had needed to hear what he said—both because I needed the prescription for seeing myself and teaching my daughter to see herself in the different paradigm and different light provided by the gospel, but also because I desperately needed to know that a man can receive a strong revelation that puts women first, without going looking for anything except what God wants His daughters to hear.

I wish I had asked his name.

This man's humility, his willingness to mourn with those he was addressing rather than instruct or inform, seemed to be keys that unlocked this woman's heart. As this example shows, sometimes the power of our words is determined not by what we actually say but by how the listener perceives us to be presenting ourselves. In this case, the listener perceived the speaker to be speaking from a place of humility, differentiating himself from the girls and women by acknowledging gaps in his understanding. In contrast, he could have claimed additional insight into their identities by virtue of his being a man and priesthood leader, which wouldn't have sat well with this female listener. It also wouldn't have sat well with this listener if he had tried to diminish differences between himself and the girls and had claimed to understand them. But because he allowed there to be space between his experience and the girls' own experiences, rather than trying to collapse that space, he actually generated an even closer bond and a greater atmosphere of trust.

Process in the Real World:
The Relief Society Missionary Service Coordinator

This chapter is about looking for practical ways to adapt meetings and Sunday practices to see, hear, and include women. Sometimes trying something new results in breakthroughs. For example, I learned of one stake that currently has the stake Relief Society president meeting regularly with the stake president *and* the local mission president. The results of these relationships are inspired and fruitful for both members and missionaries. Here, the stake Relief Society president, the stake president, and a ward member walk through the process of building relationships, determining needs, proposing solutions, and executing on those ideas.

- From the stake Relief Society president, Lisa:

   I served my mission in Russia in the 1990s and had remarkably good humanitarian service opportunities. We worked in shelters for battered women, orphanages. Someone set up all of those opportunities for us, and I have no idea who, but they were a highlight of my mission. Because of that experience, I've had a desire to replicate that for the missionaries serving in my own area.

   When I served as a ward Relief Society president, I tried to emphasize a broad representation of humanitarian efforts for our ward. We sent sewing machines to small groups of women in third world countries so they could make things and sell them themselves. We did collections of blankets. We knitted hats for Haiti. We got individual donors to ship the collections overseas. We were resourceful, since we were working under the limitations of our budget. Our power was limited because of our limited access to money. But the efforts created a level of unity that was unique. Small service initiatives made all the difference in the closeness of that Relief Society group. We felt like a cohesive group. And if women feel a base of love and acceptance and understanding and encouragement, there is nothing they can't do.

I was called as stake Relief Society president right around the time that the missionary age change was announced, so we quickly got a huge influx of new missionaries in our area. What were all these new missionaries going to do? The sheer numbers were somewhat overwhelming. One thing I had learned in the ward setting was that efforts to get the sisters serving out in the community routinely fell flat; for some reason it was really hard to get women to volunteer in the community, which is why all of our efforts had taken place within the Relief Society itself. However, the idea now came to me that maybe these new missionaries could be our bridge to the outside community. Church members take good care of our own people, and we work well with our own people, but the official fourth mission of the Church is to care for the poor and needy. We could use the resource of these new missionaries to create a bridge between our Relief Society and the poor and needy.

My stake president invites me to join him to meet with our local mission president. So when we received this influx of new missionaries, I was meeting with the mission president and hearing him discuss the challenges of finding things for the missionaries to do. Our mission president is very young, and both he and his wife are lawyers. He loves the sisters in the mission and does a wonderful job of elevating them, so we were working toward our common goal. These joint meetings with the stake president and mission president are, I feel, essential to having the missionaries work most effectively with the local members. What I was hearing at those meetings was the need to have the missionaries be productive, to get to work, to have 10 hours of meaningful humanitarian service every week. They were defaulting to baking cookies for the members and raking people's yards. I knew we could do better. I saw a need that the Relief Society could fill.

Our ward members might be uncomfortable getting out into the community themselves, but they have plenty of connections in the community with local charities and opportunities. But the charities don't trust the missionaries; there's no continuity with them. It felt like Relief Society could be the bridge between the ward members' connections and the missionaries' labor hours.

I proposed that one or two sisters from each ward's Relief Society be called as Relief Society missionary service coordinators. These women work within the wards to gather service opportunities in the community—with employers or service organizations ward members know about—and they are responsible for scheduling weekly service opportunities for our missionaries. The women make contact with the charity, schedule the missionaries. . . . We have set up a calendar and a website that details what the opportunities are and which missionaries will take those opportunities. And the charity has a consistent contact, which makes them more excited to work with the Mormons.

Even though I had the stake president and mission president's full support to have this reside exclusively in the Relief Society, it was hard to get buy off from the bishops at first. They all suggested that this should be transitioned into the ward missions. They pushed back a bit when we asked for new callings to be extended in the Relief Societies. There were two men called at first, and I said that was great if they reported to the Relief Society missionary service coordinator.

Relief Society missionary service coordinator—it's a terrible title but I don't want to give up any of those words. They're all important. Each of the ward coordinators reports to a stake coordinator who works with me. I keep in touch with the stake president and mission president. I imagine some day the mission president's wife could oversee the various Relief Society coordinators, instead of the stake Relief Society president. At our next stake conference, the mission president will do a training for all of the Relief Society missionary service coordinators.

We've used fifth Sundays to have trainings too. The Relief Society missionary service coordinators have been working with all ward members to gather opportunities for the missionaries. This isn't about men or women; this is about the ward getting behind the Relief Society and the missionaries. The ward members are the eyes and ears in the community, and we now have a system in place where members and missionaries are benefitting from each other because of the Relief Society missionary service coordinator.

Overall, we've had a positive response from the wards. Younger women are more supportive than older women. The most supportive group is men under age 35. I throw up my hands sometimes. There is a hesitancy to get to work and build. But the missionaries and the charities love it! The missionaries have rebuilt playgrounds, planted flowers in city spaces, worked with kids in foster care, and we had a massive river cleanup that brought 60 missionaries and that many members working alongside them. Our mission president was committed to have the 10 hours be purely service, not proselytizing. We needed that guarantee for the members too so that they wouldn't be nervous about sending the missionaries into their workplaces or with their colleagues. The missionaries have been trained about how to reach out to someone later to teach them, not at the service project. It has been a rewarding journey for all of us.

- From a Relief Society missionary service coordinator, Melissa:

It's been exciting to help Lisa and the other leaders figure out how this program is going to work. It's a pilot program, so we're learning as we're going. It's been awesome to feel like I'm contributing to the mission efforts in this area. I don't think about how we're leading a torch into unchartered territory.

I'm just trying to do my best job to give our missionaries meaningful service and magnify our ward's service opportunities.

I started from square one in trying to fill 10 service hours a week for the two missionaries I was assigned to. I just Googled service opportunities in my area and started cold calling. Some organizations were excited, some were nervous that the missionaries would proselytize during the service. And there have been frustrations and kinks. For example, many opportunities and organizations require a background check to serve there. We have to find opportunities that don't require background checks because of the additional cost and time. Some require donations to their organization. But we have still found meaningful service opportunities even working around those restrictions.

My missionaries regularly go to a school for the blind and a food pantry. They've cleaned up parks in our area, and we recently had a massive cleanup of the river that goes through our city. It was pouring rain on the Saturday morning, but we had missionaries and members working alongside each other. Our missionaries are so popular at the school for the blind that they invited us to come do a ward service activity there. One thing I love is that our whole ward is now more aware of service opportunities. It's really great to see ward members get out with the missionaries and have a genuine desire to get out in the community.

Because the ward members are offering some of the service opportunities for the missionaries, it's important for the missionaries to be flexible so they can meet the members' needs. The mission president and his wife have trained us Relief Society missionary service coordinators personally, and he's told us to work around the missionaries' prime teaching times. But he's also willing to make exceptions. For example, a ward member has a son with Down Syndrome, and she invited the missionaries to come help with a special needs baseball game. The game is on a Saturday, which is not their service time, but the mission president has made it clear that serving the ward members is one of their top priorities.

It makes sense to me that this work is coming from the Relief Society. One of our purposes is to provide service, but sometimes we're hesitant to get out in the community and do it ourselves. The added element of the missionaries allows us to reach out in ways that we couldn't otherwise. It's unique for me as a woman and Relief Society member to have such a personal relationship with the missionaries and to work with them in this really collaborative way.

• From the stake president:

The mission president in our area has a vision for the mission: our missionaries will do anything that will advance the kingdom of God. That meant they needed to be in places where their light could shine. They were doing service that didn't allow them to further their missionary efforts.

The mission president's wife is highly involved and with her and Lisa we all worked collaboratively to get this program off the ground. Lisa took the lead and has run with it. The mission of the Relief Society from the earliest days has been to provide relief to those who are struggling, suffering. It seems natural for them to be the ones to provide that service as part of their mission. And they are really good at it!

Members of the ward who have participated in the program have been blessed and impressed by the opportunities to serve. And, as the mission president anticipated, we've had baptisms as a direct result of this program. I see nothing but positive results.

Chapter Twelve

Perseverance

"I will go forward. . . . I will smile at the rage of the tempest, and ride fearlessly and triumphantly across the boisterous ocean of circumstance. . . . And the 'testimony of Jesus' will light up a lamp that will guide my vision through the portals of immortality, and communicate to my understanding the glories of the Celestial kingdom."

Eliza R. Snow, Relief Society General President,
Poems, Religious, Historical, and Political, vol. 1 (1856), p. 148–49

Few practices change overnight. Many of the leaders I spoke with talked about the slow process of adopting an idea, the discouragement of having to convince other leaders of a new practice's value, and the patience required to evolve generations of traditions. Revolutions, by definition, attempt to shift culture by disrupting it with force, replacing existing systems with new ones. Our process of cultural change is not revolutionary. We are an obedient people, open to drastic changes (such as the missionary age change) when initiated by our prophets, seers, and revelators, but generally putting unity, optimism, and heritage first.

So adapting practice within our culture often requires assessing, attempting, pausing, reassessing, reattempting, and building consensus, rather than just putting a lead foot down on the pedal. This may require greater patience and a longer timeline than we would like, but the only effective way we shift practices is to create new practices, and that takes time.

Encouraging positive cultural evolution is the work that each generation needs to claim as it bridges the heritage of the older generation with the expectations of the younger generation. We take the best of what we've been given and measure it against eternal doctrines and what will come ahead. The future of our own practices depends largely on the worldview of the next generation.

But sometimes talking in "generations" can seem discouraging and overwhelming. Our personal timeframes rarely have that kind of latitude.

If we are hurt today, we react today. Conversely, it can be equally hurtful to some if heritage practices are thrown out by those who no longer feel they are useful or even right. And so we participate in a controlled evolution where we persevere to adapt and improve, but we do so with an eye to the best of our heritage.

Handling Disappointment

One stake Relief Society president shared this story with me:

> Last year, March 17th fell on a Sunday. That's the birthday of the Relief Society in Nauvoo. But because it fell on a Sunday, I thought, "Why don't we have a stake-wide celebration this year by dedicating that Sunday meeting to talking about the doctrinal foundation of the Relief Society, *Daughters in My Kingdom,* and women and the priesthood."
>
> I was so excited so I went to the stake president and I said, "We should do this! We should ask each ward to spend their March 17th Sacrament Meeting talks exploring the Relief Society." He smiled and listened. He is very sweet, and I'm old enough to be his mother. But he said, "You already had a birthday party." I said, "No we didn't. We have an annual women's conference, but that's not a birthday party. Our men and women need to understand the doctrinal foundation of Relief Society. And so do all those Young Women you are worried about and want to strengthen. Our members need to know that it's always been part of the Lord's plan to organize the women into a women's quorum, that the Nauvoo Relief Society was a restoration of part of the original church. I know you don't like making things mandatory for the bishops, but if I were you I would make an exception for this." I didn't say anything more about it. I felt like I had made a well-prepared, respectful request.
>
> March 17th came. The subject of every talk that day in my ward was the sacrament. The tears came. My stake president takes notes whenever we meet and asks me how he can be more effective. But I need feedback. I want to tell him, "Do you know how scary it is for me to come to my priesthood leader and tell you that women don't understand the power of their covenants or their own Relief Society?" I need to see commitment to changing that, or else I think I have pretty bad ideas.

What do we do, as women or as men, when we don't feel heard? When our ideas are not used? When we are disappointed? Obviously, not everyone's ideas will make the cut. Is conflict then unavoidable? How do we press on in faith and with perseverance when we don't feel we are being heard or included?

The challenge of being disappointed by experiences at Church is that spirituality is relational, not transactional. Spirituality cannot be handed to us or bought. It is relationships that determine our spiritual health, including and most importantly our relationship with our Heavenly Father. But our interactions with others here on earth have the power to affect the way we feel about our faith. So when things go wrong, our relationship to our faith can take a hit if we're not adept at assessing our spiritual lives separately from our Church experiences.

Sister Patricia T. Holland has shared wise words about conflict in a church setting.

> It seems to me that if there is a conflict, it is because someone, male or female, isn't living the gospel of Jesus Christ. Now, I did not say that the person who has the concern isn't living the gospel. That may or may not be true. What I said is that someone isn't living the gospel. A woman in pain may be living the gospel the very best she knows how and yet still find herself hurting. But if that's the case, I still believe that someone in her life isn't living—or hasn't lived—the gospel: some man she knows, some men she has known, some woman, some group of women she knows. Somewhere, somehow, promises have not been kept or obligations have not been honored, and thus the hurt. But that is not a priesthood problem. The most we can say is that it's a man or woman problem. Thus, the responsibility is on us all, male and female, to live as section 121 prescribes and as every other Christlike example requires. With that kind of loving male and female relationship and with those kinds of promises, the pain and despair and frustrations of this world disappear. I believe that with all my heart.

I love Sister Holland's assertion that when a woman in the Church is in pain, *someone* isn't living the gospel. But I do not believe that that *someone* may even know they are not living the gospel; in fact, they might believe with their whole heart that they are acting in the best interest of the Church and its members. I've heard of too many good-hearted men and women who think they are doing their best to uphold the administration of the Church, and too many good-hearted people who have still been hurt. So how do we know when it is our turn to raise our hand and say, "It's me. I'm the *someone.* I could have done better"?

I've shared examples in this book of times when a woman had to go through a variety of people, wait patiently for longer than she would have liked, or been disappointed with the resulting outcome. I've talked to men doing their best but sometimes wondering if it's enough to keep their flocks together. The uncertainty, the best intentions, the sincere desire to make a difference in the kingdom of God has been palpable in each of my interviews. Men and women alike have poured their hearts out, expressing every emotion from gratitude to exasperation to hope to impatience. There is heartbreak when things go wrong or people get ignored; there is a burning witness of faith when something happens to make someone feel seen, heard, and included. In so many examples I've learned about where a practice was adapted to more fully magnify women's impact, there was a moment at which someone—a man or a woman—said to themselves, "I'm the *someone*. I could be doing better." And they take action.

To raise a hand and commit to doing something differently tomorrow than you do it today requires not only tremendous humility but initiative and dedication to the cause of faith. Every man and woman I interviewed who saw something they could improve and took action is, to me, a hero in their demonstrated belief that this is God's kingdom on earth. If they didn't believe that at least to some small degree, would they be willing to raise their hand to say, "It's me," and work to make the change? I don't think so.

We cannot, though, coerce others to raise their own hands and change themselves or the policies they believe are most effective to achieving their goals. Problems arise most often when we point to another and say, "They are the *someone*. They must change." I hope I have demonstrated in this book how important it is for men and women to patiently and imaginatively consider the gender policy adaptations they believe could be even more effective than what we are currently doing, but at some point we need to look in ourselves and ask, "What will I do if that *someone* never changes? If this policy never changes?" Will we persevere? Or will we give up? Will we insist things around us change while never changing anything within ourselves?

In one particular situation that occurred some years ago, a bishop and a Relief Society president came to a stalemate where both felt they were right and neither backed down, with tragic results. The Relief Society president, a runner, supported and participated in the formation of a relay running team, which included other women in the ward. The race covered hundreds of miles, went through the night and finished on a Sunday morning. Although the Relief Society president was able to attend church with her family that morning, many of the other racers did not. The bishop expressed his disapproval. "Though I considered a number of different ways to express my concerns regarding the situation," he says, "I finally arrived at the decision that it would be best if I discussed it privately with the Relief Society president at her regularly scheduled Stewardship Interview (which we had every month). At the end of the Stewardship Interview, I raised the issue. Needless to say, it did not go well, and she appeared very unhappy with me when she left. I felt miserable about the meeting and resolved later that afternoon to go to her home and meet with her and her husband and let them know how much I loved them and their family, which I did."

The Relief Society president remembers the bishop's response differently: "I remember that he then called me into a special private meeting with him where he had printed out general conference talks for me to read so I could contemplate what I had done wrong. I didn't want him to be angry; I wanted to repent if there was something I had done wrong, but I didn't think there was. Preparing for the race had been a wonderful experience for our women. And so there was a disconnect. He felt I had led the women astray; I felt he wasn't respecting my stewardship over half of the congregation. There was no training for me to know how to respond on confident footing. There was no mechanism for dealing with that, for reaching out and saying, 'I need help.'"

Although their conflict didn't revolve around policies regarding women, it was exacerbated by the gender dynamics at play. "I was 30 years old," the Relief Society president recalled. "I had never had a relationship conflict in my marriage or in my work. I didn't have the skills to solve deep conflict. And the bishop was my same age. We were young and I have compassion for any leader who doesn't have the training and support he needs to deal with complex relationship conflicts. But I felt he showed a misuse of power that was grating." The bishop, in his comments to me, continually reiterated his admiration for this woman, calling their partnership "one of the defining relationships of my life." Yet the dynamics were such that the woman and her family had their names removed from church records shortly after she was released from her calling.

How much trust should a bishop put in his Relief Society president's stewardship of her women? How much deference should a Relief Society president show to the bishop's authority, while still claiming her own stewardship? The *Handbook* states that bishops have the "ultimate responsibility" for all decisions affecting the ward; does this mean the woman must inevitably be the casualty of the conflict? Must she always be the one to back down, or, as in the example above, leave? Negotiating the answers to these questions can lead to disappointment if the parties don't approach each other with humility, a commitment to see the best in each other, and a restrained plan of action.

Humility, a commitment to see the best, and restraint, however, do not demand silence or acceptance or sulking. The authors of *Crucial Confrontations* offer valuable tools to those who find themselves navigating troubled waters, facing situations in which "we set clear expectations, but the other person doesn't live up to them—we feel disappointed. Lawyers call these incidents breaches of contract." The authors address their primarily business-oriented audience, but truths can be extracted for our experiences in Church communities as well. The authors say, "When problems arise, in the worst companies [or wards or stakes], people withdraw into silence. In your average company, people will say something, but only to the authorities. In the best companies, people will hold a crucial confrontation, face-to-face and in-the-moment. And they'll hold it well. This, of course, takes skill."

The authors believe that the skills for mastering these difficult conversations can be learned, and a few of the tools they offer to develop these skills have been mentioned already. They advise starting with the "Work On Me First" phase, which I have described as the Prayer phase. Next, "Confront With Safety" is achieved by describing the gap in perception with respect for the other's viewpoint. That's our People phase. Then "Move To Action" is accomplished by agreeing on a plan and following up on it. That's Process. Staying "Focused and Flexible" throughout the entire process prevents us from getting sidetracked and helps us evaluate the real priorities.

"Policies, systems, programs—any method for encouraging change—will never function fully until people know how to talk to one another about deviations and disappointments." Whether we employ these tools in the course of one conversation or a lifetime in the Church, the way we handle disappointment can help build a foundation of faith for ourselves, for those in our stewardship, and for those who come after us. We can do so graciously, with humility, and with reliance on the Spirit to direct these crucial conversations. We can press forward boldly, knowing that if we have prayed and considered the people we are involving and the process we are advocating, we are establishing a culture of respectful dialogue. When necessary, we can raise our hand and say, "I am the *someone*," and feel supported rather than judged in our humble self-evaluation and reformation. When we know how to talk to each other about deviations and disappointments, we clear a path to more clearly see the glorious communities we are building together.

Chapter 13

We Are Not Alone

*"If you experience the pain of exclusion at church from someone who is fright-
ened at your difference, please don't leave [or] become inactive. You may
think you are voting with your feet, that you are making a statement by leaving. [Some may] see your diversity as a problem to be fixed, as a flaw to be
corrected or erased. If you are gone, they don't have to deal with you anymore.
I want you to know that your diversity is a more valuable statement."*

Chieko N. Okazaki, Relief Society General Presidency,
"Cat's Cradle of Kindness," General Conference, April 1993

Over the course of writing this book, I've been particularly interested
in learning about how other faith communities are confronting some
of these same challenges of embracing contemporary sensibilities about
women while remaining true to their heritage and spiritual principles.
There can be a perception that we Mormons are wrestling with these challenges in backward isolation and that the rest of the world has figured this
all out already. Let me assure you: nobody has figured it out. And it's not
just faith communities that are navigating this path. The media attention around national business and political leaders like Sheryl Sandberg,
Marissa Mayer, and Anne-Marie Slaughter have inspired invigorating debates among the most "progressive" of our communities.

As part of my research, I read a range of articles and books from evangelical communities that explore their admittance of women into ministerial and ritualistic realms. We in Mormonism often do not realize that our
cultural conversations are being mirrored and echoed in other faith communities. For example, during the flurry of online conversations about the
Ordain Women movement before the April 2014 general conference, one
comment on a blog post said in reference to conversations about women
and the priesthood, "I'm so embarrassed by these conversations. Do you
think the Evangelicals are protesting? The Catholics? The Jews?" Well,

the answer is yes, yes, and yes. Believers of all stripes are wrestling. Over the past couple of years, the Leadership Conference of Women Religious, which represents 80 percent of the 57,000 Catholic nuns in the United States, has repeatedly made the news with its public and sometimes heated discussions with the Vatican as it publicly explores greater leadership roles for women within Catholicism. A recent conversation with a Catholic friend reminded me that lay Catholic women have *no* outlet for participating in their religious worship, and, rather than protesting, many young members are simply losing interest and leaving. In the evangelical Christian world, Sarah Bessey addresses head on the grapples of her own community in her book *Jesus Feminist: An Invitation to Revisit the Bible's View of Women*: "I want us to talk about this—really talk about womanhood, church, the labels, and where we go from here. Because the vicious arguments, the limits, the you're-in-but-they're-out, the debates, the silencing aren't working, are they? We have often treated our communities like a minefield, acted like theology is a war, and we are the wounded, and we are the wounding." In *Let Her Lead: Creating a Better Future for Women in the Church*, the senior pastor of New Life Church in Colorado Springs, Brady Boyd, also airs frustrations about his community's imperfect struggle. In discussing his thirteen-year-old daughter, Callie, Boyd says, "Given all the promise and potential awaiting Callie, how do I help prepare her for her future? And how do I prepare that future for her? These are the central questions banging around in my brain. . . . We're going to have a conversation about a topic—women in leadership—that is touchy for many people, but I'm not trying to be provocative here. I'm not trying to pick a fight. I actually want to defuse this topic that has been infused with such vitriol along the way by simply revising a few themes that have been sidelining women far too long."

Other Christian communities are taking a different path: rather than exploring potential opportunities for greater women's inclusion (and apparently experiencing "vitriol" in the conversations), a robust subculture of charismatic Christians embraces the submission of women to men's oversight. In her ethnographic study, *God's Daughters: Evangelical Women and the Power of Submission*, historian R. Marie Griffith studies the women of Women's Aglow Fellowship, the largest women's evangelical organization in the world, and explores how Aglow has taken on "the task of recasting the traditionally Christian doctrine of female submission to male authority into formulations appealing to women." In citing the work of historians Donald G. Mathews and Jane Sherron De Hart, Griffith explains that "cultural fundamentalism—as distinguished from biblical fundamental-ism—involves absolute commitment to particular 'traditional' social and cultural forms as 'sacred templates of reality,' fixed patterns that transcend ordinary historical change." Thus the women read in their group's maga-zine, "Submit to your husband . . . and you too will discover the man you've always longed for, his seeming harshness softened by your willing obedience to his demands." Even this approach doesn't bring completely smooth sailing, however; debates about the degree and type of submission rage among the charismatic Christian subculture as well.

The point is that Christian communities are approaching similar challenges from a range of angles. One of my favorite discoveries in my research was "Tefillingate," an extended debate at Haaretz.com, the on-line edition of Israel's oldest newspaper. It started like this: In January of 2014, two Orthodox Jewish girls attending Salanter Akiba Riverdale (SAR) High School, a Modern Orthodox school in Riverdale, New York, were given permission by the head of the school (a rabbi) to put on tefillin. (Tefillin are a set of small black leather boxes containing scrolls of parch-ment inscribed with verses from the Torah, which are worn by observant Jewish men during weekday morning prayers. As the physical Torah is considered sacred in any form, allowing women to "lay" tefillin is a very big deal.) We don't need to go any further than the headlines of the ar-ticles on Haaretz.com to understand the range of emotions and opinions this news excited in the Jewish community: "Teen Girls Laying Tefillin: Brave Enough To Be Different"; "You Say Women 'Don't Need' Tefillin? Here's Why I Do"; "Tefillingate Unraveled: In Orthodoxy, Women Just Don't Wear Tefillin"; "Tefillingate: Orthodoxy Must Not Reject Its Most Committed Women"; "Orthodox Jewish Women Don't Need Tefillin; We Need Real Empowerment"; and my favorite ode to the popular *Frozen* song, "Women and Tefillin: Address It, Don't Supress It."

I followed these articles at the same time that the Ordain Women group was dominating our own headlines as they prepared to ask admit-tance to the general priesthood meeting for a second time in April 2014. I was struck by the similar themes and arguments that were laid out by both the Mormon and Jewish participants in each conversation. In each, there was an effort to put a real face on the efforts of the dissenting group, to humanize the effort. Ordain Women populated a website with testi-monials and photos of real people who supported their stance. Similarly, high school girls wrote their own articles on Haaretz.com, putting a face on the practice of girls laying tefillin. In both communities, there were voices emphasizing that women already have all they need to maximize their potential. There were others claiming that including women in ritualistic practices—either laying tefillin or performing priesthood ordinances—wouldn't change an existing culture of faulty gender dynamics. "Egalitarian prayer services? Female rabbis? Lowered mehitzahs?" said one Jewish author. "That's not what Orthodox women need. We need a mentality shift that encourages girls to open their minds, voice their opinions and fulfill their ambitions." In both communities, there was a subset of harsh, condemning feedback in which those pushing the envelope were invited to leave their faith communities or were challenged to assess their obedience. A Jewish journalist said of Tefillingate, "This whole discussion has really brought out the worst in Orthodoxy. Public debates are often less about substance and spirituality and more about who is in and who is out of the 'camp.'"

We are not alone. We can be encouraged by the ways our doctrine opens doors to theological possibilities and potential that are not options in other faith communities. But we may, on the other hand, feel our community is behind the times, or we may see much in other faith communities to admire and wish we had ourselves. But whatever our perspective, we can take comfort in knowing that from the times of our earliest scripture until today, people of God have wrestled and asked for guidance and been granted a portion of His spirit to carry the kingdom through another day. Have you ever considered how much of the New Testament is dedicated to untangling disagreements and policies and cultural norms among the early followers of Christ? Paul took on everything from circumcision to what kinds of meat to eat to all sorts of other sticky issues that came from distilling gospel truths in the context of adapted Jewish and Greek practices. He begged the church members in Corinth to have charity, those in Thessalonica to hold fast to that which is good. "Stick with us," I hear him saying. "We are working this out together, and we'll be stronger for it."

Remarkable things have happened in the realm of gender practices in the Church, even within the past five years. In fact, more than once while writing this book, I found myself paradoxically panicked by the speed and scope of the changes because it meant I had to revise portions I had already written! The portraits of women in the Conference Center, female general officers sitting behind the apostles at conference, and the female general officers appearing in the center spread of the conference *Ensign* all required last-minute editing. My momentary panics about whether this book would be obsolete before it was even published forced me to return to a theme that I hope has been clear: efforts are being made at the general level to see, hear, and include women that we still have yet to mirror at the local level. No matter how many changes are made at the general Church leadership level, it will still take particular imagination and effort for those of us on the ground to echo that dedication to women in our local culture. But I have every confidence we can do it, if we recognize the importance of the mission and understand the tools at our disposal. And then this book truly will be obsolete, and that will be a happy day.

Until that day, we might be entreated by the words of Aaron Loy, the founder of Mosaic Lincoln Christian church in Lincoln, Nebraska. In an article in the Christian magazine *Relevant*, Loy evokes Paul in his own plea to Christians to stick it out through conflict, and I can imagine this is what Paul's words would sound like to us today if the New Testament were set in America of the twenty-first century:

> Wherever you find the community of sinning saints you will find conflict. Lots of it. The Church is one big family full of characters and misfits. Sometimes sisters argue. Sometimes brothers fight. Sometimes you want to bury your weird uncle in the backyard. But despite it all, family is supposed to be the place where you stick together. Even when it's hard. Especially when it's hard.
>
> Paul addressed a lot of church conflict in his letters. No where do I hear him encouraging believers to bail on one another or move on down the road to a different church where it'll be easier. Instead, much of his letters are his encouraging and coaching these ragamuffin communities in how to do this very hard and messy thing together.
>
> When we leave at first sign of real conflict, it shortchanges God's best work in our midst. It sidesteps the process of repentance, forgiveness and grace. It negates the power of the Gospel to bring reconciliation where reconciliation might seem impossible. We and those around us miss out on all of it when we just leave.
>
> I do know that not all conflict is resolvable. I know that reconciliation is impossible where there is no repentance. I get that. But remember, repentance starts with us. And so does the extending of grace. And when we resolve to stick around and keep on repenting and extending grace, I think God can do far more than we often give Him credit for. Some of God's best work happens in the mess.

Through thick and thin, I'm sticking around. Through the best efforts and the offenses and the blunders and the tender mercies and the misunderstandings and the miracles and the teamwork and the kindnesses and the hurt feelings that are all ours as God's children, I am letting repentance and grace carry me through. I'm staying right here, to cultivate my bit of God's kingdom so that both my sisters and brothers have fertile ground in which to grow. Are you with me?

References Cited

Unless stated otherwise, typescripts of all interviews are in the author's possession. All internet links were accessible at the time of publication.

Additional resources for discussing how the roles of women at church can be improved are available at womenatchurch.com.

Introduction

p. xix *"Elder Jeffrey R. Holland emphasized . . ."* Jeffrey R. Holland, "Like A Broken Vessel," *Ensign*, November 2013, available at https://www.lds.org/ensign/2013/11/saturday-afternoon-session/like-a-broken-vessel.

p. xx *"Whatever duty . . ."* Brigham Young, July 29, 1860, *Journal of Discourses,* 26 vols. (London and Liverpool: LDS Booksellers Depot, 185486), 8:137.

Chapter 1: Misbegotten Males

p. 4 *"If we narrow . . ."* Stephanie Coontz, *A Strange Stirring: The Feminine Mystique and American Women at the Dawn of the 1960s* (New York: Basic Books, 2012), 5–6.

p. 5 *"There is tremendous work . . ."* Valerie M. Hudson, "What Sex Means for World Peace," *Foreign Policy,* April 24, 2012, http://www.foreignpolicy.com/articles/2012/04/24/what_sex_means_for_world_peace.

p. 5 *"lifting of the women . . ."* "Woman's Work and Mormonism," *Young Woman's Journal* 17 (July 1906): 295–96.

p. 6 *"By proving contraries . . ."* Joseph Smith, et al., *History of the Church of Jesus Christ of Latter-day Saints,* edited by B. H. Roberts, 7 vols., 2nd ed. rev. (Salt Lake City: Deseret Book, 1948 printing), 6:248.

Chapter 2: A Brief History of the Conversation about Women

p. 8 *"it is no sin . . ."* Joseph Smith, in Nauvoo Relief Society Minute Book, March 17, 1842, 36. Available at http://josephsmithpapers.org/paperSummary/nauvoo-relief-society-minute-book?p=33.

p. 8 *"Any and all . . ."* E. R. Snow Smith, "To the Branches of the Relief Society," letter dated September 12, 1884, *Woman's Exponent* 13 (September 15, 1884): 61.

p. 8 *"If laying on of hands . . ."* Louisa Green Richards to Lorenzo Snow, April 9, 1901. Louisa Lula Green Richards Papers. For more complete explorations of women's healing blessings, see Linda King Newell, "The Historical Relationship of Mormon Women and Priesthood," *Dialogue: A Journal of Mormon Thought* 18, no. 3 (Autumn 1985): 21–32; and Jonathan A. Stapley and Kristine Wright, "Female Ritual Healing in Mormonism," *Journal of Mormon History* 37 (Winter 2011): 1–85.

p. 9 *"had become closer . . ."* Kirk Johnson, "Mormons on a Mission," *New York Times*, August 20, 2010, New York edition, AR1.

p. 9 *"My grandmother sought . . ."* Jill Mulvay Derr, Janath Russell Cannon, and Maureen Ursenbach Beecher, *Women of Covenant: The Story of Relief Society* (Salt Lake City: Deseret Book, 1992), 367.

p. 11 *"Today we have . . ."* M. Russell Ballard, "Sharing the Gospel Using the Internet," *Ensign,* July 2008, available at https://www.lds.org/ensign/2008/07/sharing-the-gospel-using-the-internet.

p. 11 *"How To Create . . ."* Ryan Morgenegg, "How to Create Your Own LDS Blog," *Church News*, January 14, 2014, https://www.lds.org/church/news/how-to-create-your-own-lds-blog.

p. 11 *"Instead of second-hand . . ."* Shira Telushkin, "The Facebook of Mormon," *The Atlantic*, January 31, 2014, available at http://www.theatlantic.com/technology/archive/2014/01/the-facebook-of-mormon/283467.

p. 11 *"Even to imply . . ."* George A. Smith to Dr. J. Raymond Cope, December 7, 1945, manuscript no. 36, box 63-8A, George A. Smith Papers, Special Collections, Marriott Library, University of Utah, Salt Lake City. Accessed via FairMormon.org at http://www.fairmormon.org/perspectives/publications/when-the-prophet-speaks-is-the-thinking-done (July 10, 2014). More detailed information on this topic can be found in *Dialogue: A Journal of Mormon Thought* 19, no. 1 (Spring 1986): 35–39.

p. 12 *"cheerful Mormon helpfulness . . ."* Elisothel, "Call to Action: Addressing the Temple 'Issue', Period," *Feminist Mormon Housewives*, February 12, 2012, http://www.feministmormonhousewives.org/2012/02/call-to-action-addressing-the-temple-issue-period.

p. 12 *"Even among . . ."* Elisothel, "Drumroll Please: Temple 'Issue' Report," *Feminist Mormon Housewives*, March 7, 2012, http://www.feministmormonhousewives.org/2012/03/drumroll-please-temple-issue-report.

p. 13 *"An online gallery . . ."* For details about this project and more insight into the modesty discussion, see mormonwomenbare.com; and Julie M. Smith, "Men, Women, and Modesty," *Times and Seasons*, February 17, 2014, http://timesandseasons.org/index.php/2014/02/men-women-and-modesty.

Chapter 3: Why Should I Be Concerned about How Women Feel at Church?

p. 19 *"Sometimes we confuse . . ."* Dieter F. Uchtdorf, "Four Titles," *Ensign*, April 2013, available at https://www.lds.org/ensign/2013/05/four-titles.

p. 20 *"It is increasingly . . ."* M. Russell Ballard, *Counseling with Our Councils* (Salt Lake City: Deseret Book, 2012), 63.

p. 21 *"entrepreneurs in Zion . . ."* Clayton M. Christensen, *The Power of Everyday Missionaries* (Salt Lake City: Deseret Book, 2013), 149.

p. 21 *"Intelligence, to a certain extent . . ."* Brigham Young, December 3, 1854, *Journal of Discourses*, 2:136.

p. 22 *"In the summer of 2012 . . ."* Neylan McBaine, "To Do the Business of the Church: A Cooperative Paradigm for Examining Gendered Participating Within Church Organizational Structure," FairMormon.org, http://www.fairmormon.org/perspectives/fair-conferences/2012-fair-conference/2012-to-do-the-business-of-the-church-a-cooperative-paradigm.

p. 24 *"One of the weaknesses . . ."* "President Uchtdorf Addresses Church History Symposium," YouTube video, 59:25, posted by *Mormon Newsroom*, March 11, 2014, https://www.youtube.com/watch?v=4rc5GyF5i3Y. See 15:06 and 19:00 in this video for the statements referenced here.

p. 26 *"I don't see how . . ."* Valerie Hudson and Alma Don Sorenson, *Women in Eternity, Women in Zion* (Springville, Utah: Cedar Fort, 2004), 11.

p. 27 *"In a 2013 Deseret News article . . ."* Joseph Walker, "Will a Woman Pray at LDS General Conference?" *Deseret News,* March 19, 2013, available at http://www.deseretnews.com/article/865576256/Will-a-woman-pray-at-LDS-general-conference.html.

p. 28 *"Scholar Melissa Inouye . . ."* Melissa Inouye, "If We Can't Fix It, It Ain't Broke," *Peculiar People*, November 11, 2013, http://www.patheos.com/blogs/peculiarpeople/2013/11/if-we-cant-fix-it-it-aint-broke.

Chapter 4: Why Are Some Women in Pain?

p. 31 *"If the gospel . . ."* Dieter F. Uchtdorf, "Come, Join With Us," *Ensign,* October 2013, available at https://www.lds.org/ensign/2013/11/saturday-morning-session/come-join-with-us.

p. 32 *"no legal rights . . ."* Stephanie Coontz, *A Strange Stirring: The Feminine Mystique and American Women at the Dawn of the 1960s* (New York: Basic Books, 2012), 5. See *A Strange Stirring* for additional references to American gender policy in 1962.

p. 32 *"I called every phone number . . ."* Sandra Day O'Connor, "First Female Justice at the U. S. Supreme Court," *Makers* video, 4:31, http://www.makers.com/sandra-day-oconnor.

p. 33 *"Strengthening the Patriarchal Order . . ."* Brent Barlow, "Strengthening the Patriarchal Order in the Home," *Ensign,* February 1973, available at https://www.lds.org/ensign/1973/02/strengthening-the-patriarchal-order-in-the-home.

p. 34 *"Equal Partnership in Marriage . . ."* Valerie M. Hudson and Richard B. Miller, "Equal Partnership in Marriage," *Ensign,* April 2013, available at https://www.lds.org/ensign/2013/04/equal-partnership-in-marriage. For a further analysis of the two *Ensign* articles side by side, see Marintha Miles, "Truth for Our Times," *By Common Consent,* March 21, 2013, http://bycommonconsent.com/2013/03/21/truth-for-our-times.

p. 34 *"the very best predictor . . ."* Valerie M. Hudson, "What Sex Means for World Peace," *Foreign Policy,* April 24, 2012, http://www.foreignpolicy.com/articles/2012/04/24/what_sex_means_for_world_peace.

p. 35 *"This statistic was supported . . ."* Sabino Kornrich, Julie Brines, and Katrina Leupp, "Egalitarianism, Housework, and Sexual Frequency in Marriage," *American Sociological Review* 78 (2012): 26–50.

p. 36 *"The diversity of persons . . ."* Dieter F. Uchtdorf, "Come, Join With Us."

p. 36 *"In my branch in Hong Kong . . ."* Melissa Inouye, "How Conference Comes to Hong Kong," *Peculiar People,* March 4, 2013, http://www.patheos.com/blogs/peculiarpeople/2013/03/how-conference-comes-to-hong-kong.

p. 37 *"where 57% of Internet traffic . . ."* "Cisco Visual Networking Index: Forecast and Methodology, 2012–2017," Cisco White Paper, May 29, 2013.

p. 37 *"1 minute of video . . ."* James L. McQuivey, "How Video Will Take Over the World," Forrester Research, June 17, 2008, http://www.forrester.com/How+Video+Will+Take+Over+The+World/fulltext/-/E-RES44199.

p. 39 *"It has been a long time . . ."* "Mormon Women Leaders Announce International Board Members," *Mormon Newsroom,* February 7, 2014, http://www.mormonnewsroom.org/article/mormon-auxiliary-leaders-announce-international-board-members.

p. 40 *"The reason [a woman praying in conference] . . ."* Joseph Walker, "Will a Woman Pray at LDS General Conference?" *Deseret News,* March 19, 2013, http://www.deseretnews.com/article/865576256/Will-a-woman-pray-at-LDS-general-conference.html.

p. 41 *"We've had stories . . ."* "Diversity and Strength of Mormon Women Highlighted in New Relief Society Book," *Mormon Newsroom,* August 11, 2011, http://www.mormonnewsroom.org/article/diversity-strength-mormon-women-new-relief-society-book.

p. 41 *"We are not here . . ."* "Apostle Instructs Hundreds in Uganda," *Mormon Newsroom,* January 27, 2014, http://www.mormonnewsroom.ug/article/apostle-instructs-hundreds-in-uganda.

p. 42 *"'Elder Ballard,' she said . . ."* M. Russell Ballard, *Counseling with Our Councils* (Salt Lake City: Deseret Book, 2012), 1.

p. 42 *"To be perfectly candid . . ."* Ballard, *Counseling with Our Councils,* 18, 62.

p. 47 *"I now turn the key . . ."* Joseph Smith, Nauvoo Relief Society Minute

Book, March 17, 1842, 37. Available at http://josephsmithpapers.org/paperSummary/nauvoo-relief-society-minute-book?p=37.

p. 47   *"As historian Claudia Bushman . . ."* Jill Mulvay Derr, Janath Russell Cannon, and Maureen Ursenbach Beecher, *Women of Covenant: The Story of Relief Society* (Salt Lake City: Deseret Book, 1992); Maureen Ursenbach Beecher and Lavina Fielding Anderson, eds., *Sisters in Spirit* (Urbana: University of Illinois Press, 1992); Claudia Bushman, *Mormon Sisters: Women in Early Utah* (Logan, Utah: Utah State University Press, 1997) Claudia Bushman and Caroline Kline, eds., *Mormon Women Have Their Say* (Draper, Utah: Greg Kofford, 2013).

p. 48   *"Perhaps the most publicized . . ."* Laurie Goodstein, "Some Mormons Search the Web and Find Doubt," *New York Times*, July 20, 2013, New York edition, A1.

p. 48   *"ordain them to preside . . ."* Joseph Smith, in Nauvoo Relief Society Minute Book, March 17, 1842, 4. Available at http://josephsmithpapers.org/paperSummary/nauvoo-relief-society-minute-book?p=4.

p. 49   *"Joseph did not presume . . ."* Fiona Givens, "A Society Meet for Male Priesthood," *Difficult Run*, January 20, 2014, http://difficultrun.nathanielgivens.com/2014/01/20/a-companion-meet-for-male-priesthood/.

p. 50   *"To women there belongs . . ."* "Some Things Our Girls Should Know," *Young Woman's Journal* 13 (June 1902): 286.

p. 50   *"In Turley and Chapman's . . ."* Richard E. Turley Jr. and Brittany A. Chapman, *Women of Faith in the Latter Days, Volume 1: 1775–1820* (Salt Lake City: Deseret Book, 2013).

p. 50   *"would trade giving prayers . . ."* Helen Claire Sievers, "What Women in the Church Have Lost in My Lifetime," *Exponent II* 33, no. 3 (Winter 2014): 18–22.

p. 51   *"Laurel Thatcher Ulrich . . ."* Laurel Thatcher Ulrich, "An Epiphany In A Broom Closet," *Weber Studies* 10, no. 3 (Winter 1993), available at http://weberjournal.weber.edu/archive/archive%20A%20%20Vol.%201-10.3/Vol.%2010.3/10.3Ulrich.htm.

p. 51   *"We might hope . . ."* Fiona Givens, "A Society Meet for Male Priesthood."

p. 53   *"honored by Latter-day Saints . . ."* Beverly Campbell, "Eve," *Encyclopedia of Mormonism*, available at http://eom.byu.edu/index.php/Eve.

p. 54   *"important historical accounts . . ."* David L. Paulsen and Martin Pulido, "A Mother There: A Survey of Historical Teachings about Mother in Heaven," *BYU Studies* 50, no. 1 (2011): 70–126.

p. 54   *"all human beings . . ."* "The Family: A Proclamation to the World," available at https://www.lds.org/topics/family-proclamation.

p. 55   *"I have heard from many women . . ."* Kristen Moulton, "Mormon Women Shut Out of All-Male Priesthood Meeting," *Salt Lake*

Tribune, October 5, 2013, available at http://www.sltrib.com/sltrib/news/56963037-78/women-mormon-church-priesthood.html.csp.

p. 55 *"In each post . . ."* These statistics come from a series of blog posts on the blog *Doves and Serpents*, written by Heather and starting October 16, 2013. See http://www.dovesandserpents.org/wp/category/columns/equality-is-not-feeling/.

p. 55 *"I'm in teacher education . . ."* "Equality Is Not A Feeling, 2.0," *Doves and Serpents*, October 19, 2013, http://www.dovesandserpents.org/wp/2013/10/equality-is-not-a-feeling-2-0.

p. 56 *"In his trip to Uganda . . ."* "Apostle Instructs Hundreds in Uganda," *Mormon Newsroom*, January 27, 2014, http://www.mormonnewsroom.ug/article/apostle-instructs-hundreds-in-uganda.

p. 56 *"men and women have different. . ."* M. Russell Ballard, "This Is My Work and Glory," *Ensign*, April 2013, available at https://www.lds.org/ensign/2013/05/this-is-my-work-and-glory.

p. 56 *"Perhaps we might look . . ."* M. Russell Ballard, *Counseling with Our Councils*, 102–3.

p. 57 *"Our Church doctrine . . ."* M. Russell Ballard, "Let Us Think Straight," Brigham Young University Campus Education Week Devotional, August 20, 2013, available at http://speeches.byu.edu/?act=viewitem&id=2133.

p. 57 *"President Spencer W. Kimball . . ."* Patricia T. Holland, "A Woman's Perspective on the Priesthood," *Ensign*, July 1980, available at https://www.lds.org/ensign/1980/07/a-womans-perspective-on-the-priesthood.

p. 57 *"within those great assurances . . ."* Spencer W. Kimball, "The Role of Righteous Women," *Ensign*, November 1979, 102.

p. 57 *"The Encyclopedia of Mormonism . . ."* Don A. Sorensen, "Equality," *Encyclopedia of Mormonism*, available at http://eom.byu.edu/index.php/Equality.

p. 59 *"Many of the Savior's . . ."* Clayton M. Christensen, "My Ways Are Not Your Ways," *Ensign*, February 2007, available at https://www.lds.org/ensign/2007/02/my-ways-are-not-your-ways.

Chapter 5: Are We Practicing What We Preach?

p. 62 *"Mormon domestic workers . . ."* Melissa Inouye, "How Conference Comes to Hong Kong," *Peculiar People*, March 4, 2013, http://www.patheos.com/blogs/peculiarpeople/2013/03/how-conference-comes-to-hong-kong.

p. 63 *"men's vision of the capacity . . ."* Jodi Kantor and Laurie Goodstein, "Missions Signal a Growing Role for Mormon Women," *New York Times*, March 2, 2013, New York edition, A1.

p. 63 *"I look over the topics . . ."* Rex E. Lee, "The Power Within: To See Life Steadily and See It Whole," in *Women and the Power Within* (Salt Lake City: Deseret Book, 1991), 20.

p. 63 *"Just as a woman . . ."* M. Russell Ballard, "This Is My Work and Glory," *Ensign,* April 2013, available at https://www.lds.org/ensign/2013/05/this-is-my-work-and-glory.

p. 63 *"Our Father in Heaven . . ."* M. Russell Ballard, "Let Us Think Straight," Brigham Young University Campus Education Week Devotional, August 20, 2013, http://speeches.byu.edu/?act=viewitem&id=2133&cid=NEApr14.

p. 64 *"We are not accustomed . . ."* Dallin H. Oaks, "The Keys and Authority of the Priesthood," *Ensign,* May 2014, available at https://www.lds.org/ensign/2014/05/priesthood-session/the-keys-and-authority-of-the-priesthood.

Chapter 6: Getting Down to Work

p. 68 *"adapt some church programs . . ."* Church Handbook of Instructions 2: Administering the Church 17.1, available at https://www.lds.org/handbook/handbook-2-administering-the-church/uniformity-and-adaptation.

Chapter 7: Identify the Audience and Walk in Their Shoes

p. 70 *"Milk, it seemed . . ."* For a complete discussion of the "got milk?" campaign, see Jon Steel, *Truth, Lies & Advertising: The Art of Account Planning* (New York: Wiley & Sons, 1998), 238–39.

p. 71 *"There exists today . . ."* W. Craig Zwick, "What Are You Thinking?" *Ensign,* May 2014, available at https://www.lds.org/ensign/2014/05/saturday-afternoon-session/what-are-you-thinking.

p. 71 *"walk in pink moccasins . . ."* Carol Lynn Pearson, "Walk in Pink Moccasins," *Sunstone,* May 2005, 21.

p. 72 *"One Sunday I asked . . ."* Rob McFarland, "New Recruits in the Armies of Shelaman: Notes from a Primary Man," *Exponent II* 33, no. 3 (Winter 2014): 25.

Chapter 8: Are We Asking the Right Questions?

p. 73 *"Looking at the market . . ."* Carmen Nobel, "Clay Christensen's Milkshake Marketing," *Harvard Business School Working Knowledge Newsletter,* February 14, 2011, http://hbswk.hbs.edu/item/6496.html.

p. 74 *"One of the most important . . ."* Clayton M. Christensen, *The Power of Everyday Missionaries* (Salt Lake City: Deseret Book, 2013), 126.

p. 75 *"In the 2012 worldwide training . . ."* "Strengthening Quorums and Members," Worldwide Leadership Training Meeting, February 2012, available at https://www.lds.org/broadcasts/article/worldwide-leadership-training/2012/01/strengthening-quorums-and-members.

p. 76 *"Sometimes we get so focused . . ."* M. Russell Ballard, *Counseling with Our Councils* (Salt Lake City: Deseret Book, 2012), 77.

p. 76 *"Much of what we do . . ."* Harold B. Lee, *Stand Ye In Holy Places* (Salt Lake City: Deseret Book, 1976), 309.

p. 77 *"Every member of the church . . ."* Church Handbook of Instructions

2: *Administering the Church* 20.2.1, available at https://www.lds. org/handbook/handbook-2-administering-the-church/priesthood-ordinances-and-blessings.

p. 81 *"Dave Blanchard . . ."* Steve Graves, Dave Blanchard, Josh Kwan, *From Concept to Scale: Creating a Gospel-Minded Organization* (Praxis Media, 2013).

Chapter 9: Prayer

p. 84 *"Work on Me First . . ."* Kerry Patterson, Joseph Grenny, Ron McMillan, and Al Switzer, *Crucial Confrontations* (New York: McGraw-Hill, 2005), 23.

p. 84 *"You can't please everybody . . ."* Sara Katherine Staheli Hanks, "'Mormon Women Leaders Announce International Board Members': FMH Responds," *Feminist Mormon Housewives*, February 10, 2014, http:// www.feministmormonhousewives.org/2014/02/mormon-women-leaders-fmh-responds.

p. 85 *"Frances Ann Adams . . ."* "Obituaries: Frances Ann Adams," *Woman's Exponent* 31 (March 1903): 78.

p. 87 *"Being rooted . . ."* Excerpt from Kris Wright, "Baking a Sacrament Prayer," *Dialogue: A Journal of Mormon Thought* 44, no. 3 (Fall 2011): 203.

Chapter 10: People

p. 89 *"He used a personal example . . ."* W. Craig Zwick, "What Are You Thinking?" *Ensign,* May 2014, available at https://www.lds.org/ ensign/2014/05/saturday-afternoon-session/what-are-you-thinking.

p. 92 *"Disagreements . . ."* Kerry Patterson, Joseph Grenny, Ron McMillan, and Al Switzer, *Crucial Confrontations* (New York: McGraw-Hill, 2005), xvii.

p. 92 *"confronting with Safety . . ."* Patterson, Grenny, McMillan, and Switzer, *Crucial Confrontations*, 89–98.

p. 95 *"Members of the Church . . ."* *Church Handbook of Instructions 2: Administering the Church* 21.1.24, available at https://www.lds.org/ handbook/handbook-2-administering-the-church/selected-church-policies.

p. 100 *"It is easy to understand . . ."* M. Russell Ballard, *Counseling with Our Councils* (Salt Lake City: Deseret Book, 2012), 62.

p. 101 *"In a 2006 study . . ."* Vicki W. Kramer, Alison M. Konrad, and Sumru Erkut, "Critical Mass on Corporate Boards: Why Three or More Women Enhance Governance," *Wellesley Centers for Women* (Fall/Winter 2006).

p. 104 *"For most women . . ."* Deborah Tannen, *You Just Don't Understand* (New York: HarperCollins, 1990), 76–77.

p. 108 *"In her analysis . . ."* Claudia Bushman and Caroline Kline, eds., *Mormon Women Have Their Say* (Salt Lake City: Greg Kofford Books, 2013), 227.

p. 108 *"bossy . . ."* Girl Scout Research Institute, *Change It Up: What Girls Say About Redefining Leadership* (2008), available at http://www.girlscouts. org/research/pdf/change_it_up_executive_summary_english.pdf.

p. 109 *"Between elementary school . . ."* American Association of University

Women, *Shortchanging Girls, Shortchanging America* (1991).

p. 109 *"One of the key lessons . . ."* Ballard, *Counseling with Our Councils*, 24.

p. 110 *"Sisters, be prepared . . ."* Ballard, *Counseling with Our Councils,* 102.

p. 110 *"Satan does not . . ."* Ballard, *Counseling with Our Councils,* 18.

p. 113 *"I believe the church . . ."* Peggy Fletcher Stack, "'Sister Missionaries' Causing A Gender Shift in Mormonism, BYU Prof Says," *Salt Lake Tribune,* March 27, 2014, available at http://www.sltrib.com/sltrib/blogsfaithblog/57738651-180/church-missionaries-women-moss.html.csp.

p. 113 *"fasting and praying . . ."* Tad Walch, "New Leadership Roles for Women Alters LDS Mission Culture, Hits at Deep, Long-Term Ramifications," *Deseret News,* April 4, 2014, available at http://www.deseretnews.com/article/865600279/New-leadership-roles-for-women-alters-LDS-mission-culture-hints-at-deep-long-term-ramifications.html.

p. 113 *"Culturally . . ."* Jodi Kantor and Laurie Goodstein, "Missions Signal a Growing Role for Mormon Women," *New York Times,* March 2, 2013, New York edition, A1.

p. 115 *"The female part . . ."* Joseph Smith, in Nauvoo Relief Society Minute Book, March 17, 1842, 39, available at http://josephsmithpapers.org/paperSummary/nauvoo-relief-society-minute-book?p=36.

p. 115 *"On one Sunday . . ."* Clayton Christensen, *The Power of Everyday Missionaries* (Salt Lake City: Deseret Book, 2013), 139.

p. 117 *"I have to say . . ."* Gregory Prince, "Interviews and Conversations. There is Always a Struggle; an Interview with Chieko Okazaki," *Dialogue: A Journal of Mormon Thought* 45, no. 1 (Spring 2012): 112–140.

p. 117 *"borrowing strength . . ."* Stephen Covey, *Spiritual Roots of Human Relations* (Salt Lake City: Deseret Book, 1970), 122.

p. 118 *"What's the practical remedy . . ."* Mary Beard, "The Public Voice of Women," *London Review of Books* 36, no. 6 (March 20, 2014).

Chapter 11: Process

p. 131 *"My interactions . . ."* Kathleen Hughes, "Kathleen Hughes on Women and the Priesthood," *LDS Living,* December 16, 2013, http://ldsliving.com/story/74542-kathy-hughes-on-iwomen-and-the-priesthoodi.

p. 137 *"When journalists . . ."* Jodi Kantor and Laurie Goodstein, "From Mormon Women, a Flood of Requests and Questions on Their Role in the Church," *New York Times,* March 6, 2014, available at http://www.nytimes.com/2014/03/07/us/from-mormon-women-a-flood-of-requests-and-questions-on-their-role-in-the-church.html.

p. 139 *"Before they turn . . ."* Bonnie L. Oscarson, "Sisterhood: Oh, How We Need Each Other," *Ensign,* May 2014, available at https://www.lds.org/ensign/2014/05/general-womens-meeting/sisterhood-oh-how-we-need-each-other.

p. 141 *"Mother . . ."* Homer, *The Odyssey,* Book 1, lines 358–59, translated by A. T. Murray

p. 141 *"result from the interplay . . ."* Deborah Tannen, *You Just Don't Understand* (New York: HarperCollins, 1990), 31.

p. 143 *"Group appreciation . . ."* I am indebted to BYU–Idaho historian Andrea Radke-Moss for working through these ideas with me. For her excellent introduction to gender studies and, specifically, the "benevolent patriarchy" I am describing here, see her "Mormon Studies in the Classroom: Mormon Women, Patriarchy and Equality," *Juvenile Instructor*, May 08, 2014, http://www.juvenileinstructor.org/mormon-studies-in-the-classroom-mormon-women-patriarchy-and-equality/.

p. 143 *"threatened to the core . . ."* Patricia T. Holland, "'One Thing Needful': Becoming Women of Greater Faith in Christ," *Ensign*, October 1987, available at https://www.lds.org/ensign/1987/10/one-thing-needful-becoming-women-of-greater-faith-in-christ.

p. 145 *"We [women] . . ."* "An Address by Miss Eliza R. Snow, August 14, 1873," *Woman's Exponent* 2 (September 15, 1873).

p. 146 *"I used to love . . ."* Helen Claire Sievers, "What Women in the Church Have Lost in My Lifetime," *Exponent II* 33, no. 3 (Winter 2014): 18–22.

p. 150 *"I wanted very Much . . ."* Richard E. Turley Jr. and Brittany A. Chapman, *Women of Faith in the Latter Days, Volume 1: 1775–1820* (Salt Lake City: Deseret Book, 2013), 159.

p. 155 *"the manner through . . ."* Sheri L. Dew, *Women and the Priesthood* (Salt Lake City: Deseret Book, 2014), 105.

p. 155 *"When I was in college . . ."* Alison Moore Smith, "Do Titles Matter?" *Times and Seasons*, March 19, 2010, http://timesandseasons.org/index.php/2010/03/do-titles-matter.

p. 156 *"I have been thinking . . ."* Sara Katherine Staheli Hanks, "'Mormon Women Leaders Announce International Board Members': FMH Responds," *Feminist Mormon Housewives*, February 10, 2014, http://www.feministmormonhousewives.org/2014/02/mormon-women-leaders-fmh-responds.

p. 157 *"President Linda K. Burton . . ."* Dallin H. Oaks, "The Keys and Authority of the Priesthood," *Ensign,* May 2014, available at https://www.lds.org/ensign/2014/05/priesthood-session/the-keys-and-authority-of-the-priesthood. The video of the talk is available at https://www.lds.org/general-conference/2014/04/the-keys-and-authority-of-the-priesthood. See 1:02 of the video for the reference to President Linda K. Burton.

p. 158 *"What concerns me . . ."* Genevieve Kelley, "Part 2 of 3: Imaginary conversations with a conservative Mormon woman about feminism and the Church," *Loveliest Year*, March 26, 2014, http://loveliestyear.blogspot.com/2014/03/imaginary-conversations-with.html.

Chapter 12: Perseverance

p. 169 *"It seems to me . . ."* Patricia T. Holland, "A Woman's Perspective on the Priesthood," *Ensign,* July 1980, available at https://www.lds.org/ensign/1980/07/a-womans-perspective-on-the-priesthood.

p. 171 *"ultimate responsibility . . ."* *Church Handbook of Instructions 2: Administering the Church*, introduction to chapter 5, available at https://www.lds.org/handbook/handbook-2-administering-the-church/the-work-of-salvation-in-the-ward-and-stake.

p. 172 *"we set clear expectations . . ."* Kerry Patterson, Joseph Grenny, Ron McMillan, and Al Switzer, *Crucial Confrontations* (New York: McGraw-Hill, 2005), 4.

p. 172 *"Policies, systems . . ."* Patterson, Grenny, McMillan, and Al Switzer, *Crucial Confrontations*, 13.

Chapter 13: We Are Not Alone

p. 174 *"Leadership Conference . . ."* For an example of the type of media coverage on this issue, see Mark I. Pinksy, "American Nuns Respond to Vatican Rebuke With Conciliatory Statement," *Huffington Post*, August 20, 2013, http://www.huffingtonpost.com/2013/08/20/catholic-nuns-vatican-rebuke-us_n_3781683.html.

p. 174 *"Jesus Feminist . . ."* Sarah Bessey, *Jesus Feminist: An Invitation to Revisit the Bible's View of Women* (New York: Howard Books, 2013), 1–2.

p. 174 *"Let Her Lead . . ."* Brady Boyd, *Let Her Lead: Creating a Better Future for Women in the Church* (Colorado Springs: Bondfire Books, 2013), 2.

p. 174 *"God's Daughters . . ."* R. Marie Griffith, *God's Daughters: Evangelical Women and the Power of Submission* (Berkeley: University of California Press, 1997), 14.

p. 175 *"cultural fundamentalism . . ."* Griffith, *God's Daughters*, 32.

p. 175 *"Submit to your husband . . ."* Griffith, *God's Daughters*, 175.

p. 176 *"Egalitarian prayer . . ."* Elana Sztokman, "Tefillingate: Orthodoxy Must Not Reject Its Most Committed Women," *Haaretz*, January 28, 2014, http://www.haaretz.com/opinion/.premium-1.571011.

p. 177 *"Wherever you find . . ."* Aaron Loy, "5 Really Bad Reasons to Leave Your Church," *Relevant*, January 27, 2014, http://www.relevantmagazine.com/god/church/5-really-bad-reasons-leave-your-church.

Also available from
GREG KOFFORD BOOKS

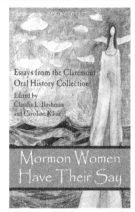

Mormon Women Have Their Say: Essays from the Claremont Oral History Collection

Edited by Claudia L. Bushman and Caroline Kline

Paperback, ISBN: 978-1-58958-494-5

The Claremont Women's Oral History Project has collected hundreds of interviews with Mormon women of various ages, experiences, and levels of activity. These interviews record the experiences of these women in their homes and family life, their church life, and their work life, in their roles as homemakers, students, missionaries, career women, single women, converts, and disaffected members. Their stories feed into and illuminate the broader narrative of LDS history and belief, filling in a large gap in Mormon history that has often neglected the lived experiences of women. This project preserves and perpetuates their voices and memories, allowing them to say share what has too often been left unspoken. The silent majority speaks in these records.

This volume is the first to explore the riches of the collection in print. A group of young scholars and others have used the interviews to better understand what Mormonism means to these women and what women mean for Mormonism. They explore those interviews through the lenses of history, doctrine, mythology, feminist theory, personal experience, and current events to help us understand what these women have to say about their own faith and lives.

Praise for *Mormon Women Have Their Say*:

"Using a variety of analytical techniques and their own savvy, the authors connect ordinary lives with enduring themes in Latter-day Saint faith and history." --Laurel Thatcher Ulrich, author of *Well-Behaved Women Seldom Make History*

"Essential. . . . In these pages, Mormon women will find *ourselves*." --Joanna Brooks, author of *The Book of Mormon Girl: A Memoir of an American Faith*

"The varieties of women's responses to the major issues in their lives will provide many surprises for the reader, who will be struck by how many different ways there are to be a thoughtful and faithful Latter-day Saint woman." --Armand Mauss, author of *All Abraham's Children: Changing Mormon Conceptions of Race and Lineage*

Common Ground—Different Opinions:
Latter-day Saints and Contemporary Issues

Edited by Justin F. White
and James E. Faulconer

Paperback, ISBN: 978-1-58958-573-7

There are many hotly debated issues about which many people disagree, and where common ground is hard to find. From evolution to environmentalism, war and peace to political partisanship, stem cell research to same-sex marriage, how we think about controversial issues affects how we interact as Latter-day Saints.

In this volume various Latter-day Saint authors address these and other issues from differing points of view. Though they differ on these tough questions, they have all found common ground in the gospel of Jesus Christ and the latter-day restoration. Their insights offer diverse points of view while demonstrating we can still love those with whom we disagree.

Praise for *Common Ground—Different Opinions*:

"[This book] provide models of faithful and diverse Latter-day Saints who remain united in the body of Christ. This collection clearly demonstrates that a variety of perspectives on a number of sensitive issues do in fact exist in the Church. . . . [T]he collection is successful in any case where it manages to give readers pause with regard to an issue they've been fond of debating, or convinces them to approach such conversations with greater charity and much more patience. It served as just such a reminder and encouragement to me, and for that reason above all, I recommend this book." — Blair Hodges, Maxwell Institute

Made in the USA
Monee, IL
25 October 2020

46070600R00132